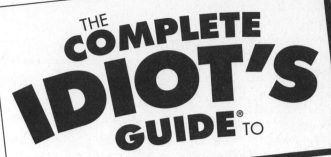

Simple Home Repair

by Judy Ostrow

ALPHA
A member of Penguin Group (USA) Inc.

This book is dedicated with love to Sam, Adam, and Rachel, my biggest cheerleaders.

ALPHA BOOKS

Published by the Penguin Group

Penguin Group (USA) Inc., 375 Hudson Street, New York, New York 10014, USA

Penguin Group (Canada), 90 Eglinton Avenue East, Suite 700, Toronto, Ontario M4P 2Y3, Canada (a division of Pearson Penguin Canada Inc.)

Penguin Books Ltd., 80 Strand, London WC2R 0RL, England

Penguin Ireland, 25 St. Stephen's Green, Dublin 2, Ireland (a division of Penguin Books Ltd.)

Penguin Group (Australia), 250 Camberwell Road, Camberwell, Victoria 3124, Australia (a division of Pearson Australia Group Pty. Ltd.)

Penguin Books India Pvt. Ltd., 11 Community Centre, Panchsheel Park, New Delhi—110 017, India

Penguin Group (NZ), 67 Apollo Drive, Rosedale, North Shore, Auckland 1311, New Zealand (a division of Pearson New Zealand Ltd.)

Penguin Books (South Africa) (Pty.) Ltd., 24 Sturdee Avenue, Rosebank, Johannesburg 2196, South Africa

Penguin Books Ltd., Registered Offices: 80 Strand, London WC2R 0RL, England

Copyright © 2007 by Judy Ostrow

All illustrations copyright © 2007 by Karen Burgess

THE COMPLETE IDIOT'S GUIDE TO and Design are registered trademarks of Penguin Group (USA) Inc.

International Standard Book Number: 978-1-59257-665-4
Library of Congress Catalog Card Number: 2007924618

09   08   07   8   7   6   5   4   3   2   1

Interpretation of the printing code: The rightmost number of the first series of numbers is the year of the book's printing; the rightmost number of the second series of numbers is the number of the book's printing. For example, a printing code of 07-1 shows that the first printing occurred in 2007.

Printed in the United States of America

Note: This publication contains the opinions and ideas of its author. It is intended to provide helpful and informative material on the subject matter covered. It is sold with the understanding that the author and publisher are not engaged in rendering professional services in the book. If the reader requires personal assistance or advice, a competent professional should be consulted.

The author and publisher specifically disclaim any responsibility for any liability, loss, or risk, personal or otherwise, which is incurred as a consequence, directly or indirectly, of the use and application of any of the contents of this book.

Most Alpha books are available at special quantity discounts for bulk purchases for sales promotions, premiums, fundraising, or educational use. Special books, or book excerpts, can also be created to fit specific needs.

For details, write: Special Markets, Alpha Books, 375 Hudson Street, New York, NY 10014.

Publisher: *Marie Butler-Knight*
Editorial Director/Acquiring Editor: *Mike Sanders*
Managing Editor: *Billy Fields*
Development Editor: *Lynn Northrup*
Senior Production Editor: *Janette Lynn*
Copy Editor: *Ross Patty*
Illustrator: *Karen Burgess*

Cartoonist: *Richard King*
Cover Designer: *Bill Thomas*
Book Designer: *Trina Wurst*
Indexer: *Brad Herriman*
Layout: *Chad Dressler*
Proofreader: *Aaron Black, John Etchison, Mary Hunt*

Contents at a Glance

Contents

Introduction

There's a truism about houses: sooner or later, whatever can go wrong, will go wrong. Most people recognize this phrase as Murphy's Law, but after twenty-five years of fixing things, I know that it's also the First Law of Homeownership.

Because stuff goes bad—often in a hurry, usually when you least expect it, and most likely when there's a tiny balance in your checking account—being able to diagnose a small problem before it's a big one, and even fix it yourself, is a very nice aptitude to develop.

That's what got me excited about writing *The Complete Idiot's Guide to Simple Home Repair.*

After about a year in our first house, we had a new baby and lots of bills, and the First Law of Homeownership kicked in. Pipes froze, the pump died, and the gutters started leaking. I noticed that moss was growing on the garage roof! My husband traveled all the time, and so the ball was in my court. I had to fix some of this stuff myself, or we'd go bust paying repair people.

So I took the next step: I started learning about my house's structure, systems, and appliances, and started down the DIY highway.

I was a bit tentative at first, but the simple repairs I completed successfully encouraged me to try others. When I did call repairmen, I asked them to explain what they were doing, and why. I picked their brains about the finer points of my house's plumbing, wiring, heating, and appliances. Pretty soon, my friends were calling *me* to walk them through the fixes for their own appliance breakdowns and plumbing disasters.

In this book, I pass along what I've learned, along with lots of good advice from fellow DIY-ers and seasoned pros. I hope you find that acquiring these skills is fun and empowering. And I hope that the knowledge will save you money; it's saved me and my family plenty!

Taking care of a home is quite a bit like taking care of ourselves; keeping it in shape requires maintenance and, when needed, tweaks and touch-ups to keep it looking and functioning at its best. Like our own bodies, a home has lots of parts and systems that need care and attention. We can do a good portion of the work ourselves. And when things happen that are beyond our scope and ability, we call in an expert.

This book will acquaint you with many modest efforts you can make yourself to keep a house in shape. It's designed as a sensible, starter volume for someone who's never worked on a house before but wants to learn. It tells you what tools you need, and how to work safely. There are no big, complicated repairs here—no major surgery. But you'll find lots of step-by-step instructions, many illustrated, to help you become well acquainted with your house and take a role in its well-being.

How to Use This Book

The Complete Idiot's Guide to Simple Home Repair contains 19 chapters and 3 helpful appendixes. Here's how it's structured:

Part 1, "Getting to Know Your House," is a beginner's guide to equip and prepare yourself for doing home repairs effectively and safely. It tells you everything you need to know about the tools, supplies, and safety equipment that anyone interested in DIY repairs should have. It also provides you with an orientation about your home's systems, and how you can control them.

Part 2, "Skin Deep: Repairing Surfaces and Openings," teaches you some basic repair techniques you'll use for your home's most visible parts. You'll find out how to make dinged and dented walls and ceilings look new, and remove some of the squeaks and bounces in floors and stairs. This section will also help you get your home's simplest moving parts—the windows and doors—moving smoothly.

Part 3, "The Circulatory System: Plumbing and Fixtures," deals with all the places where water runs through your home: kitchens, baths, and the supply lines that deliver this most necessary element to the fixtures you use every day. Tackle emergency repairs and learn the techniques to address minor problems with plumbing fixtures and fittings.

Part 4, "Mission Control: Wiring, Appliances, Heating, and Cooling," covers the systems and conveniences that make your home run like it's the twenty-first century. While your wiring, many appliances, and the heating system in your home may be complex and major repair beyond your beginner's scope and talents, you can learn some simple fixes and do some needed maintenance on your own.

Part 5, "Preventive Maintenance: Safety and Upkeep," teaches you about installing, maintaining, and using the necessary equipment for home safety. It also provides you with a routine to keep up with the maintenance of your house, inside and out, to prevent small problems from becoming larger ones.

To round out your beginner skills, you'll find a Glossary of the specialized vocabulary for house parts, systems, and repair techniques you should know; a chapter-by-chapter list of Online Resources for additional information about specific repairs, tools, materials, and training; and helpful Home Inspection Checklists that you can photocopy and use to keep track of your home's condition—both inside and out—on a regular basis.

Extras

For every repair in the book that requires tools and materials, you'll find a helpful checklist to gather what you need. And in every chapter are little helpful nuggets to further expand your knowledge without flipping back and forth in the book. Watch for them:

def•i•ni•tion

The boxes quickly clarify words and phrases related to house parts and home repair that you may not have encountered before.

Ounce of Prevention

These little "red flags" let you know when you must be extra careful, or when you can take some action to save time or money.

What Pros Know

Experienced DIY-ers and repair people who fix houses for a living know a lot of facts and shortcuts. Get their tips here!

Acknowledgments

For as long as I've been learning about home repair, I've had patient, willing teachers to guide me in learning the empowering secrets of getting hands-on with a house. And I am so appreciative that because of them, I've developed some mechanical know-how that I would otherwise have never possessed.

First there was my dad, who engaged me with the sweet smells of the lumber yard, deep bins of nails, screws, nuts, and bolts, the mysteries of his big metal tool box, and all those gadgets in the basement. He could fix anything; I am still in awe.

I bow to my first carpentry teachers, Patti Garbeck and Lizabeth Moniz, who helped me get past the noise and speed of power tools and tame, if not defeat, the fear factor. They'll both tell you that respect for your tools and what they can do is a good thing.

For learning about my own houses I owe a lot of helpful and talkative (once I got them started) contractors: Steve Sferra, Richard Gates, Bob Warner, Todd Lawson, Curt Haskell, and many others who've let me look over their shoulders.

A great hardware guy or woman is invaluable when you're looking for just the right tool, material, or part for a job. Thanks to Joe di Pietro, Jr., at Chubby's Hardware in Pound Ridge, New York. Whenever I was stumped, he could point the way. I hope everyone who reads this book can find a hardware salesperson as helpful.

On safety issues, thanks to Lorraine Carli, a spokesperson at the National Fire Protection Association, for her help with a most important subject.

For the ways of old doors and doorknobs, I thank Mike at Old House Parts, in Kennebunk, Maine.

For her pictures that saved me thousands of words, I am deeply grateful to my illustrator, Karen Burgess, whose clean and beautiful drawings will surely help any beginning repair person. And to her model, Lisa McCarthy, thanks for demonstrating some intricate repair moves that made the illustrations just right.

I deeply appreciate the editorial assistance that made the book's concept a reality. Mike Sanders at Alpha Books set everything in motion. Warmest thanks are also due to Lynn Northrup, Jan Lynn, and Ross Patty, whose thoughtful suggestions and unflagging attention made the journey through their word processors feel like a spa makeover. I am also grateful for the encouragement of my agent, Bob Diforio, without whom this wonderful project would not have come my way.

Trademarks

All terms mentioned in this book that are known to be or are suspected of being trademarks or service marks have been appropriately capitalized. Alpha Books and Penguin Group (USA) Inc. cannot attest to the accuracy of this information. Use of a term in this book should not be regarded as affecting the validity of any trademark or service mark.

Part 1

Getting to Know Your House

Of course, your house is more than the sum of its many parts: it's your *home*. But even before you start the little jobs that will make it look better or run more smoothly, you need to know some basic information.

First of all, the right tool makes common repairs easier and quicker, and you should acquire a basic assortment. Also, if you're going to do repairs yourself, you need to do them safely. There are a few important rules for keeping you, your family, and your home safe when doing repairs, and they're simple to learn. Next, you need a few basic supplies that you can use for a variety of repairs, as well as a couple of things that will serve you well in small emergencies. And finally, if your house has electric power, a gas supply, and running water, you need to know where the main controls for each system are located, and how to start and stop them.

Even if you were never a Scout as a kid, the organization's motto is a good one: "Be prepared." By the time you finish Part 1, you'll be equipped and ready for lots of the little glitches and mishaps that homeownership is sure to send your way.

"Do we have some kind of water shut-off thingy?"

Your Personal Tool Kit

In This Chapter

- When it comes to tools, quality counts
- The basic categories of tools
- Must-have tools in your starter set
- The one power tool you'll need for repairs
- How to choose the right tools for you

I've never tried it, but I could probably knit a sweater using two pencils, and coax a nail out of the wall with the tip of a metal ruler. But pencils weren't designed for knitting, and the ruler isn't really a nail-pulling tool. Having the right equipment for a task usually makes the work easier, quicker, and safer.

Home repair and improvement can be broken down into a handful of actions: measuring and marking, cutting, fastening and joining, taking apart (also known as demolition), and applying. A few tools can do more than one thing, but this way of sorting them will help you remember what their primary use is.

If you can, hold a new tool in your hand before you buy it; it should be a comfortable fit, like a good pair of shoes!

Quality Counts

You can buy a cheap set of tools, and they'll probably work fine, at least for a while. Expect to replace the bargains after a couple of years. Often made of lesser-grade metals and plastic, the tips, teeth, and edges of inexpensive tools will show wear sooner, rather than later. When it comes to tools, quality counts … and costs. Most of the well-known brand name manufacturers produce tools at differing quality levels, with professional grade being the best and most expensive of the lot. Good tools will probably last a lifetime, and you can leave best-quality equipment to your grandchildren!

Sets of multiple sizes of screwdrivers, wrenches, and the like will be cheaper than buying each item singly. However, unless you're planning to repair your whole house yourself, unassisted by friends or hired hands who have their own tools, don't go overboard. Buy the best equipment you can afford and, except for the most basic tools, buy them as you need them.

If cash is tight, and you're *really* good about returning things you borrow, neighbors and friends might loan you their equipment. Take good care of borrowed tools, and return them *promptly*. Most folks I know are very possessive of their toolbox, and want things returned in the same condition as when they were loaned. If your borrowing etiquette is poor, most lenders won't give you a second chance!

Measure Up: Rule(r)s of the Road

A sturdy 20- or 25-foot retractable *measuring tape* is indispensable for all kinds of jobs around the house. Some people opt for the lighter-weight, 12-foot model, but eventually realize that the longer one is more versatile.

These come in plastic or metal cases, and the best have a stop lever so that you can extend and hold the tape in its extended position, without holding on to the case. This is a particularly good feature when you're marking the distance of long runs around a room.

About those little tick marks along the tape: carpenters can tell at a glance whether a mark indicates $7^3/_8$ inches or $7^5/_8$. If you're not so good at fractions, get a tape with a fractional read. This measure has the intervals—eighths, quarters, and halves of inches—marked clearly with the appropriate fraction, so you don't need to guess.

Better-quality tapes also have a clasp that makes it easy to attach the case to your belt while working, so you don't have to constantly hunt for it.

A metal ruler—also known as a *straightedge*—is another handy device for measuring. It serves as a ruler and as a rigid guide for a utility knife or glass cutter when you want to score a surface. An 18" straightedge is a good size for lots of jobs. Straightedges are also available in plastic; metal is slightly more expensive but much more durable.

A *speed square* has a lot of uses in carpentry, allowing you to mark angles, then draw guidelines. One of the straight sides of this triangular device has a lip, which can fit along the edge of a piece of material (a 2×4 piece of framing lumber, for example) letting its other straight side serve as a guide for marking/cutting a piece of wood or other material at a perfectly perpendicular angle (90 degrees). Speed squares are made in metal and plastic; I like the heft and feel of the metal variety.

Unless you're planning to do lots of carpentry, you don't need a big, fancy, and expensive carpenter's level. Instead, opt for a small *torpedo level*, so called because of its shape, to check whether shelves, rods, curtain poles, doors, and other household objects are hanging straight horizontally (level) or vertically (plumb). The torpedo level is one type of spirit level, so called because the measuring device employs a vial filled with liquid, usually ethanol—the "spirit"—containing an air bubble that falls between guidelines when the instrument rests plumb or level.

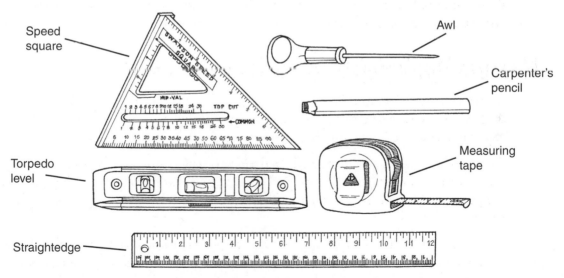

Measuring and marking tools.

Ounce of Prevention

Though its name sounds like a guided weapon, a torpedo level is easily damaged. If you drop it, it may no longer read true. So handle it with care!

Make Your Mark

An *awl* is a tool with a handle attached to a slim metal shaft with a pointed tip; it looks like a miniature ice pick. It can punch a hole in a piece of leather or a strip of wood, but for our purposes, it's a great way to scratch-mark the location for a new screw or nail on a wall or other surface.

An awl is one of those tools you can pick up for a quarter at a tag sale. Some older models have nice wooden handles. Just make sure that the shaft is firmly attached to the handle, or the tool is useless.

If you like to stash your pencil behind your ear, any sharpened #2 pencil is a good marker for your measurements and guidelines. A lot of pros think the garden-variety yellow pencil is just fine, too, but some like the *carpenter's pencil*, which can be sharpened with a utility knife and won't roll away. It looks like a regular pencil flattened by a steamroller! One disadvantage is that the carpenter model does not have an eraser attached; carpenters may not need erasers when they make marks, but sometimes newbie DIY-ers (do-it-yourselfers) do!

Sometimes using a pencil line as the guide for installing a fastener or making a cut leaves a mark that's wiggly, and leaves you scratching your head about the right location. Or, you used a dull pencil and the line is too thick to be precise. Instead, mark the right spot with a V. Put the point of the V at the spot you measured (see next figure). Then your nail or cut will be true to your intentions.

There's an old saying—a carpenter's old saw, to be precise—that goes, "Measure twice, cut once." This alludes to the importance of making good measurements, then checking them before you pick up your other tools.

When I first learned to use a circular saw, I measured twice, then turned on this most awe-inspiring power tool and made my cut. The cut was perfect, but my measurement was not; my piece was off by a quarter inch! I had to put my beautiful 2×4 in the "use later" pile for another part of the cabin I was working on.

Scrap you don't use becomes expensive trash. Until I mastered measuring, I always measured *three times*, or until I got the same measurement twice in a row. DIY 101-ers, take heed!

V-mark measurement.

The Cutting Edge: Sharp Helpers

You need just a few sharp tools for most of the cutting you'll do for basic improvements and repairs.

I don't know about your house, but in mine, *scissors* tend to migrate, like all those socks that disappear in the dryer, never to be seen again. To remind yourself to return them to your toolbox when you've "borrowed" them for another purpose, take a piece of masking tape and label your toolbox scissors ("Mom's toolbox," or "Dad's toolbox," or "My toolbox") so they aren't MIA when you need them. Sturdy scissors with 5" blades should handle most cutting tasks nicely.

There are so many uses for a *utility knife* around the house that a list of them could practically fill this book. Although you can pick up a plastic, pencil-sized, 99-cent model at most hardware checkout counters, invest in the standard, palm-filling metal model. It fits comfortably in your hand, and you can adjust and retract the blade with a simple lever. Plus, it uses disposable blades that can be stored inside the handle. It costs a couple of bucks and will last a lifetime.

Ounce of Prevention

The blade of a utility knife is very sharp. Always keep the business end retracted when you're not using the knife.

Wire cutters do what they say. In a pinch, you can repeatedly twist a wire until it breaks from all the abuse, but a wire cutter does the job in a single snip!

When you're learning repair and DIY skills, the most versatile hand saw for cutting wood is called, simply, a *toolbox saw*; it has a fairly short blade (about 15 inches or so), and is easy to use. Look for a model that can be re-sharpened, as all saws will lose their edge over time. The toolbox saw is good for making short cuts; remember only to apply pressure on your downstroke (push).

Although it may look scary, it works great. I'd never seen a *Japanese pull saw* before I took a course in carpentry for women a few years ago. The one pictured is a double-edged saw; one side has coarse rip teeth for cutting wood with the grain, and the other side has more closely spaced cross-cut teeth, for (did you guess?) cutting across the grain. It looks like a most imposing spatula, and unlike the American toolbox saw, it cuts on the pull stroke—a much easier and more elegant way to saw, to my way of thinking. And when the saw gets dull, you can buy a replacement blade.

Cutting tools.

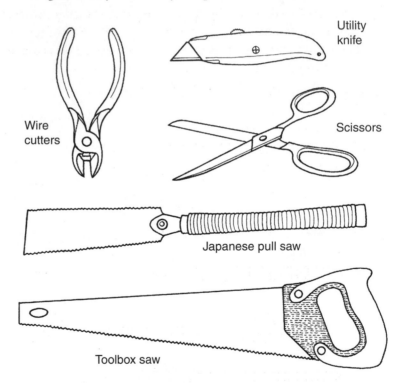

Utility knife

Wire cutters

Scissors

Japanese pull saw

Toolbox saw

What Pros Know _____

The first time I used a toolbox saw, I started hacking away, using pressure while I pushed down and pressure when I pulled back. Being a more sensitive creature than you'd think, the saw bucked and whined, and later, my husband accused me of dulling the blade. He was right! Saws cut one way; most American saws will cut on the push—the downstroke; Japanese saws will cut on the pull movement. I never noticed this little wrinkle when I was growing up, watching my Dad do stuff around the house. But now I know. If you get a chance to try before you buy, you can decide which type of saw you prefer.

Putting It Together: Tools for Fastening and Joining

Nail meets wall, screw meets joist. Putting things together is a major part of home repair and improvement. Having a good selection of tools to make this togetherness happen is an important facet of homeownership. Because, as you will discover, things meant to be together will sometimes fall apart!

Fastening/joining tools.

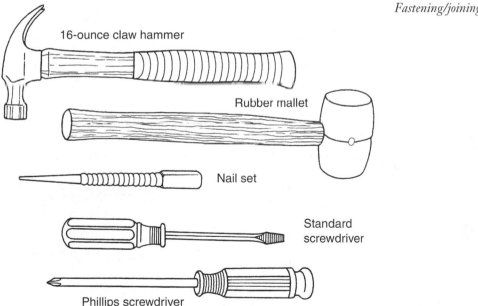

16-ounce claw hammer

Rubber mallet

Nail set

Standard screwdriver

Phillips screwdriver

Basic Tools

A hammer is such a basic piece of equipment that it should be anyone's going-away present when leaving the comfort of Mom and Dad's house, where things so magically stayed together. A *16-ounce claw hammer*, with a curved claw for pulling out nailing mistakes, is a good basic size and style. You can tell the difference between this one and the larger framing hammer (for putting up walls and other work requiring nailing above one's head, or at funny angles), because the framing hammer has a longer handle.

There is usually such an array of hammers at the home center or hardware store that you may have trouble choosing. Pick what feels good in your hand. Don't choke up on the hammer handle, but use the handle as an extension of your arm. If the 16-ounce model feels too heavy, drop down to a 12-ounce. But don't go for a cheap, wimpy, 7-ounce hammer (these are sometimes part of an equally cheap set of fastening/joining tools). This mini is good for tacks but not much else.

Sometimes you need to drive in a nail but don't want to damage the surrounding area, so the metal head of your claw hammer won't do. An inexpensive *rubber mallet* gets the job done.

Another tool that lets you drive a nail below a surface (called countersinking) while leaving the surrounding area undisturbed is a *nail set*. Often sold in sets of three or more standard sizes to match different nail heads, you can position the nail set over the nail head to drive your nail smoothly "underground."

A good selection of screwdrivers belongs in every tool kit. Composed of a shank with a flat tip that looks like a minus sign (-), called a *standard* screwdriver, or a tip that looks like a plus sign (+) called a *Phillips* screwdriver, with a handle of wood, metal, or some type of hardened plastic, screwdrivers are available in a number of point sizes. Shanks also come in a number of different lengths: long shanks let you reach into tight spaces; short, stubby shanks give you more turning power.

What Pros Know

Always use the right size driver for the fastener you are driving. Use the Phillips screwdriver for Phillips head screws (more prevalent than single-slot screws today). Use the standard driver for slotted screws. Too-big or too-small driver points can damage or deform the fastener. And don't forget this helpful saying: "Righty, tighty; lefty, loosey." Translation: tighten by turning to the right (clockwise); loosen by turning to the left (counterclockwise). It works for screws, nuts, light bulbs. Any threaded object turns on the same principle.

Specialized Tools

A good hammer and half a dozen screwdrivers will suffice for probably 75 percent of the joining and fastening tasks in your home. But other fastening tools, for grasping and turning specialized fasteners, and holding the work while you do the job, are great to have on hand.

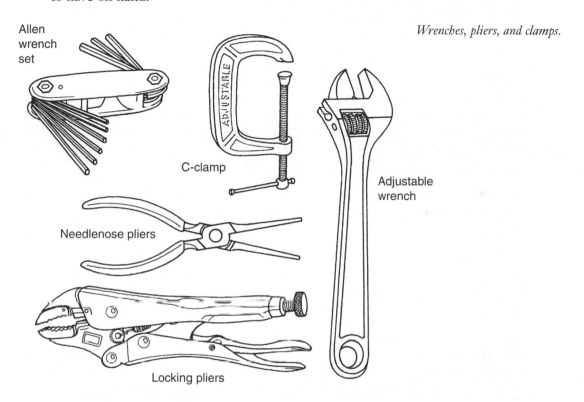

Allen wrench set

C-clamp

Needlenose pliers

Locking pliers

Adjustable wrench

Wrenches, pliers, and clamps.

Nuts, big bolts, pipes, hard-to-reach wires—sooner or later, you'll have a job that requires more specialized gear to help you grab hold of an irregularly sized piece of something, keep it steady, turn it, move it, or attach it to something else.

Sometimes, door latches, light fixtures, or other house hardware is joined with fasteners that require a hexagonal tool, called an *Allen (or hex) wrench* to attach or detach a part. Allen wrenches are sold in sets, sometimes conveniently encased in a penknife-like sheath. This is a good way to buy them, since the wrenches are comparatively small and easy to lose. Simply extend the right size wrench, leaving the others tucked away in the sheath.

An *adjustable wrench* is a great way to get hold of a nut so that you can loosen and remove it from its bolt. The jaws of the wrench hold tight to the nut with a few turns of the little adjusting gear. While you can buy a set of wrenches that fit perfectly around each size nut, often the size you need will be missing from the set. (This has happened to me more than once at crucial moments such as—gulp!—Christmas Eve, with something complicated that needs assembly.) An adjustable model is inexpensive and versatile.

If you're all thumbs, *needlenose pliers* are perfect for "grab and twist" workouts with wires of all types—phone, electrical, audio. They look just like their name sounds. If you're working with electric wires, choose a model with insulated handles, one of the many safeguards against shocks you'll learn about as you read this book.

Locking pliers are another handy tool; the most famous variety is the Vise-Grip brand, invented by a smart Danish-American from Nebraska named William Peterson. He wanted a tool that worked like pliers and could grip metal parts in his blacksmith shop "like a vise." They still do, and several manufacturers have variations on this tool, which has a lever that locks the jaws of the pliers in place. They work like a third hand for many jobs.

Ounce of Prevention

If you want to protect the surfaces you're clamping together, insert little pieces of wood or cardboard, also known as shims, between the clamp jaws and the work piece, so the clamps don't leave a mark.

When you have to glue things together and hold them tightly in place until the adhesive dries, *C-clamps* will do the job. There are a variety of other, more expensive clamping devices, and you can explore the shelves of the hardware or woodworking shop when the time comes to expand your collection.

Demolition Derby: Tools That Take Things Apart

The pros call it "demo," and they usually enjoy this part of home improvement: you see the results of your work nearly instantly. Some of you may think this sounds like your kind of fun. But before you start tearing up that 70s shag carpet in the den, remember that you'll have to figure out what to do with what lies beneath the fuzzy, matted mess. And it might not be pretty. So before you tear anything apart, think: can I live with the result for a while?

Sometimes you get lucky. In one room of our family's Maine house, armed with utility knives and small pry bars to remove the furring strips, my niece and I tore out an old, worn red carpet that was driving me crazy. It was a messy job, but we found a wax-and-buff-ready maple floor beneath.

We were not so lucky in the kitchen. Beneath the multicolor indoor/outdoor carpet was a glued-down layer of carpet padding. Beneath that was a layer of brown linoleum with yellow, red, and green spots. And beneath that was a layer of fifty-year-old gooey black adhesive. Having made this discovery in an inconspicuous corner of the kitchen, I knew my limits, and called in the pros. But it was several months before they could schedule the work and reveal the golden planks of the original maple floor.

So be careful about using your demolition tools!

Pry bars come in many different sizes; keep one that's about 8"–10" long in your tool kit. It can neatly squeeze under old tile, flooring, or carpet furring strips, and its lever action plus your muscles make quick work of many demo jobs. (One company even calls its model the "Wonder Bar," a great name for this handy tool.)

I've always been a cat person, but never heard of the handy *cat's paw* until I went to carpentry class. Like its larger cousin the crowbar, this sturdy tool is a fairly heavy (for its size) round or hexagonal bar of steel. It curves at one end to form a cup-shaped tip with a V-slot that can grip around a nail head. Hammer just above the back of the V-slotted tip, working the slot around the nail head. When the nail head is seated in the slot, rock back the cat's paw and the nail glides out (finish it off with your hammer claw). It's a beautiful piece of equipment for removing nails when you don't care how the surrounding wood looks afterwards (you can lessen the damage by sliding a shim under the "heel" of the V-slotted paw as you work out the nail). You may not need this tool right away, but when you get to taking out old work with lots of nails, this will come in handy.

A *cold chisel* is another one of those old tools that show up at tag sales on the cheap. It gets its name from the fact that this tempered steel cutter is used for cutting "cold" metals, and not used in conjunction with heat, as in torches or forges. Paired with a hammer to drive its point, it's a good tool for removing cemented tile. Just remember that when you're cutting into hard materials, these can chip and fly. Always wear safety goggles and other protective gear; see Chapter 2 for the particulars.

Demolition tools.

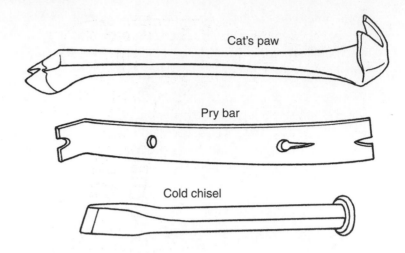

Cat's paw

Pry bar

Cold chisel

The One Tool You Can't Live Without

For the repairs in this book, you'll need just one basic power tool: an *electric drill*. Corded models have been around for years, but battery-powered drills are so improved that they are worth more than a second look. You won't have to plug into a socket with the cordless variety, so it's much more versatile. For optimum use time, buy one with a charger and two batteries (one to use, one spare to keep charged when you're doing a lot of drilling and don't want to lose power at a crucial moment).

A visit to the power tool department of your hardware or home center can be a heady experience: so many drills, lots of different prices. When considering which to buy, think about what you need.

What Pros Know

Don't forget the feel-good factor! Get a drill with the features you want, but also make sure it feels comfortable in your hands and doesn't weigh you down. If it doesn't feel right, you've wasted your good money.

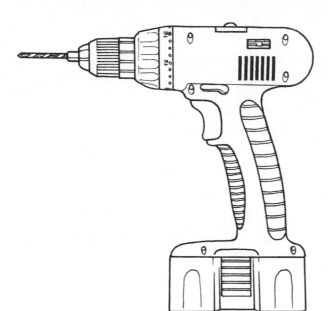

Cordless electric drill.

Power

Most DIY (not pro-grade) corded models quote power in the range of 500 to 1,000 watts. The higher-wattage models will have sturdier parts and be able to take more abuse.

Same with cordless; 9.6-volt batteries don't pack the power of a 12V- or 18V-powered cordless drill. If you are going to use the drill a lot, or want it to last, opt for the most power you can handle (the higher voltage battery packs and sturdier parts increase the weight of the tool).

There are different types of batteries for cordless drills; the most common are Nickel Metal Hydride (Ni-Mh) and Nickel Cadmium (Ni-Cd, or "ni-cad").

Speed

Single-speed drills lack versatility. If you're using large bits for big holes, the bit needs to turn more slowly or you'll wear out the bit quickly. A step-up option is a drill with two fixed speeds—there's usually a manual switch that makes this adjustment.

A variable speed control offers an infinite number of speeds up to an indicated (read the package) limit. You control the speed by a trigger, and some drills have adjustable trigger stops so you don't accidentally put the tool in overdrive when high speed is not needed.

Keyless Chuck

In the old days, bits were inserted into the business end of the drill by opening and closing the *chuck* (which holds the shaft of the bit) with a key. After a bunch of years, manufacturers realized that people always lost the key, so drills with a keyless chuck are pretty standard these days. Lots of pros love them; my dad had one, but I haven't seen a keyed chuck drill in years! $^3/_8$" is the most common chuck size, and right for the work in this book.

Screwdriving

For your drill to work like a screwdriver, it needs three attributes: variable speed, a reverse drive, and a torque control that shuts off the drill when a certain turning force is reached. You know the drill has this last feature if there's a numbered dial (up to 16 positions). Torque control prevents you from driving the screw too deeply or too tightly.

Helpful Bits About Drilling

If you've never used an electric drill before, know that it's destined to make many home repairs simpler than you can imagine. Here are a few tips for using it safely and well:

What Pros Know

If you're driving a bunch of screws, find the right turning force for the job by testing your setting and screw on a scrap piece (wood or drywall). Oh, and one more thing: to use the drill like a screwdriver you'll need screwdriver bits!

- Always wear safety goggles when you drill. That stuff you're drilling has to go somewhere, and you don't want that somewhere to be your eyes.

- Use the highest speeds for jobs that use the small bits, and slower speeds for big bits.

- Indent your drill-in point with a nail or the tip of a nail or screw. This will prevent the drill from sliding off the mark.

- Leave the motor running when you're removing the bit from your work. If the drill ever gets stuck in the work, turn off the drill and then restart it in reverse.

Put It There! Applying the Right Stuff

Lots of repairs use patching compounds, adhesives, and other stuff best applied (or smoothed) with a tool. These are almost self-explanatory:

◆ *Putty knives* come in a variety of widths; they're great for applying all kinds of goop for various repair chores. They're also quite useful for scraping, lifting, and prying in certain circumstances. A narrow one (2") and a broader one (4–6") are a good basic pair to own. Better models have metal ends on the handles that will take the force of a hammer (when you're trying to open a stuck window, for example) without breaking the handle.

◆ A 2" nylon-bristle *paintbrush* and a clean *old toothbrush* can be used to brush away dust or other particles, and also to apply various liquids.

◆ A household *sponge* is good for cleanups, but it's also good as an applicator for certain liquids. Keep a clean one handy.

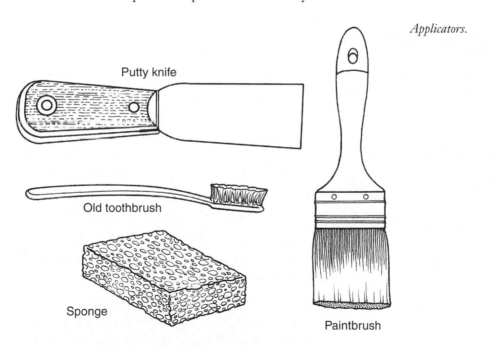

Applicators.

Putty knife

Old toothbrush

Sponge

Paintbrush

Hold It! Transporting Your Tools

Box, bag, or bucket? When you're assembling tools to do a repair job, it's good to have a container that holds everything you need. I like my canvas rigger's bag. It holds a ton of tools, was inexpensive, and is incredibly sturdy. However, you can get a tool bucket, which is an ordinary bucket equipped with a canvas tool holder that makes an incredibly roomy tool caddy. Or opt for a conventional toolbox. Go for sturdy, go for capacity, and choose a container that has enough slots for those tools you want to keep handy, or those you want to protect from other tools banging against them.

Tool bag.

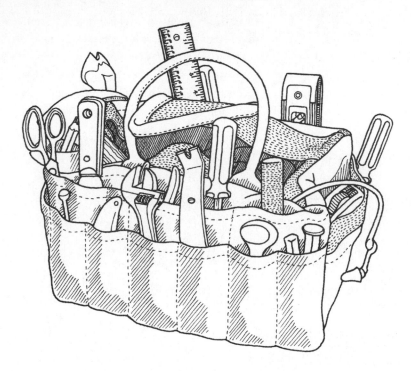

Tool belts are another personal choice. I like the simple canvas apron that costs a couple of dollars. It has a few sturdy pockets to held the fasteners I'm using and a small tool or two. I use the tool bag to carry the rest of the stuff. Too many tools around my waist weigh me down.

Some people opt for the heavy belt with leather or canvas pockets and a nice loop in which to slide the handle of your hammer. My husband bought me one of these when I went off to carpentry class. I use it sometimes, but the hammer kept hitting me in the thigh and gave me a bruise after a week of building. I did notice, however, that my carpentry teacher had a solution for this: she maneuvered the belt so the hammer hung over her backside, and whenever she needed it, she'd just reach back and pull it out. What's that old saying? Each to his/her own!

I Can See Clearly Now

No set of tools is complete without a working flashlight. Because so much repair goes on in basements, attics, and other dimly-lit recesses of the house, buy one that fits in your tool bag, make sure it lights, and stick an extra set of batteries for it in the bag for good measure!

Flashlight.

Your Work Space

Most of the repairs in this book are done on-site, where the damage has occurred. But once in a while you'll need to cut or saw something, and will need a flat, durable surface on which to place and maneuver your work.

If you're reading this book, you probably don't have a big, fancy workbench with a *vise* to hold things. The good news is: there are many fairly inexpensive substitutes for this handyman's standby.

If you're old enough to remember the film *The Graduate*, when actor Dustin Hoffman was a young man, there's a memorable scene when an old guy gives our hero a word to live by: *plastics*.

def•i•ni•tion

A **vise** is a tool with two jaws, closed by a screw or a lever to hold objects immobile.

If you've got very little space to set up a workbench, a couple of companies now make very sturdy, hardened plastic, portable workbenches that fold into a couple of inches of space in a small closet, and give you a place to set and clamp your work. This is a worthy investment.

And if you're a purist, a sheet of plywood clamped to a pair of sawhorses (you can buy a sturdy, folding, portable pair for less than forty bucks) will serve you well for most jobs, and also fits into a small space for storage.

Ounce of Prevention

Never work with a saw or other cutting device without clamping the work piece to the work surface. 'Nuf said.

The key here is sturdy, stable, and clamp-able. A work surface should support your work and keep it steady, and you should be able to hold your work piece in place with a clamp.

When you graduate from DIY 101, you can move on up to one of those big hardwood workbenches that sell for a couple of hundred bucks at specialty wood-working shops. But you won't need it right now.

The Least You Need to Know

- ◆ Cheap tools don't last long; get the basics, but get the best you can afford.

- ◆ Tools can be categorized by their functions: measuring and marking, cutting, fastening and joining, demolition, and application.

- ◆ An electric drill should be your first power tool; look for features you'll really use, and a model that feels good in your hands.

- ◆ You need a stable, sturdy surface for some DIY work where you can clamp a piece that needs cutting or sawing.

- ◆ There are portable options that are easy to store if your working space is limited.

Your Most Important Tool: The Safety Drill

In This Chapter

- ◆ Seven habits of intact DIY-ers
- ◆ What gear you'll need to stay safe when working on your house
- ◆ Ladder safety, top to bottom
- ◆ How to set your own limits, and hire a pro when you need one

Okay, so you just bought a house, and a slew of new tools, and you're ready to fix everything that seems to be ailing your new digs.

Not so fast. You've got one more little investment to make, and that's the insurance you provide for your own personal safety. I'm not talking about your homeowner's policy, but the commonsense rules you follow when you work on your house.

A few years ago, I wanted to expand my DIY know-how and signed up for a course in carpentry. I was eager to learn, and couldn't wait to get my hands on some of the terrific tools that make renovation and improvement easier to do myself. Before the course ever started, the school sent me a list of safety equipment to bring and use. And when my classmates and I arrived, our teachers sat us down for a discussion of self-protection and good work habits. Their guidance was invaluable to my class, and to any beginner do-it-yourselfer who wants to stay safe.

I've used the equipment I brought, and the rules I learned, ever since. Except for a couple of minor scrapes and bruises, the knowledge has served me well. I'll share it here.

Good Safety Habits

Basically, there are seven things to keep in mind when you work on your home. Think of them as the seven habits of intact DIY-ers:

1. **Choose the right wardrobe.** When you work with tools, don't wear anything that can get tangled up in your work. Leave off the bracelets, earrings, and anything that dangles. If you have long hair, tie it back or wear it up, or under a cap or bandanna.

   Wear comfortable work clothes. If you are working with something dusty, or something that makes debris, cover up!

   Sturdy shoes that cover your feet, with non-slip soles, will help prevent injury. Never wear sandals or flip-flops; they're an invitation to hazards like splinters and dropped tools—ow!

2. **Make sure your tools are clean and in good repair.** Inspect the cords of power tools and extension cords for signs of wear. Never work with damaged equipment.

3. **Wear your safety gear.** The goggles and earplugs will do nothing to protect your eyes and your hearing if you leave them in your bag. Carry and use your safety equipment, every time!

4. **Check your attitude.** Don't tackle a job if you're feeling tired, rushed, or upset. You're setting yourself up to lose focus, and that's when accidents happen.

5. **Take a break every couple of hours.** If you need a breather, hang out with your family, kids, or pets away from the worksite. Chit-chat can be distracting while you're working on something, so save the socializing for your timeout.

Ounce of Prevention

Sturdy shoes are good, but steel- or titanium-toed work boots are better. Spring for a pair and you won't have to worry about broken toes. These industrial-strength boots are available in men's and women's sizes. My friend Siobhan, who installed all the siding on her 4,000-square-foot house, put pink shoe laces in her steel-toed footwear for a feminine touch! She keeps the ends of the laces tucked in to prevent tripping.

6. **Keep your worksite organized and clean.** Protect nonwork areas from debris with drop cloths and/or newspaper. Carefully follow the directions for any chemicals or compounds you are using; if they say "make sure the area is well-ventilated," open the windows!

7. **When you need one, ask a friend to help.** If you're working on a ladder that needs holding, or just need an extra pair of hands, make sure you've got the assistance you need.

Lastly, trust your gut! If a little voice inside your head says, "Maybe this job is just too much for me," listen. Better to pay a pro than the bill from the E.R.

Safety Gear: The Basics

Here's a rhyming couplet to remember:

Eyes, ears, nose,

Fingers and toes!

When you finish a repair job, you want to keep all those parts I've just mentioned!

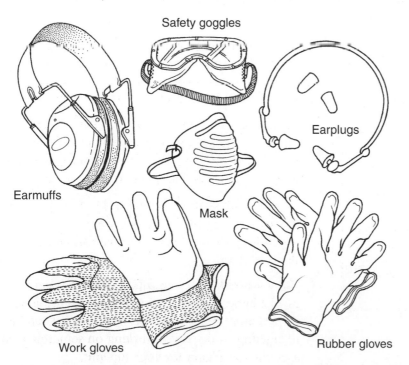

Safety gear: don't start a job without it!

Safety goggles

Earplugs

Earmuffs

Mask

Work gloves

Rubber gloves

Good *safety goggles* are not designed for high fashion, but to protect your eyes and their socket area from injury. They are usually made of high-quality plastic and won't shatter when hit; they'll also protect eyes from spilled or airborne liquids. Make sure the pair you use gives good coverage. Some styles use conventional earpieces, just like eyeglasses or sunglasses; others are secured by elastic. Just make sure the pair you select fits, and stays on when you're looking up, down, and side-to-side.

What Pros Know

At a certain age, most people need glasses to magnify close work, such as reading fine print, attaching/detaching jewelry clasps, and discerning the details of a home repair. Instead of wearing your reading glasses under goggles, which can feel uncomfortable and appear awkward, look for a pair of safety goggles equipped with magnifying lenses; these make the goggles look like bifocals. These specialized glasses are made by at least one major manufacturer of work safety equipment, in varying strengths (1.5, 2.0, 2.5, and so forth). If you can't find them in your local hardware/home center, check Appendix B for a source.

Hearing loss is a progressive ailment; it results from long-term exposure to high levels of noise. Foam *earplugs* or safety *earmuffs* should be used in noisy work environments—when power tools or other loud equipment is in use. It isn't necessary, but I also like to wear my safety earmuffs when I'm using any equipment that makes noise I don't like—the vacuum cleaner, for instance. Even though I haven't seen any evidence that proves vacuum noise can hurt your hearing long-term, it makes the experience more pleasant for me!

Wearing a *mask*, also called a respirator, to avoid inhaling dust or chemical-laden fumes is always a good idea. In order to get the right mask, you need to read the manufacturer's label. Depending on the products you are working with, you will need differing amounts of protection. Masks are labeled for the kinds of dust and fumes they filter.

There are several different types of disposable masks, which are the economical choice unless you are working repeatedly with materials that produce particles or fumes you don't want to breathe. If you're doing a lot of work that requires protecting your lungs, then it might be more budget-wise to buy a reusable respirator, which has replaceable filters, rather than a large quantity of disposable masks.

A pair of sturdy *work gloves* in a heavyweight fabric—canvas, leather, or one of the rugged new synthetic fabrics—will protect your hands when you're carrying materials that could splinter or irritate your hands in some other way. Unless you lose them, a good pair can last a lifetime. *Rubber gloves* will protect your hands from prolonged exposure to liquid, and a tight-fitting pair of surgical-style latex gloves can protect your skin from irritants often found in certain paints, adhesives, and other repair compounds. (If you're allergic to latex, use a different type of tight-fitting glove to protect your hands.)

As discussed in the previous section, wear appropriate, sturdy footwear to protect your toes!

Ounce of Prevention

Not all safety masks are created equal. The National Institute for Occupational Safety and Health (NIOSH) sets standards for workplace safety equipment. When a product is labeled "NIOSH approved," it means that the mask meets certain workplace standards for the process and/or material (painting, drywall, fiberglass) indicated.

The Job Site

If you can set up, work, and finish your repair in a day, the seven habits of intact DIY-ers should be enough rules to keep you safe.

For projects of longer duration, remember the following:

◆ Train your kids, your pets, your elders—anyone who's not working with you—to keep away from a work site unless they're invited to observe. You can show them what you're up to when you're on a break.

◆ Repair materials and tools should be safely stored away whenever you finish for the day. If toxic materials like paint and solvents or power tools are being used, keep them out of reach of children or pets, even when you just step away for a couple of minutes.

◆ Drop cloths and spread-out newspaper can be slippery for other members of your household who are not dressed for the work; pick them up and sweep at the end of a repair session. Replace the protective coverings when you start the next day (or the next weekend).

This may seem logical to most readers, but sometimes an extra step for safety—securing tools and materials *just in case* a child or pet may get curious, or carefully picking up *just in case* someone's not paying attention—seems like too much work to others. Making a mistake that someone you love might have to pay for is just too high a price.

Be safe, not sorry.

The Ups and Downs of Ladder Safety

When you have jobs in tall places, a ladder is a terrific help. But be careful! According to the American Academy of Orthopedic Surgeons (AAOS), more than half a million people wind up in emergency rooms every year because of mishaps with ladders. Don't become another statistic. Follow these tips to stay safe.

Choosing a Ladder

Safety begins when you choose your ladder. Most people start with a stepladder that's good for indoor jobs, and some outdoor work as well.

- **Materials:** Wood is traditional, but subject to rot and weathering. Aluminum is lightweight, but metal is not good for working around electricity. Fiberglass is the current preference of professionals; it is versatile, lightweight, and sturdy, but more expensive than either wood or aluminum.

- **Height:** If you have standard, 8-foot ceilings, a 5-foot stepladder will probably be fine for any indoor task, and a lot of outdoor work, too. For stepladders, the ladder's height plus 4 feet equals the height limit you can achieve.

- **Strength:** Ladders have a duty rating—the amount of weight they can carry—established by the American National Safety Institute. Type 1A extra heavy duty carries up to 300 pounds; Type I heavy duty will carry 250 pounds; Type II medium duty 225 pounds; and Type III light duty 200 pounds. Err on the side of a heavier rated model when you're in doubt as to which model to choose.

Ounce of Prevention

When you buy a stepladder, there will usually be a sticker on the pail shelf that says "This is not a step," and one on the step below the top of the ladder that says "Do not stand above this step." Take these cautions seriously. If you need to climb higher, you'll need a taller ladder.

Using a Ladder

Safe ladder use means taking a few steps in the right direction:

◆ Don't wear leather soles; they're slippery. And tie your shoelaces securely. Likewise, don't wear baggy pants or loose clothing that could catch on the sides of a ladder or nearby obstructions.

◆ Inspect your ladder before you use it. Check it for any loose screws, hinges, or rungs. Clean off any dirt, grease, or dried spills. If the ladder has defects that can't be fixed, replace it.

◆ Place the ladder on a firm, level surface. Don't place a ladder on uneven ground, or prop up with bricks or other small items under the legs.

◆ Climb or descend with your hands on the side rails, not on the treads.

◆ Never position a ladder in front of a door that opens in the direction of the ladder unless the door is locked, blocked, or guarded on the other side. If you're working while other household members are moving around, put some tape and a sign across the door frame on the inside so they don't accidentally open it and topple you!

◆ Don't stretch—move the ladder instead. Reaching or leaning too far to either side of the ladder can make you lose your balance and fall. The AAOS has a good guideline: your bellybutton should not go beyond the sides of the ladder!

◆ Move things with caution; if you're cleaning out closet or garage shelves, always keep the load in your arm small enough that it doesn't throw you off balance. Push and pull things carefully.

◆ Get help if you need it. If you feel the least bit wobbly, have someone hold the ladder. And two people should never be *on* the ladder at the same time.

When you're outside, you may need to use an extension ladder if you have tall gutters or need to reach an outside light to replace it. Learn additional rules of using long ladders in Chapter 19.

Keep your body centered on the ladder.

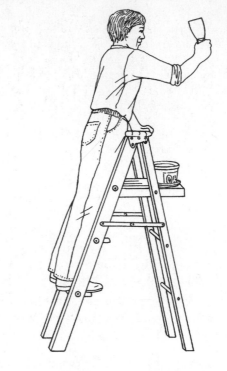

Don't lean far outside the rails of the ladder. It's easy to lose your balance in this position.

Knowing Your Limits: When to Call a Pro

Some people like to try everything; others know what they're good at, and only occasionally stray into unfamiliar territory. Only you know your own degree of risk tolerance for DIY tasks. You may really like working on walls and floors—all those nice, solid things—but go queasy at the idea of clearing the gunk-clogged trap under the kitchen sink.

It's best to start your DIY career with those jobs that you feel comfortable and safe doing. As you build your confidence, you can tackle more things.

Here are three questions to ask yourself before you try doing a new kind of repair:

◆ Do I have the time?

◆ Do I have the tools—or can I get them easily?

◆ Do I have the skill?

The tasks in this book are not large ones; they require only small amounts of labor, tools, and know-how. This is, after all, a guide to *simple* home repairs. But if any jobs in this book make you hesitate for more than a few minutes after reading the instructions, or if you have to answer "no" to any of the three questions listed above, then you're probably right to call in the pro.

And should you call the handyman, the plumber, or the electrician, watch him or her do the job. You may learn something you'll be able to do yourself—next time.

The Least You Need to Know

◆ Eyes, ears, nose, fingers, and toes all need protection when you work.

◆ Tackle repairs when you're rested and calm; working when you're tired or stressed invites accidents.

◆ When on a ladder, stay centered; when you need to lean out to reach what you're after, it's time to move the ladder.

◆ Know thyself! Make your first home repairs the ones you feel most comfortable with. Success begets confidence.

Chapter 3

Your Supply Closet

In This Chapter

- ◆ Where to store your tools and supplies for home repairs
- ◆ Which supplies solve different repair dilemmas
- ◆ The subtle differences between fasteners
- ◆ The importance of leftovers (the home repair kind)

There are a couple of rules about household repair problems and the supplies that fix them:

1. Repair emergencies usually happen at night, or on weekends and holidays when it's hard to find someone to help you.

2. A few inexpensive supplies can save a lot of money and grief.

If you can impress upon yourself that bad stuff will happen to your house at the worst possible times, you will not be stuck, as I was, trying to stop a leaky pipe with my finger while being told by my plumber's answering service that he wouldn't be back for a week. I had an infant and a 3-year-old, and had to shut off the water to the whole house while the kids and I drove to the home center at 9 P.M. for emergency repair supplies. Of course, my husband was out of town!

DIY Depot: Storing Your Repair Stuff

All the tools and materials in the world are worthless if you can't put your hands on the right item when you need it.

Lots of handy gentlemen and ladies dedicate a corner of their spotless garage to a workbench and storage area, but maybe you're not lucky enough to have such a clean corner, or even a garage.

A closet shelf, a cleared cabinet—any place you can get to easily, but also close off and make child- and pet-proof, if these wonderful creatures share your home with you, is fine for storage.

> **Ounce of Prevention**
>
> You do not want your children playing with grown-up tools, tampering with sharp objects like nails and screws, or investigating the contents of bottles of adhesives or cans of lubricants. Whatever place you choose for your repair tools and supplies, make sure it's out of the reach of children and pets. If not, secure the door of your supply storage area with a keyed or combination lock.

The Supply Side

As your home repair savvy grows, you'll be doing more jobs and adding to your supply cabinet. But for starters, here are some basic supplies to keep on hand.

Keep It Moving: Lubricants

The places where parts come together often need a bit of help to move smoothly and quietly, or to get unstuck when they haven't been moved in a while.

A spray or liquid *lubricant* can help when you've got a noisy hinge, a draggy sliding door, or a nut that just won't turn when you're trying to loosen it. WD-40 is a popular brand of lubricant that comes in a can; it has a narrow straw that attaches to its sprayer so that you can direct a stream of lubricant to a precise location.

Lubricants are useful for hundreds of chores and repairs. Special lubricants that contain a high percentage of silicon are often helpful for moving parts made of wood, vinyl, or rubber. See Appendix B for more helpful information.

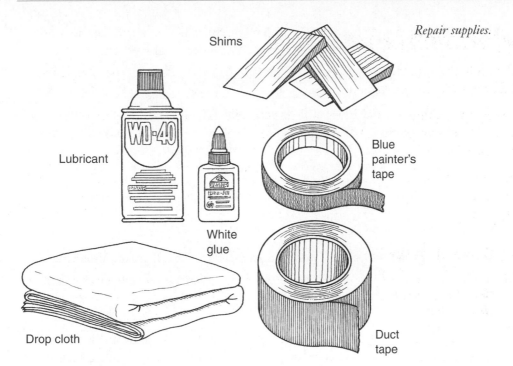

Repair supplies.

Shims

Lubricant

White glue

Blue painter's tape

Drop cloth

Duct tape

Keep It Together: Adhesives

While there are many varieties of adhesive—for every kind of material that can break or fall apart—you can start with a single basic type. *White glue*, available in supermarkets, stationery stores—virtually everywhere—is good for sticking together paper, cardboard, wood, leather, cloth, and lots of other materials. Keep a container in your supply closet. Keep in mind, however, that it's not waterproof; you'll need a different adhesive when water resistance is required.

When you start working with wood, add a container of carpenter's (wood) glue, which is usually yellow and of the same consistency as white glue.

Specialized adhesives—instant glue or contact cement, for example—are powerful products that create an incredibly tough and virtually instantaneous bond. If you use them, follow directions carefully, and keep the appropriate solvent on hand in case you stick your fingers together!

Blue painter's tape, like the familiar off-white masking tape, is a light-duty adhesive tape that is easy to apply and remove. The blue variety is called painter's tape because its adhesive is formulated to lift off a surface without damaging a new coat of paint; regular masking tape can be difficult to remove because it makes a tighter bond, and will often lift off the new paint, shred, or leave a residue if it's left on a surface too long. The blue stuff is good for holding many lightweight objects in place temporarily.

Duct tape—most people know the gray or silver-colored variety—has a strong adhesive backing because its original use was to seal gaps in lengths of flexible ductwork. (This is no longer an approved use in most building codes.) People have found thousands of uses for duct tape, and written books about it, but it's an emergency fix for a lot of breaks and tears in household objects: patching a small hole in window glass until you can replace the pane; holding two pieces of wood together while you screw or nail them. Having it in your supply closet will definitely prove handy at some point.

Fill the Gap

Small *shims* are little wedges of soft wood, usually cedar, that look like miniature shingles. They're useful for closing gaps between stair treads and risers, for example— you'll see them used in some repairs in Chapter 7.

They're also good to level out a table, couch, or chairs when your floors are uneven— just slide a couple under the wobbly leg. While pieces of corrugated cardboard will work as shims in a pinch, a package of these little wooden helpers is cheap; if you've got an older home, I guarantee you'll find uses for them.

Cover It Up

A *drop cloth* is essential for protecting the areas of your home where you're doing a repair. Many people use plastic drop cloths; they're cheap and disposable. But they're also slippery to walk on, and some are so thin that they tear with little provocation. Buy a 9'×12' canvas model and you can shake it out, fold it easily, even wash it when it gets too soiled.

Rub It Off: Abrasives

Get at least one sanding block with a combination of surfaces—a medium-grade grit (80–100) side and a finer grit (120–150) is a nice toolbox standby. It's easier to handle than sheets of sandpaper. 220-grit sandpaper or blocks are good for fine surface work such as touch-ups to floors and furniture.

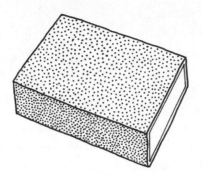

Sanding block.

Eventually, you may also want to get some files: a metal file and a wood rasp for quickly filing edges of these materials.

More Togetherness: A Quick Guide to Fasteners

A variety of fasteners for joining house parts and hanging accessories is good to keep on hand. Invariably if you have a giant coffee can full of wood screws, what you'll need are a couple of brads. Fasteners are generally inexpensive bits of metal, so a good supply won't set you back more than a few dollars.

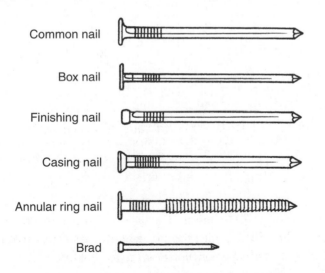

Common nail

Box nail

Finishing nail

Casing nail

Annular ring nail

Brad

An assortment of practical fasteners.

Screws.

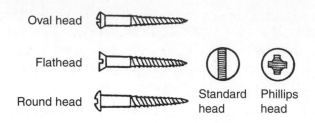

Oval head

Flathead

Round head

Standard head

Phillips head

Common nails and their more slender brothers, *box nails*, are good for general use. They have fairly large heads and good holding power; coated varieties will grip even harder.

Nails used for outside work should be galvanized (zinc coated); in high-moisture areas—by the shore, for example—stainless-steel nails will hold up to the environment best.

Because their heads are relatively large, use common and box nails when surface appearance doesn't matter.

Small-headed nails—*casing* or *finishing nails*—are good for woodwork. Both can be countersunk with a nail set, and the hole filled with wood putty to leave a smooth surface for painting or finishing. Use the smaller *brad* for nailing very thin pieces of molding or paneling.

What Pros Know

In the United States, nails are sized in "pennies," symbolized by the letter "d." This sizing system is a traditional one, going back to England a few hundred years ago. A 2d, or two-penny nail, is 1 inch long; the longest nails, 60d, are 6 inches long. The rule of thumb is to use a nail that is 2½ to 3 times as long as the thickness of the piece being fastened.

For some of the repairs in this book, you'll use *annular ring nails*, which have a grooved shaft to "bite" into wood like a screw.

Screws have great holding power, and because they can be loosened or tightened, they can be removed without undue damage to the surrounding surface. Depending on what's being fastened, you can use *flathead* (flush to the surface), *round head* (sits atop the surface), or *oval head* (usually for decorative use) wood screws.

Wood screws are available with a *standard* (looks like a minus [–] sign) or *Phillips* (looks like a plus [+] sign) driver slot. Some professionals like to use screws with a square slot (called a Robertson), which requires a matching, square-headed driver.

If you like to cover your walls with art, you'll probably have use for an assortment of fasteners for hanging pictures and other decorations. Picture hooks that feature an angled receptacle for driving in a small nail with ease—even into plaster—are good to keep on hand in a range of sizes for items of varying weights, up to about 25 pounds or so. Larger items that must be wall-mounted will use larger fasteners; check with your helpful hardware salesperson about the type and size of fastener best suited to your walls and what you're hanging.

Keep a handful of tacks—the large-headed thumbtacks and small-headed metal tacks—for hanging other small items.

Hold It: Containers

Even when you're not using liquids, a household bucket makes a good tote for tools and supplies for any DIY job. Get a sturdy, good-quality plastic model with an equally sturdy handle for those times when you do transport water (at about 7 pounds per gallon, water can be unwieldy to carry).

Also keep a supply of small lidded containers for those occasions when you need to carry around fasteners, small quantities of liquid, or other little items that can easily go astray.

A variety of containers.

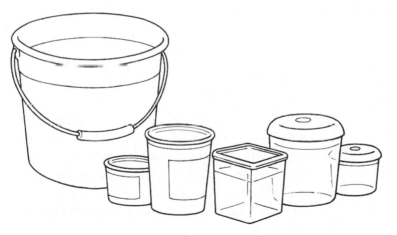

In Case of Small Water Emergencies

Between your tool kit and the supplies I've already described, you're covered for a lot of different small breakdowns in the house. And here are two more things you shouldn't neglect.

Plumbing leaks and backups are the most potentially damaging of the small home repair crises you will encounter day to day. Of course, you can always just shut off the household water at the main (see Chapter 4) and wait for the plumber. But a stopped sink or toilet, or a pinhole leak in a pipe, can be addressed with a couple of simple and inexpensive items.

A plunger, also known as a "plumber's helper," will help you clear many types of clogs in your waste water (drain) system; you can find out how to make these fixes in Chapter 10.

Plunger.

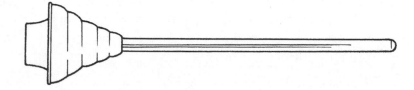

For tiny leaks in supply pipes, you can buy a package of do-it-yourself gasket material (cork or rubber is good), and a couple of adjustable hose clamps that fit your pipe (metal supply pipe is usually $1/2$") to hold back the water until your plumber arrives. This fix is also covered in Chapter 10.

Pipe leak repair supplies.

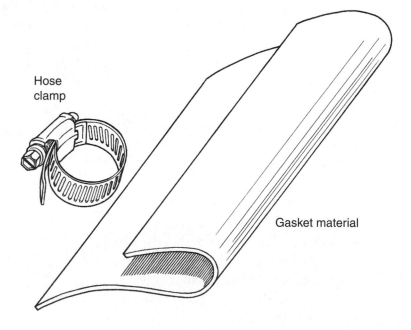

Hose
clamp

Gasket material

Storing Those Leftovers!

Whenever you or a pro do a home improvement project in your house, there's usually material left over: extra tiles, extra paint or wallpaper, carpet scraps, or resilient flooring pieces.

In most houses, there never seems to be enough closets and cabinets to hold all our stuff; those DIY leftovers feel like just another pile of junk to deal with. So too often, the leftovers are thrown out or given away.

Even if you save that last half-roll of bedroom wallpaper, or the extra tile from the bathroom re-do, the tendency is to just throw the stuff in a box and put it anywhere out of the way where the box fits. The problem with that strategy is that you probably won't find it when you need it!

If you look through this book, you'll notice that many of the repair instructions call for leftover this-and-that. So do yourself a favor you'll thank yourself for later. Buy some clear plastic storage containers and keep the leftover stuff in those. Label the containers with what's in them and which room the leftovers came from. It's an easy system, sure to save time, money, and trouble down the road.

In the case of leftover paint—great for touch-ups—you may not need the leftover half-gallon of the custom color in your living room ever again, but you might need a small amount. To have what you need to cover a future minor repair, save a half-pint or pint in a clean, airtight container; label it with the room, paint brand, color name, and color number. You'll be glad you did. Custom colored paint is usually available in gallons only, a big expense and a big waste if you're just doing touch-ups after a small repair.

Check with your local waste removal carrier (private or municipal), about the rules for paint and solvent disposal in your area. Usually, you cannot throw these substances away in the regular household trash pickup.

When you finally move on to your next place, you can give the leftovers to the next owners as a housewarming present. Having replacement parts is always handy!

Ounce of Prevention

Take care not to store certain liquids—like paint or solvents—in your home's hot spots: near a heat source or in attics. Always check the original label; most DIY liquids belong in cool, dry places, with their lids tightly secured.

Closed containers for storing leftover materials.

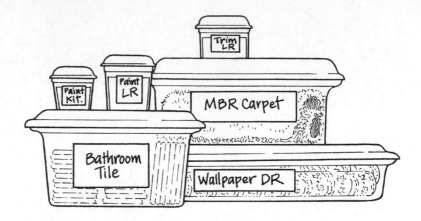

The Least You Need to Know

♦ DIY supplies and materials deserve a dedicated place in your house. Find one that's convenient for you and secure for all family members, including pets.

♦ A well-stocked supply closet includes at least one lubricant, a liquid adhesive and DIY tape, a selection of fasteners, and stuff for cover-ups and clean-ups.

♦ You'll appreciate the value of a plunger and a pipe repair kit after your first night, weekend, or holiday plumbing emergency, when pros are hard to find.

♦ Leftover DIY stuff that you organize and save is destined to be very helpful later.

Chapter 4

A Map of Your World

In This Chapter

- Locating the main controls for the systems in your house
- Starting and stopping water flow, whether it's from a well or from an outside supplier
- Controlling your gas supply, and what to do if you suddenly smell gas
- Safe handling of your electrical panel
- Creating a personal home workbook

You need a lot of information to run a house. Unless you're a person who leads a very simple life, your home has a plumbing system, an electrical system, and maybe a gas supply to heat your home or hot water. If you're out in the country, you probably have a water well and a septic field, too.

Not to mention all those helpful appliances! They have plugs, hoses, switches, gaskets … a whole bunch of parts that may someday give you grief. And when one of them breaks down, you discover that you don't really remember where you tossed that use and care manual; it might have come in handy, if you could find it!

This chapter will help you figure out how to get more control of all the equipment that helps you run your home. You'll get some ideas about how to organize everything you should know about your house in a single location. It will make taking care of things a little bit easier.

The Main Thing: Your Home's Power Centers

The least convenient time to search for the controls for your home's water, gas, and electric service is when something suddenly goes very wrong. In the case of a gas leak, not understanding where and how service comes into your house can be life-threatening. So listen up!

Go to the stationery store, or with your own creative know-how, make labels or tags that say "Main Shutoff" for the primary gas and water valves in your house, as well as for the main electric service panel. Then follow the directions below and on the following pages so you can find, mark, and use them.

Basements are not always well-lit or easy to negotiate, so you'll want to take along a flashlight for this activity. If you don't have a basement, your utilities may be in a dedicated closet, or small room close to where the wires and pipes enter the house. Unless it's well lighted, you'll need a flashlight here, too.

Finding the Flow: Your Water Supply

If your water comes into the house from a municipal or private water company, there will be an outside shutoff for the water as it comes from the main pipe under the street onto your property and into your house. Don't concern yourself with this control, as the shutoff can only be made by water company employees with special tools. (You should call the water company if an unusual flow of water near the street causes you to suspect a leak in the larger system.)

Find the water meter on the outside of your house; then look inside in a corresponding area for the water supply pipe that comes into the house.

The water control in an older home is often a gate valve with a round handle. In newer homes, the straight-handled ball valve has replaced the old-style control.

The gate valve works like any round handled faucet; a clockwise turn (or turns) shuts off the water supply, and counterclockwise turns restore the flow. There's no need to play with it if you don't need to shut off the water supply. When you do need to turn it off, if it's difficult to turn, get your can of lubricant and give the valve a little squirt. If it still won't budge, leave it alone and call the plumber.

Ball valves work differently. They are sturdy and long-lasting, and the best replacement for a worn gate valve. When the water supply is flowing, the handle is in-line (parallel) to the pipe. A quarter-turn (90°) shuts off the water. The ball valve turns off in only one direction, so don't try to force it the wrong way.

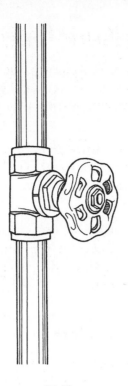

Gate valve.

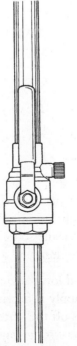

Ball valve in "on" position.

What Pros Know

Ball valves are a lot easier to operate than gate valves. Because main controls are operated infrequently, an old gate valve can become very hard to turn on and off. If you've got one of these antique numbers, and it's looking worn, consider having a plumber replace it the next time you hire him for another job. It's a nasty problem when the main gate valve starts leaking!

Once you've found your main water control, label it "Main Water Shutoff." To make it easier to see in a dark basement, you might want to mark it with fluorescent tape.

Oh, Well

If you live in the country and do not have municipal water service, you'll need to know where your well is located, and figure out where the supply pipe enters your house. The shutoffs will look the same as those for metered service, except that you don't have a meter. Instead, you've probably got an electric pump, positioned deep in your well, that pumps water into holding tanks, and from there into your house.

A well supplies the water for my own house, but fixing the pump is not my kind of work. And the pump always decides to give us trouble on the holidays, when our well service man is otherwise engaged. Fortunately, these pumps are built to last, and breakdowns don't happen often.

However, if a there's a water leak in your house and you want to stop the flow of water, there's an additional water/off option. You can use the main shutoff at the pipe, just as you would shut off the municipal supply, *or* you can go to your electrical panel (see more about this control later in the chapter) and shut off the circuit that controls the well pump.

Where the Well Water Goes

It has to go somewhere, and if you have a private water well that serves your home, chances are your wastewater goes to a septic tank and septic field on your property.

When you bought your house, if you have a septic system you should have gotten a map showing the location of your tank and field. If not, one should be on file at your county Board of Health.

The good news about septic systems is that they work very well—until they don't. If you don't have a company to pump out your septic tank, you should get one and use their services at recommended intervals. (These intervals are based on the number of occupants of your home; the Board of Health sizes septic fields based on the number of bedrooms.) Most septic service companies will put you on a schedule and call when you're due for a pump-out. Do not neglect this regular service!

A septic system is a mess to repair, if the waste (effluent) is blocked from leaving your house via the waste line. And a failed septic system is a huge expense to replace. So make friends with a reliable septic system service company.

Your Gas System (Outside the House)

If you use natural gas for your heating system, hot water, clothes dryer, or stove, your supply also comes in from the street through a pipe that registers your usage at a meter outside the house. Just before the gas meter, you will see a shutoff valve that usually looks like a small, rectangular handle. When this control is parallel to the pipe, it means the gas is flowing. When it's turned perpendicular (90°) to the gas pipe, the gas is turned off.

The outside gas main control requires a wrench to turn it on and off. Like other outside controls for municipal and private utility service, in most cases the outside gas shutoff should only be turned on and off by gas company personnel, or the fire department.

If You Smell Gas

When natural gas comes out of the ground at its source, it has no color or smell. Companies that supply gas to consumers and businesses add the very noticeable odor of rotten eggs to gas so that a leak is easy to detect.

This is very important. If you should ever smell a *strong* odor of natural gas, do not use any devices that might make a spark. Light switches, phones, even turning on a flashlight could ignite the gas and cause an explosion.

Leave your home immediately and take anyone else in the house with you, including pets. Once you're *safely out of and away from the house*, call the gas company or 911 from a neighbor's house or your cell phone, if you've got one.

Other Gas Controls

There is sometimes a gas supply main control inside the house, in addition to the valve outside before the meter. It should be located close to where the gas supply comes into the house. This one (if you've got one) is usually a ball valve, operated in the same way as a water supply main ball valve: parallel to the pipe means the gas is flowing, and perpendicular to the pipe means the gas is off. Label this one "inside main gas control." Like the water supply valve, you may want to use fluorescent tape on the label so it's easy to see in a dark space.

Inside main gas supply control.

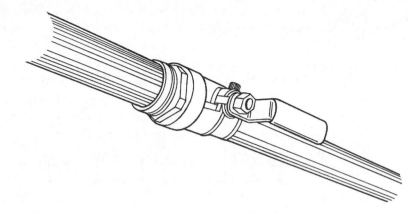

There are also individual controls for every gas appliance in your home. Usually they're located on the metal supply pipe, where it connects to the flexible pipe that supplies the appliance. While the gas *supply stops*, as they are called, may have a slightly different look than the main supply ball valve, they work the same way.

def•i•ni•tion

Supply stops, also known as supply valves, are on/off controls found along household utility supply lines, managing the flow of gas or water to individual fixtures and appliances. Gas supply stops usually work on the principle of the ball valve, with the position in line with supply pipe indicating "on," and a position perpendicular to the pipe indicating "off." Supply stops for water fixtures usually work by turning the stops clockwise for shutoff, and counterclockwise for the open/on position. (Remember: righty, tighty; lefty, loosey.) The handles of water supply stops are usually round or oval, but sometimes older stops look like the gate valve pictured earlier in this chapter.

Propane is a gas derivative of the production of petroleum and natural gas, which is then compressed into a transportable liquid. Many rural homeowners who do not have access to natural gas pipelines use propane to power their gas appliances. Propane is stored in a tank outside the house and piped inside. There is a shutoff at the tank (reserved for the use of the propane service that you pay to keep the tank filled). Inside the house, appliances using propane will have supply stops at the juncture of the supply line and the appliance's gas line. These stops will work the same way as supply stops for natural gas.

Propane is just as flammable as natural gas, and is treated to have the same rotten egg odor if it leaks into the air. If you detect the strong smell of gas, use the same extreme caution as you would with natural gas. Don't fool around, get outside quickly, and call for help.

Your Electric Service

Before you reach for your flashlight to go figure out your home's electrical system, remember that you need to use common sense when working around electrical wiring. Do not even touch the electric service panel if there is standing water in the room where it is located. Don't use both hands to explore the panel; keep one at your side. Touching both hands to the panel completes a circuit (you!), and you don't want to be the recipient of current gone astray. Take care!

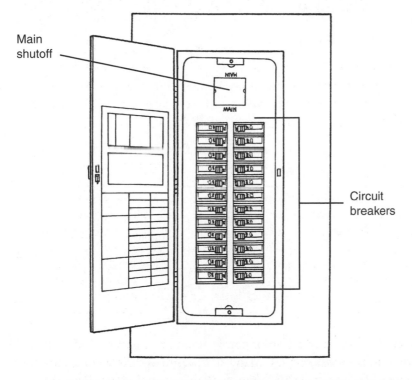

Main shutoff

Circuit breakers

Electric service panel: circuit breaker panel.

Depending upon how old your home is, your electrical controls will be located in a metal box containing fuses—which look like tubes or glass-topped plugs—or toggle switches, called *circuit breakers*. The toggle-switch type of circuit breaker meets current electrical code requirements and has been around for more than 40 years; you'll find fuses in an older house. This metal box is connected to the large insulated wires that come into your house from the electric meter outside, and the electric company's power grid beyond it. The box, called an electric service panel, or "breaker box," is control central for the electric current that powers all the switches, receptacles, and light sockets in your home.

Fuse panel (aka fuse box).

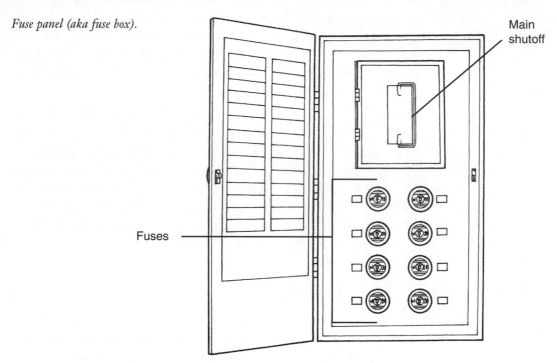

Main shutoff

Fuses

def•i•ni•tion

A **circuit breaker** is a device that stops the flow of electricity in a circuit if there is too much current for safe operation. Both the toggle switches and the fuses used in the two types of service panels act as circuit breakers, but only the toggle-switch type are commonly referred to as circuit breakers. Toggle types move automatically to "off" in an overload. Fuses "blow"; that is, the metal strip inside the fuse melts from the overload. You will have to replace it with the same size and type of fuse.

If you have toggle-type circuit breakers, the main control that turns on and shuts off all the electric current for the house is often (but not always) located at the top of the service panel, above all the other circuit breakers. Sometimes, as in the previous illustration, the main toggle switch is enclosed with a little access door; open the door, and flip the switch to "off" to shut off. If you have fuses, you'll find the main fuse at the top of the box. The main toggle in the circuit breaker panel will usually have a number on it, indicating the type of service coming into your home. This service is measured in *amps* (amperes), so you will usually see the main toggle marked 100, 150, or 200.

Occasionally the main control for the service coming into your house will be located in a different metal box, and sometimes a different location, than the service panel containing the toggle switches or fuses for separate circuits. If you can't locate the main control—if it's not obvious—then you need to call an electrician. They may be nice enough to direct you to the main by instructing you over the phone, or you may need to hire one to explain your system. Either way, you're talking about electricity, so knowledge is much safer than ignorance here.

If you're lucky, someone has taken time to clearly identify all the circuits in the house for you; each toggle switch or fuse is labeled with the rooms, switches, and receptacles, or appliances that each breaker or fuse controls. If not, or if they're labeled ambiguously (for example, the previous owner marked a switch "Grandma's bedroom," so you can't identify it), it's a good idea to create a "map" of all the circuits in your house, then label the switches or fuses in the service panel or fuse box. When the lights shut off from a current overload in the future, you'll be glad you took the time to do this. You'll find instructions for creating a circuit map in Chapter 13.

A Workbook for Your Home

When something goes wrong with the workings of your house, you'll find a lot of solutions in this book. But as you read, you'll find that some instructions contain the words "often," or "usually," or "consult your owner's manual." That's because every mechanical system and appliance may have parts or works that diverge from a certain reliable standard. Perhaps the switch you're looking for is on the back of the appliance, not the front, where it is on 90 percent of the models most people see.

The more information you make available to yourself about your house, its systems, and all the appliances and conveniences it holds, the better able you will be to troubleshoot problems, judge which ones you can handle, and quickly assign the tough chores to the pros.

So, put it all together. Get yourself a 3-ring notebook with a wide spine (3 inches or more). The D-ring style holds pages flat most easily. If you have a lot of notebooks, buy this one in a color you can find quickly (red or yellow are highly visible). Fill it with those clear plastic sheet protectors—the kind that hold multi-page documents. If you want to be really organized, buy a pack or two of dividers, and label them with the name of each room and section of the house: kitchen, baths, bedrooms, living room, basement, attic, garage, and so on.

What will you put in this notebook? Let me give you a few ideas of basic things you can keep in it.

Appliance and Fixture Use and Care Manuals

Not every equipment problem signals the need for a repair or a service call. Sometimes you may have forgotten to turn a switch on or off. Maybe you've tried to start the device improperly. Use and care manuals contain instructions for assembling (when necessary), starting and stopping an appliance or fixture, and using it properly and safely. This handy guide usually has an illustrated diagram of the device, complete with the names and location of all its parts, including the label that will provide the model and serial numbers for your specific piece of equipment.

Often there's a handy section on troubleshooting—that is, strategies for figuring out what's wrong if something's not working properly, usually followed by the manufacturer's 800 helpline number or website URL. In addition, you'll find a listing of authorized service representatives.

These manuals are great. If you've got them all in a drawer somewhere, transfer them to the sheet protectors in your notebook. If you're really organized, file each one behind the divider you've labeled with the name of the room where the equipment is located.

If you're not very organized, now's the time to start. Those little instruction booklets can save you a lot of time!

What Pros Know

Can't find the use and care manual for an appliance or piece of equipment? If you can locate the manufacturer name, model number, and serial number (usually listed on a label somewhere on the device), you may be able to find the manual from the manufacturer's website. This is very possible if your equipment is fairly new, less so if it's more than five to seven years old. Once you find the manual online, you can download and then print a hard copy of it to file in your workbook. (Be sure to have plenty of printer paper and an almost-full ink cartridge before you try to do this.) If an Internet search proves fruitless, try calling the manufacturer's 800-number consumer help line.

Receipts and Manufacturer's/Dealer's Warranties

When something breaks down not long after you've purchased it, it may be covered for service or repair by the existing manufacturer's warranty, or a warranty you purchased from the retailer when you bought the equipment. File your purchase receipt and a copy of the warranty with the use and care manual. If your device is covered, your tool kit can stay in its storage location. In fact, *never try to repair something yourself when it is still under warranty; you'll void the warranty.* Call the number listed on the warranty; or call the dealer, if you purchased the warranty through the retail store.

Some manufacturers guarantee their equipment for life. I never believed I'd take someone up on this promise, and was doubtful that what was promised was indeed true (I can be cynical). But most companies who make this pledge turn out to actually mean it. When my very expensive, guaranteed-for-life kitchen faucet came apart after just a year, I called the manufacturer, and two days later, they had a new one delivered to my door!

Now, there must have been some serious flaw in the design (or in the user—me!) but the faucet broke again about two years later. And, true to its word, the manufacturer sent me another new faucet.

Make use of your lifetime guarantees! They'll save you money and time.

Equipment Manuals or Schematics

Heating and cooling devices (furnaces, central air-conditioning units), water treatment units, and other big items that figure in the major operations of your home, may have been installed long before you arrived. In that case, you may be out of luck on obtaining a manual or a detailed drawing (called a schematic) that illustrates the equipment with labels for its parts. If you've got a drawing or manual, pop it in your workbook. It will help you when something goes wrong with your big systems. Down the road, if and when you sell the house, the buyer will appreciate this documentation.

A Circuit Map of Your Home

If your circuits are clearly labeled, copy the information on a piece of paper to keep in your home workbook. If they're not, you should go to Chapter 13 as soon as you can and learn how to create this valuable map.

Service Records

When you do a repair on any equipment in your home, save the receipt. Make sure you or the professional service person notes the scope of the work and the date it was done. That way if a repair fails you've got a record, and you'll know if you've got a chronic problem with something in your house.

File these records right behind the manuals and warranties you keep for the equipment.

Other Workbook Items

When you do a home improvement—install new carpet, paint a room, upgrade your kitchen—you can put the records and specifications, receipts, and manuals in the appropriate section of your workbook. This is particularly helpful when you're looking to match paint or other materials to do a repair later on.

If you take the time to start it, and use it as information central for all the important components of your house, your personal home workbook will save you hours of time, and probably lots of money!

The Least You Need to Know

- The proper time to find out where to find the controls for your water, gas, and electric service is before there's a problem—that is, *right now*.

- Label all the main shutoffs to make them easy to see and read.

- If you can't locate your main controls, don't hesitate. Call a pro who can help you find them.

- For easy reference, for saving time and money, and for troubleshooting problems, create a home workbook to keep your manuals, diagrams, and service and repair records in one place.

Part 2

Skin Deep: Repairing Surfaces and Openings

Walls, floors, ceilings, stairs, windows, and doors are the first things you see when you look at a house. If the heating system and appliances are like its vital organs, a home's surfaces are like its skin. And although neglecting surfaces will not usually make a house fall down, they're components that everyone notices.

Unfortunately, like our own skin, these parts of the house show signs of aging and the bruises of long and continued use. Your house may have little indicators of time passing—nicked walls, bumpy floors, doors and stairs that squeak and sigh. It's inevitable, just like wrinkles.

But if you're not yet ready for the face lift—a full-tilt, expensive renovation—there are a lot of small repairs and cosmetic fixes that will brighten this top layer of your house, and help you enjoy it more. Part 2 gives you lots of ideas and plenty of instruction.

"Make my day."

Chapter **5**

Walls: From Trash Talk to Smooth Talk

In This Chapter

- ◆ Making minor repairs to drywall surfaces, and patching a larger hole
- ◆ Repairing small cracks in plaster
- ◆ Replacing grout, and removing and replacing a cracked or broken ceramic tile
- ◆ Making minor repairs to wallpaper

Unfortunately, your walls *do* talk. Every bump with a furniture leg, hit with a hockey stick, and bounce of a ball where it shouldn't be can make a mess of your nice, smooth walls. Sometimes, a scuff will wash away with soap and water, but sooner or later, deeper evidence of close encounters of the worst kind will need treatment.

In this chapter, you'll learn to work with joint compound and other soft stuff: grout, tile cement, glue, and other materials to make beat-up walls look clean and new. And working with all this goop may bring back nice memories of your sandbox days!

Minor Drywall Repairs

Drywall is the most common type of base wall material, and what you'll usually find in houses less than fifty years old. It is made by sandwiching a gypsum core, which is fire resistant, between layers of paper. Sometimes known as Sheetrock, wallboard, or gypsum board, this material is also made in a water-resistant variety for use in damp areas such as basements and bathrooms.

You may not want to fix dings, dents, or popped fasteners every time they happen; if you've got an active family or an enthusiastic pet, little nicks and dents are bound to occur frequently. But sooner or later, your walls will get that tired, worn-out look. If possible, wait until your room is ready for its next paint job.

These little repairs are easy to do but take time because there are several steps. Between each step, you must wait for the patching medium to dry. Normally this means waiting 8–12 hours (or overnight) to go to the next step. Unless you're that rare bird with time on her hands, make all the wall repairs in one room on the same weekend, or successive days, so that all the fill-ins dry in one waiting period, are primed at one time, then painted at one time.

With little repairs, work gently. A bold, heavy hand will make a small flaw larger.

Ounce of Prevention

Be sure to wear safety goggles and a dust mask whenever you sand to protect your eyes and lungs. Maybe you think it's wimpy to protect your eyes, nose, and mouth for simple, small repairs. But I think my vital parts are worth protecting, no matter how few small particles are flying. Over time, little particles add up to bigger problems, and tiny crumbs of plaster in the eye can create a big problem. So be safe when you sand! I also hate sweeping and dusting, so the newspapers or drop cloth are my constant home repair sidekicks; they're much cheaper than a cleaning service.

Repairing Dings and Dents

You'll need the following:

- ❏ Sanding block or sandpaper (80–100 grit and 120–150 grit)
- ❏ Utility knife
- ❏ Clean sponge or cloth

❑ Putty knife

❑ Joint compound

1. Lay newspaper or a drop cloth below the repair site to catch debris. Put on safety goggles and a dust mask when you sand to protect your eyes and lungs.

2. Using the 80–100 grit sanding block or paper, *lightly* sand the dent to remove little flecks of the drywall or paint that hang on the surface.

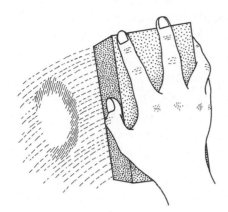

Sand the dent.

3. *Gently* cut away any torn pieces of the drywall that remain at the repair site with a utility knife.

4. Wipe the dent with a damp cloth or sponge to remove any bits that remain in the dent area.

5. With the putty knife, fill the dent with joint compound, and smooth the surface of the repair. Wipe off and clean the putty knife. Allow the repair to dry (usually overnight; see joint compound package directions).

Fill the dent.

6. When the repaired surface is dry, sand with the fine (150-grit) sandpaper.

If the surface looks rough or bumpy, or if any of the dents can still be seen, you'll need another cycle of compound application/drying time/sanding. If you're satisfied with the repair, wipe it off with a damp cloth or sponge, or vacuum the repaired area using the brush tool. You are ready to prime and repaint.

What Pros Know _____

When applying joint compound, your result should blend into the surrounding wall. While the recesses caused by denting and nicking should be filled, you don't want the surrounding walls to look like a relief map of the Rockies. Aim for a finished repair that is as flush to the intact drywall surface as you can make it. Think of the compound as a thin glaze, not fluffy frosting!

Popped Nails

While most pros now opt for screws and power drivers to install drywall, nails used to be the fastener of choice for attaching wallboard to the wall studs (lumber that creates the frame for the walls). A drywall/wallboard nail (they may be called by either name) has little rings on its shank and a flat, round head. Even though they're designed to stay put, these sturdy fasteners do pop out from time to time. Here's how to keep them in their place.

You'll need the following:

❏ Claw hammer

❏ Drywall nails

❏ Putty knife

❏ Joint compound

❏ Sanding block or sandpaper (150-grit)

❏ Clean sponge or cloth

1. Lay newspaper or a drop cloth below the repair site to catch debris. Put on safety goggles and a dust mask when you sand to protect your eyes and lungs.

2. Hammer the nail back into the drywall so it's flush with the wall. With a second hit, create a small dimple in the wall around the nail. Don't pound hard; you want a dimple, not a tear. Then drive a second nail next to the first, to hold the popped one in its place, and create a second, overlapping dimple.

Create dimple.

3. Using the putty knife, apply joint compound over the nail heads and dimples. Clean the putty knife and allow the compound to dry. When the repair is dry, sand the area and wipe off any remaining dust. You are ready to prime and repaint.

Apply compound to dimples.

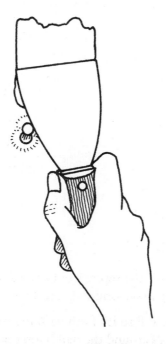

Patching Holes

Oops! I know you didn't mean to put your hammer (or the shower rod, or some other object) through the wall, but there it is: a nasty-looking void in the drywall. It used to be that fixing this kind of damage meant ripping out a section of drywall between studs and doing a (very) labor-intensive repair. Hardware stores now stock a great invention for holes of relatively small diameter: a mesh patch you can place over the hole. It's got a sticky back that adheres to the intact wall surface around the cavity. These patches are available in sizes up to about 8 inches square.

You'll need the following:

❏ Utility knife

❏ Sanding block or sandpaper (80–100 and 120–150 grit)

❏ Mesh wall patch (about 2× the area of the hole)

❏ Tray to hold compound

❏ Joint compound

❏ Putty knife (4" or wider, depending on the hole)

❏ Clean sponge or cloth

1. Cover the floor with newspaper and place a drop cloth on the surrounding area to protect furnishings. (This job may raise more dust than the others!) Put on safety goggles and a dust mask when you sand to protect your eyes and lungs.

2. Prepare the surface for the patch. Use the utility knife to cut away any protruding or hanging pieces of drywall. You might also want to sand the edge of the hole gently with the coarser grit (80–100) sandpaper. The idea is to make the surface of the hole flush with the wall, not to make the hole bigger!

3. Peel away the backing paper from the mesh patch and center the patch over the hole; then stick it down, smoothing the edges.

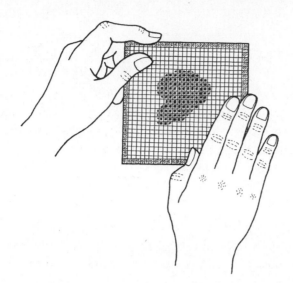

Apply the mesh patch.

4. Load your tray with joint compound. Use the putty knife to apply the compound over the patch. Cover the mesh area completely, applying compound beyond the borders of the mesh. Smooth on the compound from side to side, top to bottom, corner to corner. When you're finished, clean and dry the knife and tray.

Apply compound to patch.

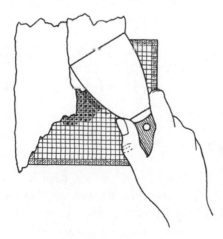

5. Let the repair dry—like other drywall repairs, this one will take 8 or more hours. Then sand the dried area with the coarse (80–100) sandpaper. Wipe away any dust with a damp sponge or cloth.

6. Apply a second coat of compound as in Step 4. Let the compound dry. This time, use the fine sandpaper (120–150), and clean up as before. You're ready to prime and paint.

What Pros Know

Small flaws—dents, popped nails, and the like—can usually be covered with a 2" or 3" putty knife, and joint compound applied right from its small container. If you've got holes or a lot of imperfections to cover, you'll probably want a larger bucket of compound and a broader knife, 4" or wider, to cover the hole(s). To keep the compound from drying out, transfer the quantity you think you'll need into a tray (you'll find trays near the joint compound in the hardware store or home center). Then reclose the lid on the compound bucket to preserve the rest. Professional drywall installers work quickly, and waste neither time nor words. They call joint compound "mud," an apt description that saves two syllables!

Loose Drywall Tape

Drywall seams are joined and sealed by means of drywall tape, now a nice, self-stick product that usually stays put. But the drywall seams in your house may be put together with the old, paper product. This sometimes lifts off, and you can smooth it down with a new strip of 2-inch drywall repair tape, then go over it with joint compound and your putty knife, just the way you repaired everything else in this section.

If the old drywall tape is lifting all over the place in a section of a room, or rooms, this may be an indication of a moisture problem behind the sheetrock, and that's not funny.

Moisture in the walls not only damages drywall. It could degrade insulation, cause mold, and on and on. If you repair lifted tape and the problem keeps popping up, call in a pro.

Repairing Cracks in Plaster

Plaster is a beautiful wall surface; intact plaster has a smooth, hard finish that is beautiful to the eye and the touch. If you've got an old house, your walls may be covered with this material, which is traditionally applied in three coats over a layer of *lath* that is attached to the wall studs. But houses settle, and that's when the fun begins. Sooner or later, cracks and other defects may appear.

For all of us in DIY 101, the cracks are what we'll deal with. Bigger jobs are for the pros.

Spackling compound is a bit thicker than joint compound, and is good for repairing hairline cracks in plaster.

You'll need the following:

❏ Lever-type can opener

❏ Clean sponge or cloth

❏ Spackling compound

❏ Sanding block (150-grit)

def•i•ni•tion

Lath is the foundation for plaster, or sometimes for tile. It is traditionally a framework of thin wood strips, or, more recently, wire mesh.

1. Lay newspaper or a drop cloth below the work area to catch debris. Put on safety goggles and a dust mask when you sand to protect your eyes and lungs.

2. In order for the compound to make a good bond with the wall and the underlying layer of plaster beneath the crack, a hairline crack should be opened to about $1/8$" wide. Do this by running the tip of a lever-type can opener (or the tip of the blade of a table knife) down the length of the crack. Brush away any crumbs of plaster that remain with a damp sponge or cloth.

Open plaster crack uniformly.

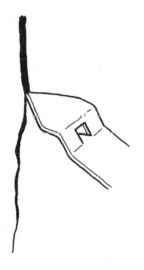

3. With your forefinger, push the spackling compound into the crack using smooth strokes until the crack is filled, end to end. The repair should overlap the wall slightly, creating a bond with the plaster.

Apply spackling compound.

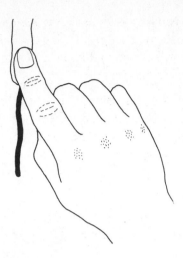

4. Wash your hands, and let the repair dry (up to 24 hours; check the spackling compound package directions). When it's dry, if the patch seems to have shrunk into the crack, repeat Step 3, filling the indentation until the patch is flush with the wall, then let the area dry completely.

5. Sand the dry surface of the repair, and wipe away remaining dust. You're ready to prime and paint.

Because plaster is usually composed of three layers—a base coat, a second thicker coat, and a top coat (the beauty part), damage below the surface layer and beyond small cracks can be a tough DIY project. If you're patient, don't mind a *lot* of dust, and have plenty of spare time, see Appendix B for some sources of help for larger repairs.

You may prefer to call in a professional. Plasterers are artisans, but since drywall has so overwhelmingly replaced plaster in modern construction, masters of this craft are disappearing. It may take some time and sleuthing to find a good one.

Grout and Tile Crackups

Attractive, quite sturdy, and easy to clean, tile is a great wall covering in bathrooms, on kitchen backsplashes, and anywhere moisture can settle. A sponge or damp cloth wipes away dust and grime. It's wonderful stuff!

Over time, though, the grout (cement filling) between the tiles can become dirty and start to degrade; little bits of grout can chip or crack, and then it's time to renew the offending seams. If grout is falling like rain, you may want to call a pro. Doing a whole wall or a whole room could be more work than you bargained for.

Sometimes, bad stuff happens to good walls. A single tile will develop an obvious crack, or fracture from too many hits with a pot, or the vacuum cleaner. Replacement is fairly straightforward if you've got some leftover tile stashed away.

You'll need to remove the grout around the broken piece before you remove the tile.

Ounce of Prevention

If the grout in the tiled areas of your home still looks good, a great little weekend project would be to seal it. Your local tile dealer stocks sealers that are easy to apply, and will protect the surface of the grout; just follow the package directions. If you seal the grout every couple of years, you may be able to skip this section for a while!

Replacing Grout

Finding grout to match what's already there may be the hardest part of this small job. Before you start, chip out a little sample of grout from the crumbling area with a utility knife, and bring it to the tile store. If you can't find a perfect match, ask the tile dealer about grout dye, which is applied like paint, with a brush, to the replacement grout. You may find just the right shade to make your repair invisible.

Oh, and if you've got a match, after you take what you need, be sure to close the package containing the remaining grout. Store it in an airtight container, labeled with the color and where it is used in your house. Love those leftovers!

You'll need the following:

❑ Masking or painter's tape

❑ Utility knife or grout saw

❑ Grout to match what's already there

❑ Clean sponge or cloth

❑ Grout sealer

1. Removing grout will create some debris in the area below the damage; spread newspaper or a drop cloth in the work area. Put on safety goggles to protect your eyes from flying debris.

2. The surface of ceramic tile is vulnerable to scratching and chipping. If you're removing grout, or a cracked or broken tile, you'll want to mask the edges of the surrounding tiles with masking or painter's tape so the repair you're doing won't create more work!

Mask around the repair.

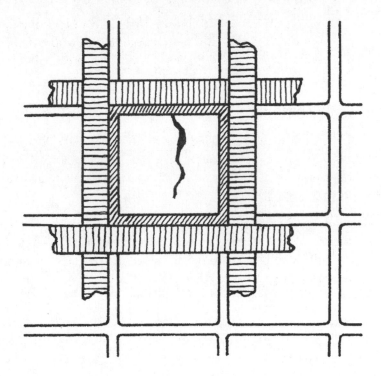

3. Remove the old grout with a utility knife or a grout saw. Ceramic tile is usually ¼" thick (or less) so work carefully and don't cut into the surface of the wall.

A grout saw looks like a large utility knife with an offset handle. It is useful for cutting grout, especially if grout seams are wider than ¼". A utility knife is fine for cutting narrower seams.

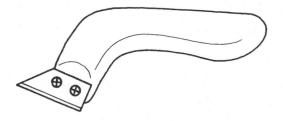

4. Make sure the seams are free of the old grout, then mix the new grout according to package directions.

5. You won't be needing the masking at this point, so remove it from around the open seam(s). Apply the grout to the open seam(s); smooth it with your finger.

6. When the seams are completely filled and look smooth, you can wipe away any grout remaining on the surrounding tiles with a damp sponge or cloth. Let the grout dry, then seal it with a grout sealer according to package directions.

Replacing a Ceramic Tile

If you're only replacing one or two tiles, you will only need a small quantity of tile adhesive, also called mastic. Bring the replacement tile with you, or ask the tile dealer when you buy a replacement which adhesive is suited to the job. Purchase that variety.

You'll need the following:

❑ Masking or painter's tape

❑ Utility knife or grout saw

❑ Metal straight edge

❑ Glass-cutting tool

❑ Nail set

❑ Hammer

❑ Cold chisel

❑ Putty knife

❑ Tile adhesive/mastic

❑ Replacement tile

❑ Wood block

❑ Grout to match what's already there

❑ Clean sponge or cloth

Ounce of Prevention

If your broken tile is over the bathtub, you'll want to protect the surface of the tub from flying shards of tile. Cover the whole tub with a drop cloth. Bits of tile can be very sharp and downright dangerous when they become airborne. In addition to your goggles, protect your arms with long sleeves—button sleeves if they have buttons so loose cuffs won't be in your way.

1. Protect surrounding tiles with masking or painter's tape, and cover the floor around the work area with newspapers or a drop cloth. Put on safety goggles to protect your eyes from flying debris.

2. Remove the old grout; follow the instructions in the repair just described.

3. Using the straight edge as a cutting guide, and the glass-cutting tool, score the damaged/broken tile with an X mark, corner to corner on the diagonal.

The glass-cutting tool is not only good for cutting glass; you can use it to score many hard, brittle materials.

Score the crack.

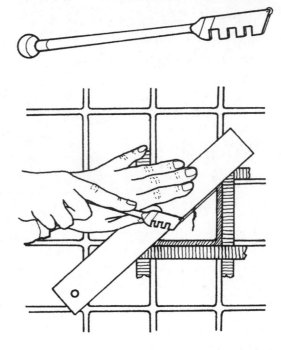

4. Position the nail set at the center of the X, and tap with the hammer to loosen the cracked tile.

5. Using the hammer and the cold chisel, carefully chip out the tile. Once you have gotten enough small pieces out, you can hammer the end of the putty knife (if it's got a metal end on the handle) to carefully work out the tile. Take care not to gouge the underlying wallboard. Hold the chisel or knife at an angle so that you're lifting tile but not denting or tearing drywall.

Chisel out broken tile.

6. When all the tile bits are removed, scrape out the remaining dried tile adhesive with the putty knife, also taking care to leave the underlying wall intact.

7. If you do make a gouge in the wall, go back to the drywall repair section of this chapter and make the repair. You'll have to wait for the compound to dry, then sand it and wipe away any remaining dust before you set the tile. (Remember to wear a dust mask when you sand.)

8. Using the putty knife (be sure it's clean and dry), "butter" the back of the tile with adhesive, and position it where the old tile was set. Wipe away any mastic that squishes up from beneath the tile.

9. Using a wood block to protect the surface of the new tile, hammer the block gently so that the tile is level with the surrounding work.

10. Hold the tile in place with masking or painter's tape while it dries (tape it up and down, side to side, to the adjoining intact tile work).

Secure the new tile in place.

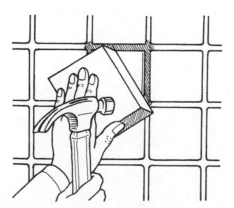

11. Once the tile is set (adhesive should usually set for 24 hours; check the directions on the adhesive packaging), grout the seams around the tile, and wipe any excess grout away with a damp sponge.

Replace grout.

12. When the grout dries, apply a sealer according to package directions.

What Pros Know

Uh oh! You have no leftover tile and there's nothing resembling it at the six or seven tile stores you've visited. (Did you check their discard piles of extras from old jobs? Don't forget to try.) If you're willing to sacrifice a few intact tiles, and the field (your tile wall) isn't too large, you can make lemonade out of this lemon of a dilemma. Buy a few contrasting tiles that fit the color scheme in your room, or a few pretty art tiles that will complement the décor, and install them randomly. This replacement method will look like a design, not a repair, if done well. If this sounds like too much work, it won't take a pro long to replace a few tiles with substitutes, and the price will beat a complete retiling.

Minor Wallpaper Repairs

After he graduated from the crib to a big-boy bed, my son lulled himself to sleep by picking at the wallpaper where his bed aligned with the wall. Cleverly, he did this below the level of the mattress, so I didn't notice until he had removed a fairly large patch of paper. To give him an alternative sleep aid to peeling wallpaper, we went shopping for a new fuzzy stuffed friend, and then I learned to patch. Fortunately for me, the paper was a simple grid pattern; it was easy to line up the pattern and cut a patch along the grid lines. And my son loved Jerry, his new bear!

Even though you can return unused rolls of wallpaper and get a little money back, save at least one roll of leftover paper from any wallpaper project for unexpected mishaps, and store it with your other leftover supplies. Most wallpaper patterns go out of production after a couple of seasons, and if you've got a tear or hole in a prominent position that you can't cover with a hanging picture, you will regret being penny-wise!

Bursting Those Bubbles

Unlike popping balloons, getting rid of air bubbles beneath wallpaper is a delicate maneuver.

You'll need the following:

- ❏ Utility knife
- ❏ All-purpose glue
- ❏ Toothpick
- ❏ Clean sponge or cloth

Carefully make a slit in the bubble and press it flat with your fingertip. If it won't stay down, put a little all-purpose glue on a toothpick, and carefully spread the glue underneath the lifted area. Press down, and wipe away any excess glue with a damp sponge.

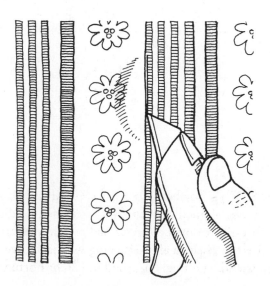

Flatten a wallpaper bubble.

Flattening Flappy Seams

A good paperhanger takes care to match and flatten each strip of wallpaper so that the pattern—not the strips—are what you see when you walk into the room. Over time, the adhesive that once kept the edges down may dry out sufficiently that the seams begin to lift off the wall in places. And these little "lift-offs" can tear if someone brushes against them. A little first aid will keep your seams straight!

You'll need the following:

- ❏ All-purpose glue
- ❏ Toothpick
- ❏ Clean sponge or cloth
- ❏ Wallpaper seam roller

As with the burst bubble, put a little glue behind the tear or the lift. Use a toothpick for gluing very small lifts. Press down, making sure the repair lines up properly with the adjoining pattern. Wipe away any excess glue that blobs out from under the repair with a damp sponge. Roll the seam with the seam roller for a neat, flat finish.

Glue a wallpaper seam.

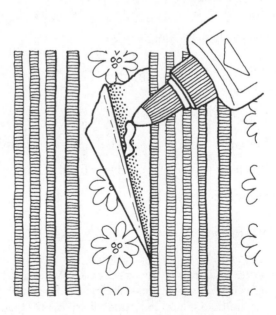

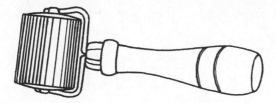

A wallpaper seam roller will glide over your repair without hitting a snag. It's also great for smoothing anything else you have to glue and flatten.

Patching a Torn Section of Wallpaper

That leftover roll of wallpaper is key to this repair. You'll need to make your patch line up with the existing paper, to make it less visible. It's best if the corners of the patch wind up inside the pattern, rather than on the plain background of the paper, so the repair is less visible. If the paper is a very busy pattern with little or no plain background, the corners should disappear nicely.

You'll need the following:

- ❑ Utility knife
- ❑ Blue painter's tape
- ❑ Straight edge
- ❑ Putty knife
- ❑ Wall sealer (for repair area)
- ❑ Bucket of lukewarm water
- ❑ Sponge
- ❑ Leftover matching wallpaper
- ❑ Wallpaper adhesive, or a shallow pan of water
- ❑ Brush for applying wallpaper adhesive, if necessary
- ❑ Wallpaper seam roller

What Pros Know

Dipping it for about ten seconds in a pan of water activates the adhesive on pre-pasted wallpaper. Unpasted wallpaper is applied with wallpaper paste. Which kind is yours? Sometimes the manufacturer will tell you by printing the information on the backside of the paper. If you can't figure it out, dip a scrap of paper in water and see if it will stick to a wall surface. (Unless you want to keep it there, remove immediately after checking and wipe away the residue with a sponge!) Expensive designer papers, meant to be installed by pros, are often unpasted. If you're still in doubt, bring a scrap to the wallpaper store and ask.

1. Spread newspaper or a drop cloth below the work area to catch debris.

2. With the utility knife, remove any bits of wallpaper that are hanging loose. Cut a piece of wallpaper from your leftover roll that covers the torn or damaged area with a generous border around it.

Cut the patch.

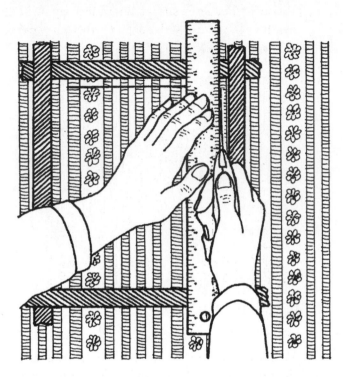

3. Carefully match the edges of the patch to the existing wallpaper, and tape it flush to the wall with blue painter's tape.

4. Using the utility knife and your straight edge, cut out a square or rectangular patch inside the taped edges that also encloses the torn area. You will be cutting the patch and scoring the existing paper at the same time. Take care not to gouge the wall. (If you should slip, you can always repair the underlying drywall with the skill you learned earlier in this chapter!)

5. Set aside your newly cut patch for the moment. Dampen the scored area around the torn area and use the putty knife to scrape away the wallpaper. You may have to apply warm water to the paper and let it soak for a few minutes to make removal easier.

   If your old paper is strippable (it may say so on the back of the paper), you can just lift the corner of the paper with your putty knife and pull it back, holding the paper at a sharp 10° angle. Peel *carefully.*

Remove old paper.

6. When all the paper is removed from the area you will patch (with your "custom fit" replacement), apply wall sealer (from the wallpaper store; ask the dealer) according to package directions, and let it dry.

7. If you're using a prepasted wallpaper, dip it in water and then install it over the opening you've prepared, taking care to line up the pattern and the seams. Use the sponge to wipe away excess moisture. (If using unpasted paper, apply adhesive to the back of the patch according to directions. Wipe away any excess adhesive from the edges of the repair.) Smooth the paper from the center to the edges, taking care to keep the pattern in line.

Install the patch.

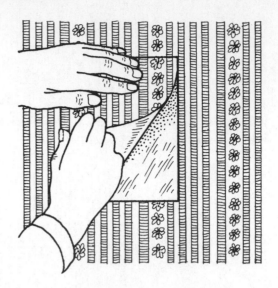

8. When you're satisfied with the fit, run the seam roller along the edges for a nice, flat edge. Let the patch dry.

The Least You Need to Know

♦ Wall repairs take time because many patch products dry slowly. The good news: you don't have to watch! Do something else while you wait.

♦ Save and label leftovers from renovation projects. You never know when you'll need an extra tile or piece of wallpaper.

♦ A heavy hand in wall repairs makes more work. Light and easy does it!

♦ Always protect your eyes, mouth, and nose when sanding.

Chapter 6

Floors and Ceilings: Beneath Your Feet and (Not Really) Over Your Head

In This Chapter

◆ Making small repairs to hardwood floors, and replacing a laminate floorboard

◆ Replacing a vinyl or ceramic tile or a small area of resilient flooring that's been damaged

◆ Cleaning stains and replacing a section of wall-to-wall carpet

◆ Smoothing a ceiling that's starting to show its age

There's a trend today for people to take care of their floors by adopting the Japanese custom of leaving their shoes at the door. It's a nice idea if your family can live with it; it will certainly cut down on the sweeping/ vacuuming schedule. Of course, if you have pets who track in all kinds of debris, and you're not compulsive about making your guests and your UPS delivery man remove their shoes, your floors will sooner or later suffer the same indignities as any shoe-wearing household.

When really bad things happen to floors—deep gouges, extensive water damage, I'm talking disaster here—you'll have to opt for refinishing or replacement. But barring a crisis, there are lots of things you can do to maintain an old floor's—or its covering's— attractive appearance. Read on.

Wood Floors: Skin Repair

Water marks, burn marks, and scratches all affect the appearance of your hardwood floors. They're like blemishes; some people don't mind them, but others rush for a cover-up. If you choose the cover-up strategy, it's best to deal with them as soon after they happen as possible. When you're trying to fix a minor flaw, you'll need to use a wax stripper to remove the protective finish from the damage site. Check with your hardware store associate about the appropriate stripping product for the finish on your floor. When you're finished with the repair, you can rewax or oil the area.

> **Ounce of Prevention**
>
> The liquids used for oiling, waxing, and repairing blemished floors may be flammable and toxic. Read the directions on the product container, and use and store these substances according to manufacturer's instructions. When you're working and the stuff is wet or drying, close off your work area from children and pets. Be sure to wear snug-fitting rubber or latex gloves to protect your hands from these liquids.

Water Marks

I know everyone in your house is supposed to use a coaster under their drinks, but if Dad set a glass of water on the floor and forgot it, try this fix.

You'll need the following:

- ❏ Fine steel wool (#0000)
- ❏ Paste wax or liquid floor wax
- ❏ Wax stripper
- ❏ Clean soft rags (or *cheesecloth*, cut into little pads)
- ❏ Odorless mineral spirits

1. Open the windows when you're using waxes and other floor repair products. Some people like the smell, but it's really not good to expose yourself to these fumes in an unventilated area. Wear gloves when you're using the liquids.

2. Using a wax stripper, remove the finish from the stained area.

3. Rub the water marks with the steel wool and a little paste or liquid wax.

def•i•ni•tion _____

> **Cheesecloth** is a light, gauzy fabric originally used to strain and hold cheese. In the absence of a good supply of soft, clean rags, and folded into palm-sized pads, it's a great substitute if you've run out of old flannel shirts and pajamas. Hardware stores and home centers sell it in inexpensive and generous packages.

4. If the marks don't disappear, wipe up the wax with a clean rag or cheesecloth pad. Rub the area again with the steel wool, using a small amount of mineral spirits.

Wipe clean, let dry, and rewax or reoil the area.

Burn Marks

Grandpa's lit cigar fell on the floor and left a mark in the finish. Now you've got a good excuse to make him take his habit outside! But you still need to repair the floor. You'll need the following:

- ❏ Fine sandpaper (220–400 grit)
- ❏ Clean, damp rag
- ❏ Utility knife
- ❏ Putty stick or stick shellac to match the floor surface

If a burn has just darkened the surface of the wood, you can sand it with fine sandpaper, and wipe up the sanding dust with the damp cloth. (Wear a dust mask when sanding to protect your lungs from particles.) Finish as desired; you may want to give the area a light coat with the putty or shellac stick before you reoil or rewax the spot. Use the sticks according to manufacturer's directions.

For a deeper burn, follow these steps:

1. Carefully scrape out the burned area with the tip of your utility knife; be sure the blade is sharp (if in doubt, pop in a new one first).

2. Apply one or more coats of the putty stick or stick shellac.

Rewax or reoil the spot.

> **What Pros Know** _____
>
> Putty sticks, stick shellac, and small containers of wood putty are sold in different colors to match different wood finishes. Without a spare piece of wood to make a perfect match, use your digital camera to take a photo of your floor and bring your snapshot to the hardware store. When in doubt about the color, go lighter rather than darker. You can always cover the lighter filler with a darker shade, but too-dark material will create another blemish.

Scratches and Gouges

You don't have to be too compulsive about this; if you've got dogs and kids, you'll be fixing scratches every other day. But before routine waxing or oiling of your floor, and after stripping the protective finish, you can spend a little time touching up the scratches with your handy putty stick or stick shellac, then rewax or reoil the area.

For a deeper gouge, you may get a better result by using wood putty from a can to fill the gouged spot. When it dries, you can feather the edges with fine sandpaper. If the patch is too visible, touch it up with the putty stick or stick shellac. Then rewax or reoil the spot.

Preventing Blemishes

If you dislike housecleaning as much as I do, you won't like this advice. But it works. I've already discussed the no-shoes strategy. But if you can't deal with that, the best defense for your floor's finish is frequent sweeping or vacuuming. Surface dirt is the real culprit in floor wear.

Floorboard Fixes

Wobbly wood floors are annoying and dangerous: that thing that goes bump in the night could be you! Here are a few common problems, and how to solve them.

Drilling Pilot Holes

Before you drive a screw or nail into hardwood floors, you must first excavate one or more of what's called a *pilot hole* with your electric drill. The drill hole acts like a "pilot" for your nail or screw, literally directing it toward a tight, clean insertion. Pilot holes are your insurance that you won't chew up the flooring with a poorly hammered nail or a screwy screw . Many instructions in this book call for pilot holes. If you're unfamiliar with using the drill, practice on a piece of wood that you clamp firmly to a work table (careful, don't drill the table). Wear safety goggles when you drill. Drill holes until you get a feel for the tool. (If you're having trouble, refer to the drill's use and care manual for further guidance.)

Split or Cracked Boards

You'd be amazed at what falls in the cracks! One Christmas, my husband gave me a beautiful pair of earrings, and I lost one. It was tiny, and I'd given up ever finding it again. But when I repaired a crack in a dining room floorboard, what do you think I found?

You'll need the following:

- ❏ Electric drill
- ❏ A combination pilot bit (its shank should be slightly shorter than the depth you drive your nail)
- ❏ Annular ring nails, long enough to go through the floorboard and almost through the subfloor when countersunk (your nails can be about 2" for standard $^3/_4$" floor and subfloor)
- ❏ Claw hammer
- ❏ Nail set
- ❏ Wood putty or wood filler
- ❏ Finish to match your floor

A combination bit, or screw pilot, is the right bit for drilling a pilot hole and countersinking the fastener. The bit is graduated to a larger diameter at the top, allowing the fastener head to be countersunk with a nail set (if it's a nail) or a screwdriver (if it's a screw). If you're not sure of bit length, check with your hardware store salesperson.

1. Wearing safety goggles, drill pilot holes at an angle every few inches along both sides of the crack.

Countersink pilot holes along a floorboard crack.

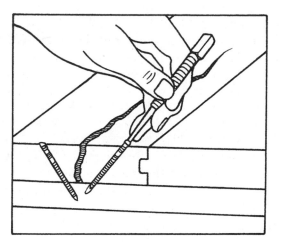

2. Drive in the annular ring nails, then countersink them using the nail set.

3. Wearing snug-fitting rubber or disposable latex gloves if you don't like putty on your hands, fill the nail holes and the crack with wood putty; let it dry.

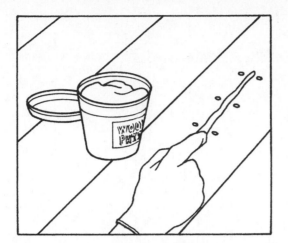

Fill crack and nail holes with putty.

4. If a better match is needed, apply a color putty stick or stick shellac, or finish to match the surrounding floor. Let it dry, then wax or oil as needed.

More Bit Bits

This and upcoming chapters call for the electric drill and various bits. I don't know about you, but I have trouble sometimes judging whether a bit is "slightly smaller" than my fastener. I'm at that stage of life where I need reading glasses for all close-up work. If you also have trouble when comparing bits and fasteners, keep a drill gauge in your pocket or purse when you buy fasteners and corresponding bits in the hardware store or home center.

Your fastener should fit through the *next size larger* hole in the gauge than the correct hole for your drill bit. (The following illustration is a sample of what a gauge looks like; real gauges have the fractional sizes of each hole marked.) The fastener should be larger than the pilot hole, because you want the fastener to grab the wood (or other material) that surrounds the pilot hole. You want that fastener to fit tightly. With a drill gauge there's no more guessing.

Fractional drill gauge.

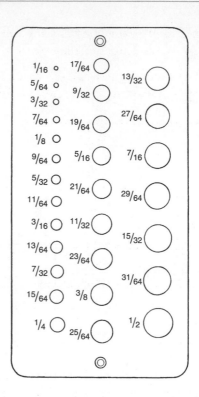

Warped Boards

You may notice warping boards in the winter, when your heating system starts to dry things out, and wood fiber starts to shrink as it loses its natural moisture. If this is a persistent problem in your house, you may want to put more moisture into the air by using humidifiers in winter months.

This is a fix for a *badly* warped board; it doesn't yet look like Mount Everest, but creates a slight rise that looks weird and presents a possible tripping hazard.

You'll need the following:

❑ Electric drill

❑ Combination bit sized for your screws

❑ Standard screwdriver

❑ Slotted wood screws ($1\frac{1}{4}$"; you'll be driving them straight)

❑ Wood putty

❑ Finish to match the floor

1. Wearing safety goggles, drill pilot holes every few inches at the high point of the warp along the length of the warped board.

2. Insert and then tighten the screws in each hole. Take care not to tighten so hard that you deform the screw head. Be firm but gentle.

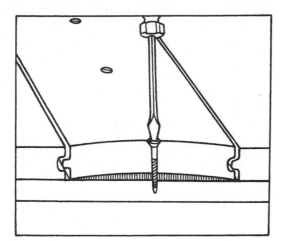

Drive screws into the warp.

3. Wearing snug-fitting rubber or disposable latex gloves if you don't like putty on your hands, cover the holes with wood putty and then apply finish to match the surrounding floor.

Loose Boards

Loose boards are a fairly easy fix. If you can get to them from *underneath*, the solution is invisible, but this is only possible if you've got an unfinished ceiling below the floor, as in a basement or garage.

If you are so blessed, you'll need the following:

- ❏ Stepladder

- ❏ Electric drill

- ❏ Corresponding bit for your screws (no need to countersink these, aesthetics are not an issue)

- ❏ Screwdriver (standard or Phillips, depending on the screw heads)

- ❏ Measuring tape (for marking the drill bit, and locating the loose boards)

- ❏ Wood screws (1¹/₄" for standard ³/₄" floor and subfloor; the screws should be ¹/₄" shorter than the thickness of the two layers)

- ❏ Masking or painter's tape

1. The worst part of the job is locating precisely where on the ceiling the loose floorboard above is located. You can have a friend jump on the loose board, watch the movement in the subfloor and locate it that way, or you can do a measuring job to find it. (If walls above and below match up, it's easier.)

2. Once you've located the spot, put on safety goggles to protect your eyes, and drill several pilot holes straight up from below, then insert and tighten your wood screws. It will help if your friend stands on the loose board, putting some downward pressure on the board as you tighten each screw. Your friend can also make sure that the screw does not break through the surface of the hardwood floor.

What Pros Know _____

When you're drilling holes from below the floor, you don't want screw points coming up through the floorboards. You can buy drill bits with stops that you can adjust to the desired drilling depth, or wrap a piece of painter's or masking tape at the correct point on the bit so you don't drill past it. Use either strategy whenever you want your drill holes to be a specific length.

Fix loose board from below.

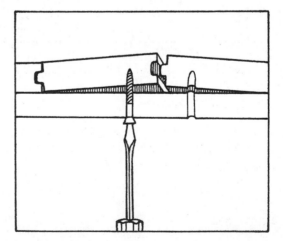

After all the effort it took to find the right board, the good news is, you don't have to cover the screws on the unfinished ceiling with wood putty. Phew!

To fix the loose board from above, you'll need the following:

- ❏ Electric drill
- ❏ Combination bit sized for nail diameter and countersink
- ❏ Claw hammer
- ❏ Nail set
- ❏ Annular ring nails
- ❏ Wood putty
- ❏ Finish to match the floor

1. Wearing safety goggles, drill pilot holes as shown in the following illustration, angled in from the board edge, through the board and into the subfloor.

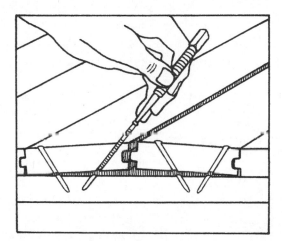

Nail loose boards from above.

2. Drive in nails with a hammer and countersink them with a nail set.

3. Wearing snug-fitting rubber or disposable latex gloves if you don't like putty on your hands, fill the nail holes with wood putty, and apply finish to match the surrounding floor.

Stopping Squeaks

Squeaks are caused by pieces of flooring rubbing together. When my children were teenagers, I never bothered to fix the squeaks in the floor. In fact, I liked them. The more they squeaked, the easier it was to detect the patter of adolescent feet, sneaking in past curfew.

Here are two ways to try to silence a squeaky floor. For the first strategy, you'll need the following:

❑ A block of wood (a foot-long piece of 2×4 framing lumber is good; your local lumber yard may have some scrap if you don't)

❑ A piece of felt, scrap carpet, or other thick fabric to cover the block

❑ Claw hammer

❑ A few common or box nails

1. Cover the faces (not the ends) of the block of wood with your heavy fabric or carpet and nail the material snugly in place on one long end of the block, leaving you three cushioned sides to work with.

2. Starting in the center of the room and moving around and outward in a path toward the edges of the room, position the long, unnailed face of the fabric-covered block flat on the floor, and perpendicular to the floorboards, and tap it sharply with the hammer. Doing this may help ease the floorboards, which may have dried and shifted, back into place, so they don't rub together so noticeably.

For the second strategy you'll need the following:

❑ Glazier's points (the little metal pieces used to position glass in a window frame)

❑ Graphite

❑ Claw hammer

❑ Putty knife (2")

Coat the glazier's points in graphite, and then hammer them between offending floor-boards. To do this, tap the hammer on the edge of the blade of the putty knife, using the opposite edge of the putty knife to push the points between the boards. Make sure the points don't protrude from the spaces so that they stick out above the boards (ouch!). The graphite-coated points act as space holders to keep the boards away from each other.

Getting at Squeaks from Down Under

If the offending floor is in a room above an unfinished basement or garage, you can try to stop squeaks with yet a third strategy.

You'll need the following:

- ❑ Stepladder

- ❑ Claw hammer

- ❑ Wood shims

Again, you'll need a friend to walk around upstairs to locate the squeaky parts of the floor. Wherever the floor is squeaking, tap a shim into the space between the *joist* and the subfloor. Be sure to wear safety goggles to protect your eyes from falling debris.

def•i•ni•tion

A **joist** is the framing that supports a floor or ceiling.

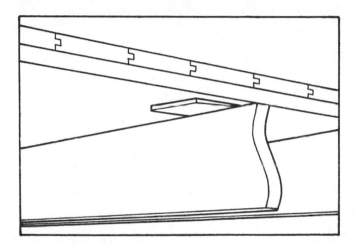

Silence a squeak from down under.

Resilient Floor Fixes

Vinyl flooring in sheets and tiles is everywhere; it holds up to a lot of hard wear, which is probably why it's known as *resilient*. Cork and asphalt tile are also known as resilient flooring, but vinyl dominates.

The routine for maintaining a resilient floor is fairly simple: regular sweeping, vacuuming, damp-mopping, and occasional waxing to renew the surface when its factory-applied wear layer starts to wear thin. But sometimes, bad stuff happens to perfectly good floors.

At our house we had a bad habit of bringing home the pizza and putting it in the oven on a low setting to warm it up, still in its box. One day, my son was home alone and tried to warm up the pizza I'd left on the counter. It was still in the box; I don't know the oven temperature he set.

The box caught fire, my son threw it on the vinyl floor and doused it with water and baking soda. No one was hurt, and the only damage was a nice, 2" square burn mark in the middle of the kitchen floor. You can be sure that no one in my house ever put a pizza box in the oven again! My heart still beats fast when I think of the dumb example I set for my children.

We were years away from renovating the kitchen, but fortunately I had some leftover tile. Here's how I made the repair.

Replacing a Vinyl Tile

You must have a replacement tile for this one. Bring your replacement tile to the floor or hardware store and get the right adhesive and solvent.

You'll also need the following:

- ❑ Kitchen towel
- ❑ Steam iron
- ❑ Putty knife
- ❑ Notched trowel
- ❑ Adhesive for the tile
- ❑ Appropriate solvent to clean excess adhesive
- ❑ Clean rag to apply the solvent

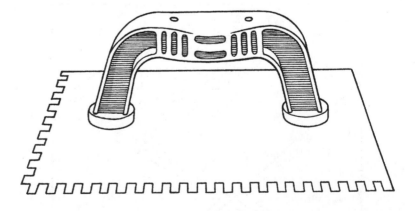

A notched trowel is used to apply adhesive for all kinds of tile and other flooring materials. Its notches leave a swirled pattern.

1. To soften the tile, place a towel over the damaged piece and iron it on a medium setting until the tile (and underlying adhesive) is very warm and begins to soften.

2. Remove the damaged tile by prying it up at one corner with the putty knife; gradually and carefully pull it up and off. (If you need to soften it more, lay it back down and apply more heat with the iron over the towel.)

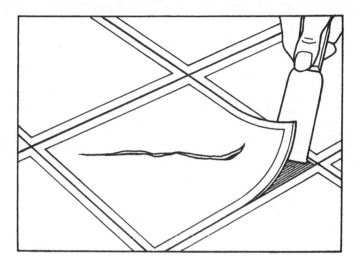

Remove the damaged tile.

3. Let the adhesive cool and harden, then scrape up the dry adhesive with the putty knife until the subfloor is smooth, clean, and flat.

4. Using the notched trowel, apply the adhesive to the clean, dry, flat subfloor. If any adhesive settles on the adjacent tiles, clean them up with the solvent, according to the directions.

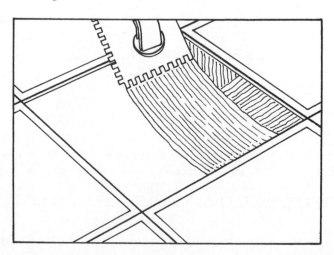

Apply adhesive for tile replacement.

5. Position the replacement tile above the adhesive-covered opening; make sure you've got the pattern, if there is one, going in the right direction.

6. Set two adjacent edges of the new tile against two adjacent tiles surrounding the repair; again, make sure the pattern matches. Press the tile into place.

If any adhesive comes up between the new tile and the adjacent ones, clean it with the solvent according to directions. Set the new tile level with the surrounding pieces; if it's too low, pull it up and add more adhesive.

If it's too high, press it down hard, and clean up any excess adhesive that squishes up at the edges with the solvent. Don't walk on the floor until the repair dries completely (check drying time on the adhesive container).

Patching Sheet Flooring

If you look at the illustrations for patching a hole in wallpaper in Chapter 5, this repair is done in a similar way, just with a different material. Again, you'll need a left-over piece of flooring, enough to cover the damage and match the pattern.

You'll also need the following:

❏ Utility knife

❏ Straightedge

❏ Painter's or masking tape

Many floor patterns have imprinted seams in the shapes of blocks, bricks, or other geometric forms. Try to make your patch so the edges fall within the pattern's seams; it will be less noticeable.

1. Cut a piece of the leftover flooring with a utility knife and a straightedge. Work on a protected surface so that the utility knife doesn't damage bare wood (or the good portion of your floor!).

2. Position the replacement piece over the damaged area and match up the pattern. Secure this piece to the surrounding floor with painter's or masking tape. Cut a patch large enough to cover the damaged area by using the straightedge and utility knife to cut through both the replacement flooring and the old flooring, around the damaged area. Set aside the replacement patch you've just cut. Now you're ready to remove the damaged piece of flooring.

Removal and replacement are exactly the same as the fix for replacing a tile. Use the same tools and materials, and follow Steps 1–6 for "Replacing a Vinyl Tile," described earlier. You'll be substituting your patch for the replacement tile, but the procedure is the same.

Ceramic Tile Floor Repairs

If you drop a pot or a tool and break a tile, or if the grout is chipping away, you can handle replacement and grout repair by following the instructions for wall tile repairs in Chapter 5. It will actually be a bit easier working on the floor instead of the wall!

To keep your floor grout in shape, you should treat it every year or two with sealant. This will make it easier to clean; it also keeps out the water you use when mopping—repeated soaking will degrade unsealed grout.

Carpet Capers

Wall-to-wall carpeting feels great under your feet on a cold morning. And manufacturers have worked hard to perfect carpet technology so that this stuff is more stain resistant than ever. When you have new carpet installed, be sure to ask the dealer or installer to provide manufacturer's specifications for cleaning the type of fiber your carpet is made of (file it in your home workbook!); knowing this info will help you when someone drops something nasty on it down the road.

Taking Up a Wall-to-Wall Carpet

Sometimes you just have to get beneath your carpeting—a squeaky floor, perhaps, or a run of pipe that's in a crawl space the plumber can't get to from below.

Wall-to-wall carpet is usually attached around the perimeter of your room by means of narrow *furring strips* that are nailed to the subfloor along the walls. These furring strips are treacherous! The carpet sticks to them by means of dozens of protruding carpet tacks. So lifting the carpet for any reason can hurt you if you're not prepared.

def·i·ni·tion

In construction, **furring strips** are thin, narrow pieces of wood used to provide backing to support a finished surface. In the case of carpeting, the strips are prenailed with carpet tacks, making a base to hold down the edges of the carpet. The carpet padding is cut to fit within the perimeter of the strips, then the carpet is laid on top. It's all very neat.

You'll need the following:

- ❑ Pry bar
- ❑ Wood shims
- ❑ Rubber mallet

You'll also need to move any furniture that obstructs the area you're trying to get at. Ease the heavy lifting by asking a friend or family member to help you with the moving. Four hands are also better than two when you're trying to move carpet. Its backing material—the stiff burlapy stuff that holds the fiber—is tough and sometimes heavy.

The process is simple.

1. Wearing a pair of heavy, good-fitting safety gloves, start in a corner of the room that's nearest to the spot on the floor you want to reach, and use the pry bar to loosen the edge of the carpet from the tacks, then pull the carpet up at its edge. If you've got base molding around the perimeter of the room, you can place a shim behind the heel of the pry bar to protect the molding from getting blemished or nicked as you pry up the carpet. Peel back as much carpet as you must to get to the problem; you'll probably have to weight the carpet ends with a pile of books or piece of furniture to keep them from snapping back at you.

2. Once you've got the carpet pulled back, you'll also have to deal with the padding, usually nice, light, springy foam stuff that's not too hard to handle. Fold this back too, and do your repair.

   Be aware of the tacky furring strips. You don't want to put a bare hand down on them; the tacks can also snag your clothes.

3. When you finish your repair, first replace the padding; make sure it's nice and flat before you pull the carpet down.

4. Press the carpet in place along the furring strips, using a rubber mallet to hammer the carpet (gently) back in place on the tacks.

Dealing with Spots and Spills

Many years ago, I was invited to a cocktail party at the home of a very famous writer and his equally illustrious wife. They lived in a beautiful brownstone townhouse in Manhattan. It had just been decorated: white rug, white upholstery—it was a blizzard in there! I made the mistake of taking a glass of red wine, and of course someone bumped me from behind. The full glass of red wine began to seep ominously into the pristine carpet. I was horrified, and sure that replacing the rug would take all of my salary for a year or two.

Fortunately, the hostess was as smart as she was famous, and also most gracious to a young, clumsy woman (me). She quickly retrieved a towel and a bottle of club soda from the kitchen and blotted up the red wine. The blotting, the towel, and the club soda did the job perfectly. Her rug was saved, as was my equilibrium.

In addition to keeping plenty of clean towels and club soda on hand for clumsy guests at cocktail parties, here are the ABCs of spot and spill cleaning:

- **Act quickly.** The sooner you can take action to remove a substance from the carpet, the more likely you'll be to prevent a permanent stain.

- **Blot, don't rub.** Rubbing at the spill only sticks the mess more securely to the carpet fibers.

- **Continue.** You may have to repeat the process more than once. Persistence usually pays off.

You should keep a bottle of carpet spot remover with your cleaning supplies just in case of spills. Read the label, as not all removers work for every type of spot.

There are hundreds of substances that can leave their mark; refer to Appendix B for some good websites with further information on treating different kinds of stains.

Here are a couple of general guidelines:

- When you start trying to remove a spot, whether liquid, gooey, or solid, work from the outside toward the center of the spill, so you don't spread the mess around.

- Pudding, peanut butter, melted chocolate, and other gooey, semi-solid spills can be gently scraped up and lifted with a spoon or table knife. Remove as much of the stuff as you can with this technique, then use your spot remover and blot with paper towels. Don't rub. Repeat until you've done your best. When you're finished, rinse the area with water and

Ounce of Prevention ___

When you buy a bottle of spot remover, don't wait for the first spill to see if it's compatible with your rugs. Apply some (follow the package directions) to an inconspicuous corner of the carpet, and blot it up with a paper towel. If you see the carpet color on the paper towel, the remover and your rug are not compatible. Try another brand.

blot with paper towels. You can leave some dry towels on the spot and weight them down to soak up the water. When the towels have done their job, let the area dry some more.

◆ With ground-in dry solids, break them up with a fork or table knife and vacuum. Use the spot remover, followed by the blotting technique, for whatever residue remains.

When Spot Makes a Spot

Pet urine can really mess up a carpet. I won't get into the psychology of why cats and dogs suddenly lose their manners. That's a subject for another book, but here's what you can do to take care of this business, pronto.

For stains that are still wet, follow these steps. You'll need the following:

❑ Paper towels

❑ Newspaper

❑ Bucket of cool water

1. Place a thick layer of paper towels on the wet spot; on top of this put a nice thick layer of newspaper. Weight the area with some heavy books, or stand on top of the newspaper/towel layers for a couple of minutes, then remove the dampened paper, and repeat the process.

2. Rinse the area with cool water (warm or hot water will set the stain). Remove the water by blotting it up with paper towels. Let the area dry and, if an odor remains, use the product recommended below.

For stains that have already dried, try this:

Go to a pet store and find an odor neutralizing product and follow the instructions. These special solutions contain enzymes that work on the odor caused by urine. My friends and I, pet owners all, swear by a liquid neutralizer called Nature's Miracle, but there are other enzyme-based cleaners that also do the trick. The key is to follow the directions and repeat applications if needed. And repeat after me, *blot* the spots, don't rub them.

If Spot or Fluffy returns to the "spot," it means you haven't gotten rid of all the odor. Repeat the process, or go to the more radical solution, described next.

Replacing a Stained or Damaged Section of Carpet

When all else fails, a badly discolored stain, a burn, or a tear in your wall-to-wall carpet can be cut out and replaced with a patch. This technique works on cut pile carpets; a patch is hard to hide on a looped pile rug. If you've got the latter, it's time to call in the professionals, or put a nice area rug over the bad spot.

This repair requires a piece of carpet that matches what you've got. Hopefully, you've saved your leftovers from the installation. If not, and you've carpeted a closet with the same material, cut a piece from a back corner or from under a piece of furniture. I'll never tell!

In addition, you'll need the following:

- ❑ Utility knife
- ❑ Straightedge
- ❑ Hot glue gun
- ❑ Carpet tractor

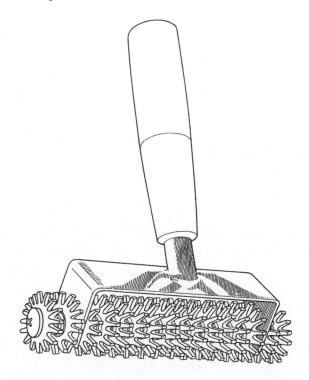

If it were any larger than a hand tool, a carpet tractor would look like an instrument of torture. Rolling it over the seams between pieces of carpet hides the seams and blends the carpet fibers together. It's not cheap—about $30—but it's a lot cheaper than a new carpet.

Crafters know all the wonderful ways a hot glue gun can pull things together. Available in corded or cordless (battery powered) models, these little heater/applicators use small sticks of glue that are heated and then squeezed out of the nose of the gun.

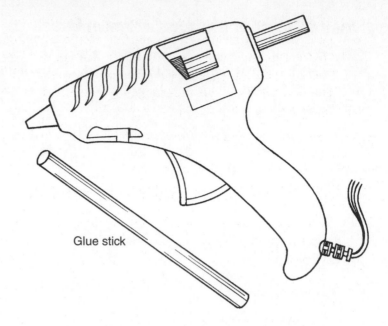

Glue stick

1. Use the utility knife to cut out a square around the stained area; guide the knife with your straightedge, and leave a border of 2"–3" around the damaged spot. Try to cut between the fibers so you only cut the backing, and take care not to cut the padding underneath.

Cut out the damaged area of carpet. You'll use the damaged piece as a template for your patch.

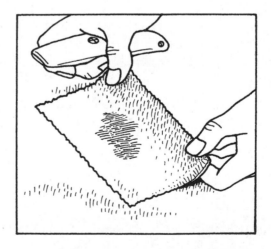

2. Use the damaged cutout as a template to cut the replacement patch from your leftover piece.

3. Apply glue to the edges of the patch, and set it into place. (Be careful of the gun's tip; it's hot when turned on. And keep the gun in an upright position when you're using it; laying it on its side can damage this little tool's thermostat.) As you set in the patch, work the glue into the edges of the carpet and the backing. Check the seams to see that they're well glued. If there are any gaps, carefully remove the patch, add glue, and reset.

4. Use the carpet tractor to roll the seams of the patch.

First Aid for Floating Laminate Floors

With a finish that's tougher than hardwood, floating laminate floors are a homeowner's dream. It's really difficult to hurt them. Manufacturers sell repair kits to hide any surface flaws that develop.

If a strip gets punctured or badly scratched and needs to be replaced, here's how to proceed.

Fortunately, damage most often occurs in the hard-wear areas of a floor: at entryways and along high-traffic hallways. Because floating floors actually "float"—their tongue-and-groove, snap-together design is resting, but not nailed on an insulating underlayment—they can be removed without pulling nails or sawing them apart.

If the damaged piece is close to a wall, the replacement is something like taking apart a jigsaw puzzle, then putting it back together. All you need to do is carefully and gently remove the baseboard molding and, starting with the piece closest to the walls, disengage the tongues from their interlocking grooves until you reach the piece that needs to be replaced.

To do this repair, you'll need a replacement piece to match the damaged one. And to remove baseboard molding, you'll need the following:

❑ Pry bar

❑ Wood shims

❑ Hammer

❑ Nail set

1. Start from the corner of the room nearest the damaged board. Move all furnishings, rugs, and obstructions from the area to clear your working space.

2. The baseboard molding is generally nailed at its seams and where the molding passes over an underlying framing stud. First, wearing work gloves, pry the molding at these nailing points, then pry the molding carefully from the wall with your pry bar, putting a shim under the heel of the pry bar to protect the wall.

3. Starting closest to the wall and the corner, remove the floorboards one by one until you get to the damaged piece. Remove the damaged piece, and click in the new one. If it is an end piece and has been cut, you'll need to saw the new board to the same size. Measure carefully, and be sure you cut the right small end of the board—one end has a tongue, the other a groove; check before you cut!

4. Click the rest of the floor back together and replace the molding. Use a shim between the hammer and the molding when you nail it back in.

What Pros Know

If a board has been ruined, and it's in the middle of the floor, the repair is a time-consuming process. The board needs to be cut out, removed, and a new one fitted and glued, so the floor no longer "floats" in 100 percent of its area. This is a painstaking and tedious process. I suggest picking up the phone and calling your installer for this fix.

If you've bent any nails, drive them through the backside of the molding, using the hammer and a nail set that matches the nail head. Drive in a new nail to replace the one you've removed. Countersink the nail; you can repair the nail holes with wood putty. When the putty dries, paint or use a wood-tone putty stick to match the baseboard.

Ceiling Repairs

Most ceilings are composed of drywall; in older homes, they may be plaster. You can use the same techniques used to repair wall flaws that are described in Chapter 5, with one difference: you'll be working on a ladder. This means that you need to always wear goggles and some head protection (a cap or bandanna) to shield yourself from any debris that falls when you're working. Follow the rules for ladder safety in Chapter 2. Be sure your stepladder is tall enough for you to work comfortably; remember, the rule of thumb is that a ladder gives you its height, plus 4 feet, as its total comfortable upward reach.

Some ceilings are in terrible trouble. Plaster is chipping, and perhaps the cracks or holes you already repaired are not holding their own. There may be underlying structural damage, or a leak somewhere above the ceiling. Water stains are a clue that the damage extends beyond wear and tear; moisture is coming from a leaky roof or pipe.

Badly damaged ceilings take a lot of work and time, and you should call a pro if your ceiling's "time" has come.

The Least You Need to Know

♦ Hardwood floors sometimes stain, spot, squeak, and warp, but you can fix a good portion of what ails them.

♦ Pilot holes are the best way to get a nail or screw into hard materials. If you're in doubt about which drill bit matches the fastener you're using, bring the fastener to the store and ask the hardware guy—or gal—to help you pick it out.

♦ You can soften up a vinyl tile with a steam iron and a towel to make it easier to remove.

♦ Removing stains from carpets requires quick action and no rubbing! Also, if at first you don't succeed, repeat the removal process. When all else fails, you can repair a small damaged area with a replacement patch.

♦ Repair of drywall and plaster ceilings is quite similar to fixing flaws in walls. Just use your ladder safely!

Chapter 7

Stairs: A Few Steps to a Happy Landing

In This Chapter

- ◆ The anatomy of a staircase
- ◆ Silencing annoying, squeaky stairs
- ◆ Fixing a loose tread
- ◆ Securing handrails and balusters
- ◆ Making your stairways safe for elders and children

Fixing a staircase is usually a matter of tightening up its parts. Most stairs are constructed of wood, and wood is a responsive material: it expands when the surrounding humidity increases and shrinks when its environment is dry. Even though we can't see it happening, these tiny movements in the wood, coupled with human contact—you, your family, and your pets, walking, stomping, and bounding up and down, every day—loosen the parts of a staircase. Eventually, the stairs begin to talk, as only stairs can: they squeak.

If the joints of your staircase are not as snug as they once were, you can help them settle down.

Stairs can also be a hazard for the elderly and for small children. I'll talk about a couple of fixes to improve safety, too.

Parts of a Staircase

It has more parts, but for our purposes, this is what you should know about staircases. Let's start with what we step on: the horizontal part of a step is called the *tread;* the vertical part is the *riser.* The *banister*—what we hold onto going up and down—has three main parts: the *handrail* that we grasp, the vertical posts spaced evenly along its length, which support the handrail, called *balusters,* and a larger, supporting vertical piece at the bottom of the handrail, called a *newel post.*

Anatomy of a staircase.

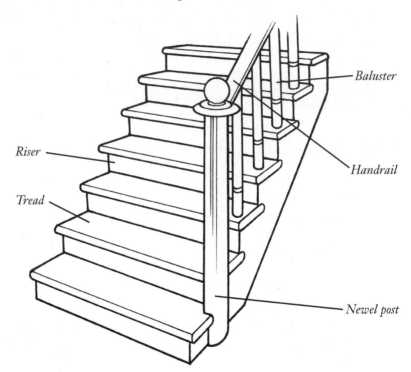

Baluster

Riser

Handrail

Tread

Newel post

Silencing Squeaks

Squeaky stairs signal loose joints, and they're fairly easy to fix. We'll start with the simplest procedure, and go from there.

A Lube Job

This doesn't make it easier, but if you must, remove carpet and padding from the steps to get to the stair. (Find out how in Chapter 6.) Follow the directions and watch out for furring strips, which may be located not only at the top and bottom of the stair run, but also at an interval or intervals where seams of the carpet start and end.

To mark the offending steps, you'll need your roll of painter's or masking tape.

Ask the heaviest member of your family (no offense intended) to walk up and down the stairs so you can locate the protesting tread or treads. Mark them with a piece of tape.

You'll also need some powdered graphite, which comes in a little squeeze bottle. You can squeeze the graphite out of the container and into the offending, noisy *joints*. In the case where the joint is between the top of the riser and the tread, you might want to hold a piece of cardboard underneath the graphite bottle to catch the falling powder, then blow it off the cardboard into the joint.

This will lubricate the joints, and may be all you need. If not, try the next procedure.

def•i•ni•tion

In carpentry, a **joint** is the intersection of two pieces of wood. There are many different kinds of wood joints.

Repairing Squeaks from Below the Stairs

Like the wood floor fixes in Chapter 6, taming squeaks is much easier if you can get to them from under the stairs.

You'll need the following:

- ❏ Hammer
- ❏ Wood shims
- ❏ Carpenter's glue (yellow)
- ❏ A small block of wood for driving the shims

1. Put on safety goggles to protect your eyes from falling debris. Since you've already marked the offending stair(s), have your friend stomp on the squeaky treads, so you can see what moves.

2. Coat the wood shims with glue, and tap them, thin end forward, into the joint between the offending tread and its riser. Drive the shims in by placing the wood block between the butt end of the shim and the hammer head.

What Pros Know

Basements can be dark, and sometimes it's hard to position a flashlight and work simultaneously. If your work area is poorly illuminated, buy yourself a work light. It's essentially a light bulb in a socket, surrounded by a little plastic cage, with a long cord, that you can hook or hang where you're working. Just always be aware of the cord so you don't trip yourself.

Silence a squeaky stair with wood shims.

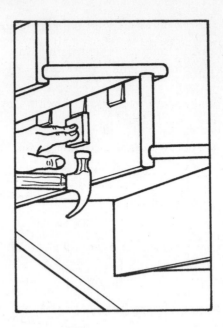

Fixing the Squeak or Loose Tread from Above

You can tighten the joint between tread and riser by drilling straight down through the tread into the riser, and inserting and tightening the screw.

Be sure to mark the location for your drill bit carefully, and keep your drill bit straight—that is, perpendicular to the surface you are drilling. You don't want the screw to go through the tread and miss the riser!

You'll need the following:

- ❑ Measuring tape
- ❑ Pencil or awl
- ❑ Electric drill
- ❑ Combination bit sized for the screw you're using
- ❑ Screwdriver
- ❑ Flathead wood screws ($2^1/_2$")
- ❑ Wood putty
- ❑ Sandpaper (220-grit)
- ❑ Finish or paint to match stair surface (not important if the stairs are covered)

1. Measure carefully if your stair tread is not flush with the riser; most treads extend at least $1^1/2$" from their supporting risers. The edge of a standard riser where it meets the tread is $3/4$" thick, and ideally you want to drill into the center of the riser. Mark the spot with a pencil or awl.

2. Wearing safety goggles, drill two or three pilot holes; insert and tighten screws below the tread surface.

Insert screws from above.

3. Fill the holes with wood putty; wear gloves to protect your hands if you don't like to handle the putty. Let the putty dry, sand, and finish as desired.

Another way to fill the gap left by a countersunk fastener is to buy a package of small, round wooden plugs, the same size as the screw head. These are called *dowel plugs*, because these small wood wafers are cut from a wooden dowel. Coat one side of the plug with glue and insert the glued side in the hole; then finish as desired. Some people like to use these plugs; others prefer the putty fix.

Getting a Grip on Handrails

With use, time, and fluctuations in humidity, the vertical balusters sometimes loosen in the *mortises* where they join the handrail, causing a shaky situation that's not good when you're negotiating stairs—the handrail should support *you*, not the reverse.

Here are two ways to tighten the relationship between handrail and baluster.

For the "shimy" solution, you'll need the following:

❑ Wood shim

❑ Carpenter's glue (yellow)

❑ Small wood block (to drive the shim)

❑ Hammer

❑ Utility knife

def•i•ni•tion

A **mortise** is a hole or slot cut into wood or other material so that a projecting piece (called a tenon) can be precisely inserted. In woodworking, a mortise and tenon joint creates a good bond between two pieces of wood.

1. Coat the wood shim with glue.

2. Using the small block as a driver, hammer the shim into the joint between the baluster and the handrail. Don't try to drive the two pieces apart, just drive the shim until it closes the gap between handrail and baluster.

3. Using the utility knife, trim the shim flush with the banister. Shims are pretty easy to cut; they're softwood.

For the "screwy" solution, you'll need the following:

❑ Electric drill

❑ Combination bit sized for the screw you're using

❑ Screwdriver to match screw head

❑ Flathead wood screws

❑ Wood putty

❑ Sandpaper (220-grit)

❑ Finish to cover repair (wood finish or paint)

1. Wearing safety goggles, using the combination bit, drill a pilot hole up through the baluster into the handrail at a 45° angle.

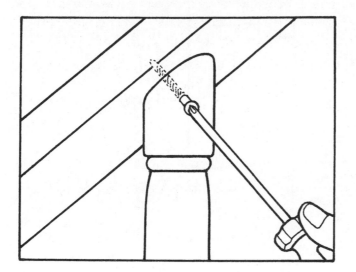

Angle a screw through the baluster and handrail.

2. Drive in, countersink, and tighten the screw.

3. Fill the hole with wood putty; let it dry. Sand the repair and finish as desired.

Off-Base Balusters

Sometimes the baluster gets loose in its bottom mortise—its joint with the stair tread. You'll need another pilot hole and countersunk screw for this one.

You'll also need the following:

- ❏ Electric drill

- ❏ Combination bit sized for the screw you're using

- ❏ Screwdriver to match screw head

- ❏ Flathead wood screws

- ❏ Wood putty

- ❏ Sandpaper (220-grit)

- ❏ Finish to cover repair (wood finish or paint)

1. Wearing safety goggles, drill the pilot hole at an angle through the baluster and into the tread.

Tighten a baluster with a screw support.

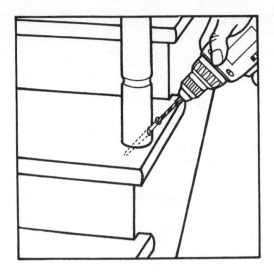

2. Drive in, countersink, and tighten the screw in the predrilled hole.

3. Fill the hole with wood putty; let it dry, then sand and finish.

Safe Stairs

For elders and children, a staircase can be a hazard. A secure handrail and stair treads tight to the risers are great first steps, but the young and the frail may need extra help.

Ounce of Prevention

Equip the electrical receptacles (outlets) in your stair halls with night lights. They use a miniscule amount of energy but make the way safe for anyone who's moving around when the house is dark. Keep a supply of the little bulbs with your other light bulbs, so you always have a spare when this little "night watchman" suffers a burnout.

Elder Safety

Falls are the leading cause of life-threatening, debilitating injury for the elderly, and falls on stairs are a common culprit. If you have an older person living with you, you want to make sure that they can *see* the steps.

You'll need the following:

- ❏ Scissors

- ❏ A roll of reflective tape (it glows in the dark, a plus at night and during power outages and other emergencies)

1. Make sure the stairs are clean and dry so the tape will adhere.

2. Cut each strip of tape so that it will extend the entire length of the tread.

3. Secure the reflective tape to the top, front edge of the tread. Make sure it is lying flat. Place the tape on the top front edge of the stair landing, and every stair in the staircase.

If there are any step-ups or places where the floor is uneven—sills in doorways, for example, where an elderly person might trip—mark these step-ups and sills with reflective tape as well. Even a half-inch rise in the floor surface could create a problem for someone with poor mobility or vision.

Kidproofing the Stairs

Child safety gates have been around for years. They're an inexpensive way to keep active and curious youngsters from an accident on the stairs, or any other place where they might find themselves in harm's way.

When my son was just 10 months old, he was quite the little bruiser, built solid and full of energy. We had put safety gates on our stairs, but at that time, what was available was a fairly simple design that clamped to the sides of the stairway by means of pressure. There were no fasteners on the thing that I could screw into the wall.

One day, my boy was cruising around on the upper floor in his little walker, careening against the walls (why I learned to repair drywall). He worked up such a head of steam that, in a split second, he crashed against the pressure-installed gate and was on his way down the steps when I grabbed him, and the walker, preventing a disaster. Within an hour I was at the hardware store, looking for the right straps and screws to secure the gate to the walls. We rigged our own safety setup. And the walker went, as my son would say when he couldn't locate something, "bye-bye someplace."

Pressure mounted gates are still around, but the Consumer Product Safety Commission does not recommend their installation at the top of stairs, because children (like someone I know) can push them over and fall down the stairs. Select gates with hardware mounts, screw them into the wall securely, and periodically check the screws to see that they are still tightly fastened.

The Least You Need to Know

◆ A staircase is made up of the tread, riser, handrail, balusters, and newel post.

◆ You can make invisible repairs to the stairs if you can get at them from underneath.

◆ Wood shims and countersunk screws tame squeaks and tighten wobbly parts.

◆ Add safety insurance to your stairs: night lights in the hall, reflective tape on the treads for your elders, and hardware-mounted safety gates for your tots.

Chapter 8

Getting Clear About Windows

In This Chapter

- Parts of a window
- How double-hung windows work
- Smoothing the passage of sticky windows, and tightening up loose ones
- Dealing with the pain of broken panes
- Common screen repairs

Your home's windows are its (and your) eyes on the bigger world. In addition to lighting your interiors, keeping fresh air flowing in good weather, and shutting out the elements when it's foul outside, windows that work and look good make a statement about you. So subdue that stubborn sash, banish those broken windows and torn screens, and give your home a clean, bright face.

What a Pane! Parts of a Window

There are many kinds of windows, but nothing's better for your *fenestration* vocabulary than learning the names of the parts of the most common window style—the double-hung. Now you can talk the talk!

def•i•ni•tion

Fenestration is the term architects use for the design and placement of windows in a building.

Let's start from the top. The *header* is the top horizontal piece of the frame. The *jamb* refers to the vertical side pieces of the frame. The *sill* is the horizontal part at the bottom of the frame. (Looking at the window from outside, you'd see the stool where the sill is, often supported by a small board called an apron.)

Now let's get to the real business of this window. Double-hungs have two moving pieces, called the *sash*. The piece on top is the *upper sash*, which can be lowered from its closed position, and on the bottom is the *lower sash*, which can be raised. The rails are the horizontal part of the sash frame and the stiles are the vertical parts.

The sash, upper and lower, hold the glass portion of the window. A single piece of glass is called a *pane*. A sash can have one or more panes; the dividers between the panes are called *muntins*. On both vertical sides of the sash are *channels*, which guide the sash up or down in a straight line. The small molding piece that runs up the front, at the sides of the lower sash is called the inside *stop*, which keeps the sash running smoothly in its channel. The sashes lock together by means of a two-piece *latch*, positioned atop the upper rail of the lower sash, and the bottom rail of the upper sash.

If your windows look like double-hungs, but the upper sash doesn't move, these are called single-hung windows.

Are you getting clear about windows yet? Don't worry; review the illustration if you forget some of the names referred to in the repairs.

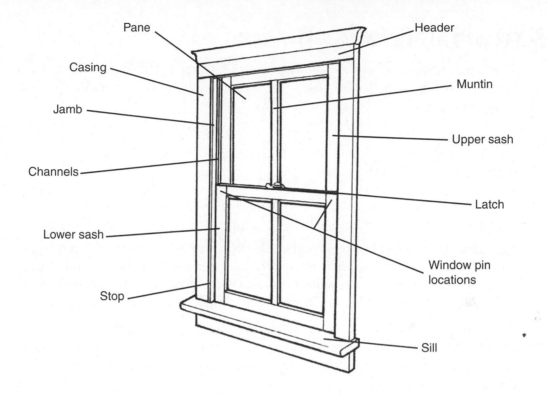

Parts of a double-hung window, as it looks when viewed from inside.

How Double-Hung Windows Work

Modern double-hung windows are truly things of beauty. Double glazed, weather-stripped, and vinyl-clad at the factory, they need very little maintenance. In the spring and fall, you just clean the channels, and spray and wipe the moving parts with a little lubricant.

When it's time to wash the glass parts, the real benefits of modern double-hung windows are even more apparent. The sash of most good-quality double hung windows can be removed from their channels and washed. No more ladders, no more freezing fingers as you try to clean them from the outside. Technology can be a blessing.

However, this part of the chapter is not for owners of fabulous, new, easy-care windows. It's for the rest of us who have sticky, drafty, balky, and unrepentant old wood windows that need more than their fair share of attention. So let's get busy!

Stubborn Stuck Sash

This section proceeds from a no-load solution to some nitty-gritty ideas.

Wait and See

This is not often the case (it's too easy), but sometimes the only problems with your windows is that it's been hot and humid for days. If the windows worked well before the heat wave, you may want to leave them alone temporarily.

Once a dry spell arrives, your windows may go up and down as before.

Don't take drastic action to sand or plane windows during humid seasons. While they may be sticky in the spring and summer, the cooler, drier months could set your newly sanded windows rattling in the jambs because you removed too much wood. If you are trying to make balky windows glide to your tune in summer—when you need to open and close them frequently—try the less invasive fixes.

Gentle Tap, Tap, Tapping

Before you disturb the paint on the windows with any type of prying tool, you can try this little wake-up call. This technique works best if you can work both sides of the window; you may need a helper if the windows are on the second floor and require a ladder to reach their exterior side.

You'll need the following:

- ❏ Small wood block
- ❏ Piece of heavy cloth
- ❏ Duct tape
- ❏ Claw hammer
- ❏ Sponge
- ❏ Lubricant or silicon spray

1. Make sure the sash is unlatched. Wrap the wood block in a piece of heavy cloth or felt to protect the finish on the windows. Keep the cloth in place on the block with some duct tape, if you like.

2. Place the block against the frame along the bottom rail of the lower sash and gently tap it with the hammer along the width of the sash. If your windows are on the first floor, go outside and do this to the same rail on its exterior side. Gradually work along the stiles of the sash, inside and out, working upward until you reach the top of the window.

3. If this frees the sash, move it up and down, and examine the channels. Clean out any debris and dirt with a damp sponge. Let dry, and spray some lubricant or silicon spray in the channels.

What Pros Know

If your windows are stuck because they've been painted shut, use a utility knife to carefully score the paint that has bonded any window parts together: between stop and sash, between upper and lower sash, between sill and sash. You'll only do more damage to the paint if you skip this step before trying to move or pry the windows.

Don't Want to Pry, But ...

If gentle tapping doesn't work, you'll need a stronger approach. You'll need the following:

- ❏ Putty knife
- ❏ Rubber mallet
- ❏ Pry bar
- ❏ Shim or thin block of wood

To pry the window from inside:

1. Make sure the sash is unlatched. Insert the blade of a putty knife into the crack between the stile of the lower sash and the stop, tapping it lightly with the rubber mallet to free the window. Do this along both stiles.

Pry open a tight sash from the inside.

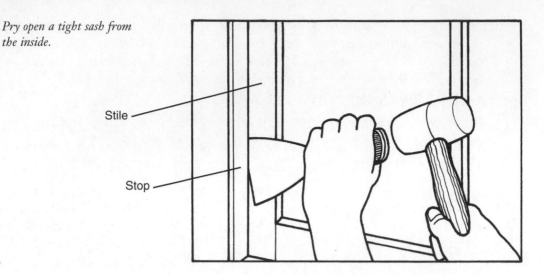

Stile

Stop

2. If this frees the sash, move it up and down. Work the putty knife into any spots that are still resistant.

Once the window is moving freely, examine the channels. Clean out any debris and dirt with a damp sponge. Let dry, and spray some lubricant or silicon spray in the channels.

To pry the window from outside:

1. Make sure the sash is unlatched. Using a thin wood block or shim to protect the stool from the pry bar, insert the pry bar into the crack between the stool and the sash. Work first at one end of the sash, then the other, so that the sash will move up evenly.

Pry open a tight sash from the outside.

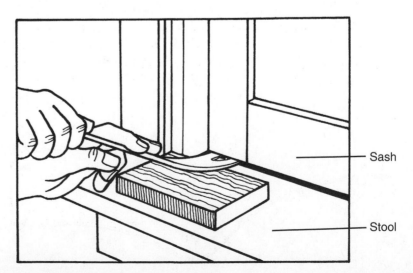

Sash

Stool

2. If this moves the window, go back inside and open it. Examine the channels, then clean and lubricate them.

Windows That Won't Stay Open

You can prop up a window that won't stay open with a stick or a ruler, set in the channel below one side of the sash. Or you can install some hardware, as described next. But neither of these "make do" fixes really corrects the underlying problem.

A sash that's loose in the jamb, and won't stay put when it's opened, usually means that its raising/lowering mechanism has failed. In old, single-paned wood windows, this is often a rope-and-weight pulley system; your window won't stay open because the weights have come loose from the rope, or the rope has simply broken from age and wear. If you look at the top of the jamb, you'll probably see the little pulley.

Some rope-and-pulley controlled windows have access panels in the jambs that allow you to get to the weights without removing the window casings. Even when you can get to them, though, this is a delicate, often frustrating (the weights fall down inside the walls!), and time-consuming job. Remember, these old, single-paned windows are probably leaky, and they're costing you for the extra money you have to spend on heating and air-conditioning your drafty house. The best fix is to start saving for new, energy-efficient sashes that can be fitted in the old jambs, or spring for completely new windows.

In the meantime, you can apply weather stripping at the joints of your windows: between sash and sill, between the sash and the stops, anywhere air is leaking in (put your hand at one of the joints on a cold, windy day and you'll feel the cold air passing through).

And to keep the windows up when you do want fresh air, you can install little stainless steel controls in the channels of the lower sash that provide some resistance to your weight-less window. They work like the stick or the ruler, but they're a bit more sturdy, and only cost a couple of dollars.

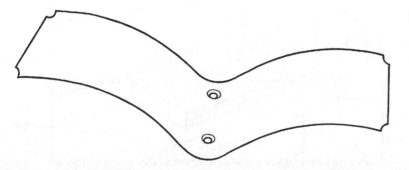

Window control.

To install them, you'll need the following:

❑ Ruler or dowel (to hold up the window while you work)

❑ One pair of window controls per loose window

❑ Claw hammer

❑ Box nails

❑ Measuring tape

❑ Pencil or awl

1. Raise the lower sash as far as it will go, and secure with the dowel or ruler; you may want to prop it on both sides for safety.

2. Position the control in the lower sash channel so that the nail holes (which have little burrs on the backside where they meet the channel) are about an inch below the highest opening you want for your window. Nail in one control.

Window control in place.

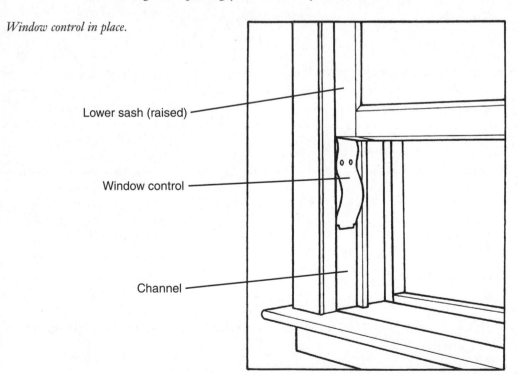

3. Nail in the control on the opposite side of the window. Measure and mark the location of the nail holes for the second control with the pencil or awl, so both controls are nailed at the same height in the channel.

4. Remove the supporting dowel or ruler and carefully lower the window so that the top sections of the controls are between the sash and channel as you lower the sash (see the previous illustration). The controls are flexible, so they act like springs to tighten the movement of the sash.

When Windows Break

Modern windows—the double-glazed, gas-filled, or tempered variety—are pretty sturdy. But when they break, you'll need a professional glass installer to fix them. Current building codes require that door glass (for *sidelights* and other door panes) be tempered. If it breaks, it does so harmlessly into about a million little chips per pane. I know this because my lawn guys got too close to our French doors with a weed-whacker, and it was doomsday for the bottom right pane. Specialized glass products have a little seal imprinted in a lower corner of the glass, which is your indicator that all such panes need professional replacement.

When tempered or other specialty glass breaks, you'll have to do a temporary repair until the glass man arrives. Even when you're just picking up glass chips, take precautions when you clean up the glass.

You'll need the following:

❑ Newspaper

❑ Painter's, masking, or duct tape

❑ Putty knife

❑ Measuring tape

❑ Utility knife (to cut cardboard make-do)

❑ Sheet of corrugated (box) cardboard, or sheet of transparent acrylic plastic, cut to fit opening

def•i•ni•tion

A **sidelight** is a window positioned next to a door. Usually doors with sidelights have one on either side of the door. Tempered glass has been heated and cooled repeatedly in a controlled environment to give it more strength than conventional, single-layer window glass.

To clean up a broken specialty glass window:

1. Sweep up and discard any chips of glass on either side of the window (interior and exterior). Tape a piece of newspaper on the inside of the opening so more glass does not fall inside. Wearing heavy gloves and safety goggles, and working from outside, use the putty knife to carefully knock off any remaining pieces of glass; put the debris in a supermarket paper bag (it's thick), and discard.

2. Measure the dimensions of the now-empty opening, and cut a cardboard template that you can put in place with duct tape or masking tape from the inside. (You can also take your measurements to a hardware store and get a piece of Plexiglas cut to fit, for a more aesthetic make-do.)

Ounce of Prevention

Large panes of glass are too heavy to handle. If your panes are larger than a foot-and-a-half square, leave replacement to the pros. You must handle glass carefully, by its edges, or it will easily crack. Start small if you want to learn to work with glass!

For small window panes that are single-glazed (one layer of conventional glass, no little imprint in the lower corner), you can replace them yourself. I don't recommend cutting your own glass unless you've had a lot of experience with a glass cutter (it's best to test your skill with a small pane first). Do the cardboard make-do fix, and take your window frame measurements to the hardware store so they can cut your glass.

You'll need all the tools and materials mentioned earlier for removing tempered glass and installing a temporary make-do (cardboard will do until you get your replacement glass).

In addition, if you're doing the replacement, you'll need the following:

❏ Pliers

❏ Sandpaper (100–150 grit)

❏ Sheet of glass (see Step 6)

❏ Glazing putty (sold in ropes so you don't have to roll your own)

❏ Glazier's points

❏ Touch-up paint (for repaired window frame)

1. Unlike tempered glass, shards of single sheets of glass are very sharp. Work from outside and, as with tempered glass, tape newspaper on the inside of the window.

2. Wearing heavy gloves and safety goggles, remove the large pieces of glass first. Use the putty knife to knock out remaining small bits of glass.

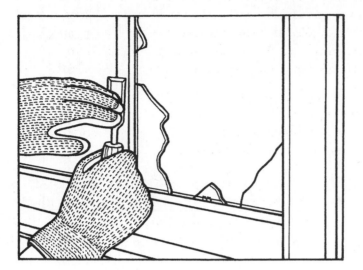

Remove a broken single-glazed pane.

3. Remove the old glazier's points with pliers.

4. Lightly sand the edges of the opening to get rid of any remaining putty.

5. Measure the window opening; measure and install the cardboard make-do.

6. Take your opening measurements (remember, measure twice, cut once) to the hardware store and get a piece of glass cut. Tell them that your measurements are the actual size of the opening; they'll cut the glass $1/8$ of an inch less than the total width and length.

Once you have your replacement glass, you can proceed with the next part of the repair:

1. Remove the cardboard make-do. Working from outside, press a rope of glazing putty, about $1/4$ inch thick, around all the edges of the window opening. This is your setup for installing the glass.

2. Carefully press the pane into place, then insert the glazier's points into the frame, pushing them in with the putty knife. Use two points on each side if it's a small pane. If the glass is longer than a foot in length or width, insert the glazier's point's every four to six inches.

Insert glazier's points into frame.

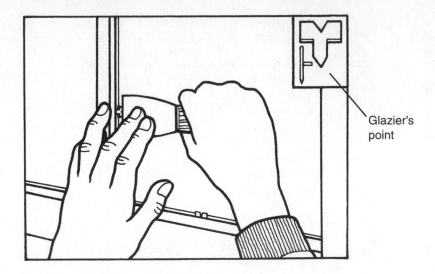

Glazier's point

3. Apply another ¹/₄-inch rope of putty around the edges of the opening. Use the putty knife to smooth the putty and form a good seal with the window frame.

4. When the putty is dry, you can paint it to match the surrounding wood.

Screen Test

The screen and storm windows at our ancient house are heavy and cranky. They're in wood frames—no nice little slide-out or pop-out aluminum framed stuff. Our least favorite weekends in spring and fall are those when we have to change from storms to screens, and from screens to storms. But before we do any of the really tiresome leg work and ladder climbing, the stored windows must be cleaned. You clean storms the way you clean any window: with glass cleaner and clean rags or paper towels. And the spring changeover is the time to replace any storm window glass. If it's the single-glazed variety of storm window, you can follow the previous directions.

This is also a good time to clean the frames, if your storm/screens are of the slide-out variety. Clean the runners and the channels where they fit, and lubricate them with a lubricating oil or silicon spray—they'll go in and out more easily.

To clean dirty screens, simply spray the screens with your garden hose and clean them with the sponge (or a wire brush) and soapy water. Rinse, let dry, and hang 'em!

Screen Repairs

Once the screens are out, you may notice some defects: a loose screen here, a little hole there. Last spring while cleaning her window screens, my sister noticed that her big red Persian cat, Gizmo, had been slipping out of the house the previous summer because one of the screens for the living room windows had come loose from its frame. She had to replace it, or Gizmo would be doing his warm-weather wandering once again!

Here's how to handle common screen defects.

Small Holes

Holes in the screens let in all kinds of unappealing critters when your windows are open: mosquitoes, moths, flies, and other little creatures will take advantage.

To some of us, little repairs in a screen door might look a bit tacky, so if it bothers you to have a patch at your door, you might want to go all the way and replace the whole screen (see how in the next section; door screens work just like the window screens). But for window screens that don't get as much scrutiny as a front or back door, you can patch; it's a less time-consuming fix.

You'll need the following:

- ❏ Scissors

- ❏ Screen patch (these come in various sizes, available at most hardware stores; make sure the color/material is a close match to your screen—some are metal, some are fiberglass—or it really will show)

- ❏ Glue for fiberglass screen (ask the store salesperson for a good, waterproof variety)

You'll notice that screens are composed of lengths of fine, interwoven metal wire or fiberglass *filament*.

1. Cut a patch to fit over the hole in the screen; the patch should extend at least 1"–2" around the circumference of the hole.

def•i•ni•tion

A **filament** is a slender strand of fiber or other material. The thin wire that is the light-producing element of a bulb when electric current passes through it and the element that emits electrons in a vacuum tube when current is passed through it are also known as filaments.

2. You'll want to remove a wire or filament (or two) from each side of your screen patch to give you a little bit of extra length to make the fix.

3. Position the patch over the hole on the interior side of the screen. Insert the wire ends of each side of the patch into the intact screen holes around the tear or hole you are covering. Bend the wire ends so they grip the intact screen. You may want to use needlenose pliers or even a nail file to help you bend the wires—they're tiny, and tough to work with if you have big hands. If the screen is the soft, fiberglass filament type, you won't bend the ends—they'll lie on top of the edges of the repair. You can glue the ends to the existing screen with the waterproof glue.

Replacing Screens

If a screen has big holes or tears or has become loose and taken on a "wavy" look, you'll want to replace it. Even if the old screen isn't torn, if it's bulging in places it may be weakened by the stretching. You may as well get new material to work with. Use the old screen for patches (store it in one of your "leftovers" bins).

The most common window and door screens are attached to the screen's frame with a flexible, vinyl rope known as *spline*. The spline fits into a groove where mesh meets frame. If you look carefully at the corners of the screen, you may also see little plastic pieces that help fit the spline snugly in each corner.

def•i•ni•tion

Spline is a piece of wood, metal, or plastic that is used as a connecting or framing piece between two sections of material. Spline can be used to hold a screen in its surrounding frame; the material that frames caning in a chair seat where it meets the wood or metal part of the seat is also known as spline.

If the screen is mounted in the window (or door), you'll need to detach it from the surrounding frame. In the case of window screens, you'll probably just need to pop or slide them out. A door screen may be mounted to the frame with screws; if so, unscrew the screen from the frame, take out the screen, and put the screws in the screw holes in the window or door with a couple of turns so they don't fall out. Loose screws are always rolling away and getting lost!

You'll need the following:

❑ Needlenose pliers

❑ Narrow putty knife or flat-tipped (standard) screwdriver

- Mesh screening
- Measuring tape
- Scissors
- Spline tool
- Utility knife
- Replacement spline
- Plastic corner pieces, if you have these in the corners

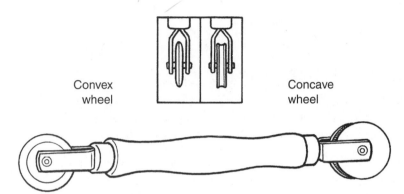

Convex
wheel

Concave
wheel

A spline tool is a hand tool with a wheel at each end. One wheel has a convex (∪) rim, for pushing the screen into the spline channel; the other wheel has a concave (∩) rim, for pushing the spline down over the mesh and into the channel.

While setting in the mesh and inserting the spline, an extra set of hands is helpful for holding the mesh in place. Or you can hold the mesh down at the corners you're not working on with a wood block or two.

You will need to bring samples of your mesh screening, old spline, and plastic corners (if they're used for your screens) to the hardware store so that you can buy the exact match of each material. There are different types of all three.

You will also need to measure the screen so that you buy replacement screening of sufficient size to cover the screen opening. Also, measure the perimeter of the window opening(s) so that you buy a sufficient length of spline.

 What Pros Know _____

Remember geometry? If you do, skip this tip. If math gave you a rash, read on. It's not necessary to measure all four sides of a rectangular opening to find the distance around it. Perimeter = length + width times 2. Aha, applied mathematics! Your geometry teacher told you it would be useful, and the time has come!

1. Lay the screen flat on a sturdy work surface. Starting in one corner, remove the little plastic corners (if they're there) with the needlenose pliers, or pop them out with the screwdriver tip. Pry out the spline with the putty knife or screwdriver, going corner to corner. The spline may be dirty or gunky, so the edge of the knife or tip of the screwdriver can assist you in getting it out cleanly.

Remove old spline.

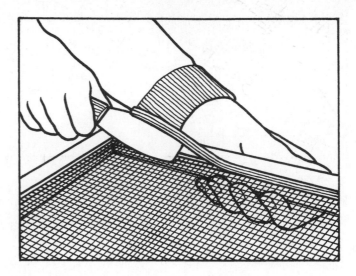

2. If you're saving the old screen, roll it up and set it aside. Otherwise discard it. Check the channels from which the old spline and screen have been removed. If they're clean, go to Step 3. If they're dirty, get a bucket of warm water, a sponge, and some paper towels, clean them and let them dry.

3. Lay the new mesh screen over the window (door) frame. Make sure the mesh is lying square to the frame; check at the edges to see that the gridwork of the mesh lines up with the frame so it doesn't look crooked.

4. Measure the frame's outer dimensions, and with the scissors, cut the mesh to this size. Cut a little square out of each corner of the cut piece, no wider than the frame. This will keep the mesh from bunching in the corners when you install it.

5. Starting in a corner, push the mesh into the spline channel with the convex (∪) wheel of the spline tool. Go all the way up and down one side. You're trying to create a light indentation, not scrunch down the mesh. The spline will do the holding.

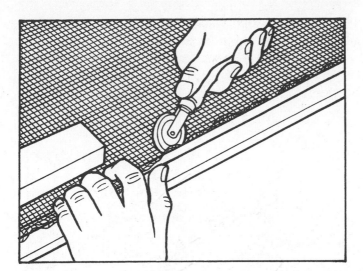

Use spline tool (convex wheel) to insert mesh in channels.

6. Starting in the same corner where you began Step 5, using the concave (∩) wheel of the tool, push the spline into the channel over the mesh. Put your other hand on the screen, or have your helper hold it, so that the tension on the screen is even and it doesn't bunch up. When you've fully inserted the spline on one side, follow Steps 5 and 6 to install the spline on the other three sides.

7. Once the spline is set around the perimeter, use the screwdriver to push the spline into all four corners; trim the end of the spline with the scissors. Trim any mesh that still overlaps the frame with the utility knife. If your original screening had plastic corners, install the new ones.

You're done! Put the screen back in the window or door opening.

Installing Security Pins in Windows

In areas of your home that are hidden from view on the ground floor, it's easy for someone with bad intentions to break a window, undo the latch, and make mayhem. If you have a perimeter security system installed, that's one way to safeguard unwanted entry. Security gates (not window guards, which protect children from falling out) for windows will do the job, but will also make you feel like you're living in a prison. I had these in one apartment in Manhattan where my bedroom windows opened on a fire escape. I hated the feeling of being locked in, and moved out within months.

If you don't have the budget for a security service, you can add a layer of protection from forced window entry using the simple method of drilling holes through the lower sash of your double hung windows and installing window security pins, common nails, or eye bolts that prevent the window from easily being raised, even if a pane is broken out.

You'll need the following:

❑ Measuring tape

❑ Awl or pencil

❑ Electric drill

❑ Window pins, eyebolts, or common nails; one pair for each window

❑ Drill bit slightly larger than pins, bolts, or nail you are using

❑ Masking or painter's tape, or bit stop to fit your bit

❑ Lubricant or silicon spray

Ounce of Prevention

If you can only find window pins that operate with a key, don't buy them; use bolts or nails instead. In case of fire or other emergency, you don't want to be looking for a misplaced key!

1. Fully close and lock the window you'll be drilling; you want the upper rail of the lower (inside) sash, and the lower rail of the upper (outside) sash to be parallel. (The double-hung window shown at the beginning of this chapter shows it in locked position.)

2. You don't want to drill through both sashes completely, because this will enable someone to foil your security plan from outside! So measure the depth of the two sashes in locked position, and mark your drill bit to $3/4$ of that measure with a piece of masking tape or a bit stop. You will stop drilling when the bit gets to this mark.

3. Find the center of the top left and top right corners of the lower sash; mark it with the awl or pencil; the awl is good for this mark, because it "grounds" the drill as you begin drilling. (Security pin hole locations are marked on the window illustration earlier in this chapter.)

4. Wearing safety goggles, hold the drill straight, drill into the window at the marks. Keep your grip firm, because you're drilling through two wood rails and possibly some weather stripping between them. Stop drilling when your bit is inserted to the stop or masking tape mark.

5. When both holes are drilled, lubricate your fasteners before you insert them in the holes. The fasteners should be a little loose so you can remove them easily.

The Least You Need to Know

◆ Some sticky window problems are merely the result of sticky weather; don't apply invasive measures unless you must.

◆ Old wood windows that have lost their weights can still be controlled by installing devices in the channels.

◆ To fix screens mounted with splines, an exact duplicate material is needed.

◆ Window pins are a simple addition to your home's security.

Chapter 9

Doors: An Open-and-Shut Case

In This Chapter

- ◆ Parts of a door
- ◆ Silencing the talkative door, and making the stubborn one respond
- ◆ Getting a grip on doorknobs with a couple of easy repairs
- ◆ Keeping balky sliders on track
- ◆ Installing a peephole in a windowless outer door

Do you have door slammers at your house? I do. They announce themselves with a bang, not a whimper, which is okay, except that our back door gets a workout. Screws loosen, the strike plate wobbles, and pretty soon it's time to get out the screwdriver for a couple of minor repairs.

Throughout her teenage years, our daughter would voice her displeasure with a resounding bang of her bedroom door. The last slam came when she broke one of the ancient hinges clear through its cast iron body—I believe the term is metal fatigue, and I'm sure it was very tired. Replacement hinges set Rachel back several weeks of allowance money, so she's become much gentler with doors ever since.

Even without a resident slammer, doors get a workout over the years, and some at your house may be showing signs of age or hard wear. This chapter will teach you all the important parts of doors, and how to make them swing to *your* rhythm—and eliminate wobbles, squeaks, drags, or rattles.

Of course, you can avoid many of these little repairs by insisting that all members of your household close doors with their hand *on* the knob: no slamming! It's the best preventive maintenance I can think of.

Anatomy of a Door

You may notice some of the same words that are also used to describe a window. The *jamb* is the vertical part of the door frame—the opening in which the door is installed. The frame's top piece is called the *header*; the bottom piece is the *sill*. On exterior doors, the sill may have another piece over it that spans the sill; this is known as a saddle (not shown).

The door itself has horizontal parts, called the *rails*; and vertical parts, called *stiles*. The *hinge stile* is the vertical piece where hinges are attached; the *latch stile* is the vertical piece that holds the latch, doorknob, and/or lock, if there is one.

Parts of a door.

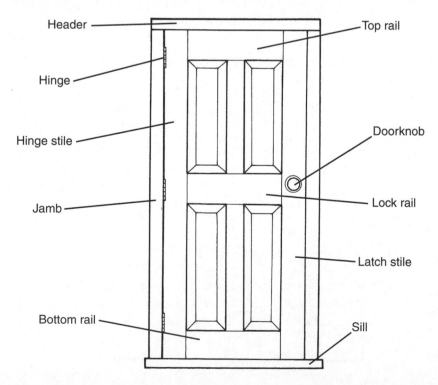

Header — Top rail

Hinge

Hinge stile — Doorknob

Jamb — Lock rail

Latch stile

Bottom rail — Sill

What Pros Know

The previous illustration shows the door from the outside; because the hinges are on the left side of the door, it is known as a *left-handed* door. Looking at the door from the outside, doors that are hinged on the right are known as *right-handed* doors. Knowing whether a door is right- or left-handed is important if you are buying or replacing a doorknob that can be locked, also known as a lockset, that works with one or the other, but not both. Since you want the key to be on the outside of the door and the push- or turn-button lock on the inside, you need to buy a right- or left-handed lockset, depending upon the door in which it will be installed.

Many older doors are composed of rails, stiles, and panels, like the one shown in the illustration. Other, newer doors may not be solid wood; they may be made of thin layers of wood or metal applied over a core of rigid foam or other material.

Silencing the Talking Door

A door that squeaks usually needs attention to its hinges—the metal hardware that attaches the door to its frame. There are lots of different kinds of hinges, but the principle is the same. The two sides of the hinge, called leaves, connect to each other by means of a pin threaded through interlocking knuckles.

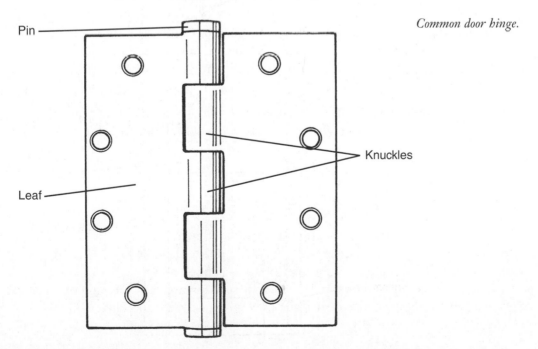

Common door hinge.

Pin

Knuckles

Leaf

Squeaks are usually eliminated by applying a little lubricant—a penetrating oil is good, though some people have told me that vegetable oil is also effective!

You'll need the following:

- ❏ Newspaper to put under the hinges (oil can spot the carpet!)
- ❏ Small-tipped nail set or thin-shanked standard screwdriver
- ❏ Claw hammer
- ❏ Can of penetrating oil or similar lubricant, equipped with a straw for applying a narrow stream
- ❏ Clean rag or sponge

1. Lay newspaper under the door to protect the carpet. Open the door and look at the hinge. You'll want to lubricate the area where the pin meets the knuckles of the two hinge leaves.

2. If you know which hinge is squeaking, start there. But lubricate all the hinges and you'll have silence longer!

3. In most cases, you can loosen the pin by driving the nail set or screwdriver tip into the hole at the bottom of the hinge joint. Wearing safety goggles, use the hammer to drive the pin up from between the leaves an inch or so.

4. Spray a little lubricant into the pin hole at the top, where the head of the pin has been raised. Give the oil a minute to seep down inside, around the pin and the knuckles. Wipe off any excess or drips of lubricant with your rag. Reset the pin and try the door.

5. If the door is no longer squeaking, repeat this exercise with the other hinge or hinges. If it's still squeaking, drive up the first pin again and repeat Steps 2–4 until you achieve silence.

Tightening Loose Hinges

Time, use, and wear can make two things that belong together—the hinge and its screws—come apart. Tighten screws as soon as you notice they are loose. The longer loose screws are left untightened, the greater the likelihood that they'll widen the screw holes or wear (strip) the screw threads and need replacement. Because of the law of gravity—the weight of the door that the hinges support—the top hinge will most likely exhibit loose screws first.

If you've got loose screws, here are a couple of suggestions.

Fix #1: Gum Up the Holes

This quick fix will work for repairing loose screw holes for hinges of lighter-weight doors. For heavy doors, skip to Fix #2.

You'll need the following:

- ❏ Screwdriver (standard or Phillips, whichever fits)
- ❏ Book of cardboard matches
- ❏ Wood glue
- ❏ Utility knife

1. Open the door wide and wedge something under it so the door's weight won't stress the hinge.

2. Remove the loose screw or screws from the hinge leaf. Dip one or two cardboard matches in the wood glue and put them in the loose screw hole. Cut away any bits of matchstick that stick out of the hole with the utility knife. Reinsert the screws and tighten.

Fix #2: Longer Screws

If you already have the right-size fasteners, this is even easier than Fix #1.

You'll need the following:

- ❏ Screwdriver
- ❏ 2 $1/_2$" wood screws, same diameter as the old ones (you may want to use Phillips head screws rather than standard head screws; most people think they're easier to tighten and loosen)

1. Prop up the open door as in Fix #1.

2. Replace the loose screws one by one.

What Pros Know

When you go to the hardware store and look at door hinges, you'll notice that the hinges are sold with fairly short screws. By using a longer screw, you'll fasten the hinge more deeply into the door jamb.

Sticking Doors

Sometimes a door binds because the door itself is swollen from humidity; if binding doors are a problem in this kind of weather, you may want to lightly sand and refinish the latch edge of the door, particularly if the door is peeling paint—bare wood swells more than finished material. Or you can take the lazy strategy, and wait for cool weather. Several of the interior doors in my old New York house bind in summer when it's very warm and sticky; I just don't close them. They work perfectly in winter, when I want to keep them closed, anyway.

And sometimes, there's a bit of a hardware problem. If the hinges are loose, the door may bind along the latch jamb (the doorknob side). Tightening the hinge screws may cure the problem. Or the problem may be located on the opposite side of the door.

Open and close the door slowly, and look at the strike plate; that's the little square or rectangular gizmo that has a hole in its center (the strike) which holds the latch or bolt that's released when you let go of the doorknob and the door is shut. If the strike plate is loose (continual slamming can loosen it!), get out your screwdriver and try Fix #1 or #2 described previously to tighten the screws into the latch jamb.

Strike plate.

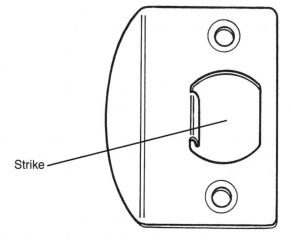

Strike

Doors That Won't Stay Closed

First, test the doorknob; the latch or bolt that fits into the strike plate may be sticking, and thus not releasing and engaging with the strike. You can probably fix this by lubricating the latch with a little graphite or penetrating oil.

The tale of the mysterious shrinking door is actually not very mysterious. If the weather is cold and dry, or if the humidity level in your house is very low, a wooden door will shrink in response. In turn, the latch or bolt may no longer engage with the strike, and the door won't close.

This is a job for shims! It's a good idea to use a fix that can be reversed, in case the door swells up again.

You'll need the following:

❑ Screwdriver (to match the strike plate screws)

❑ Cardboard (file folder stock makes good shims for this purpose)

❑ Pencil

❑ Scissors

On an interior door, shimming the strike plate works fine, and you don't have to mess with the hinges. Here's what you do.

1. Unscrew the strike plate and put the screws in a safe place so you don't lose track of them.

2. Trace the strike plate on cardboard; make a few copies. Cut out the cardboard templates.

3. Position one cardboard shim behind the strike plate, and screw the shim and plate back into its mortise. Then try the door. If the latch holds, you've solved the problem. If not, insert additional shims until the door closes properly.

On an exterior door, shimming out the strike plate can create a problem with door security. In this case, you can shim out the hinges. If you follow the direction suggested by the following illustration, you'll be able to shim the hinges without removing the door.

In addition to the tools and supplies listed for the strike plate shim fix, get a thin piece of paper so you can trace the outline of the hinge. You will also need something to support the door—wood blocks, shims, books—while you are tinkering with the hinges.

1. Open the door and, using pencil and paper, trace the outline of the hinge on the door jamb, including the screw positioning. Close the door when you're done and continue to Steps 2 and 3.

2. Using the tracing as a template, make a couple of cardboard shims for each door hinge (many modern doors have two hinges; others three, some four).

3. Cut the hinge shim like the illustration, with slots cut to the edge of the template so you can slide the shim under loosened screws.

Placing a cardboard shim behind a hinge may fix a door that won't stay closed.

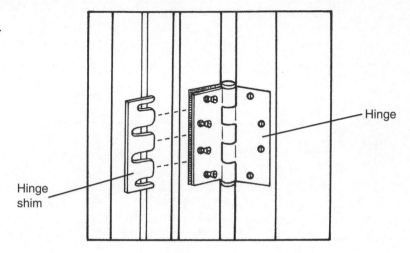

Hinge

Hinge shim

4. Open the door wide, exposing the jamb side of the hinge. Loosen one hinge at a time, slide in a shim, and tighten; shim all the hinges. Add shims until the door latches properly.

Getting a Grip on Doorknobs

There are four basic types of doorknobs:

1. *Dummy* doorknobs don't turn and are often used just for appearance.

2. *Passage* doorknobs turn, but have no keys or locks; these are often used in children's bedrooms or playrooms where a locking door could be a problem.

3. *Privacy* doorknobs lock and can be unlocked only from the inside; these are good for adult bedrooms and bathrooms. If someone should accidentally lock themselves in, you can quickly free them (see how later in this chapter).

4. *Keyed entry* doorknobs mean what they say; to gain entrance, you must unlock them with a key.

Tighten a Loose Knob

Modern doorknobs—the ones you'll find in a house that's less than fifty or sixty years old—are fairly simple to tighten. On these models, the whole works may be jiggling—from trim to knob. Usually you'll find two surface-mounted screws on the face of the inside doorknob trim piece that is mounted flush with the door—it's traditionally called a rose. Sometimes the screws are concealed under the trim piece. In this case, you'll have to pry off the trim piece to get to the screws. The screws actually pass all the way through the door to the trim piece on the other side.

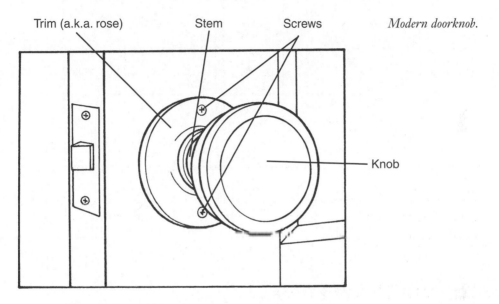

Trim (a.k.a. rose)   Stem   Screws   *Modern doorknob.*

Knob

You'll need the following:

- ❑ Screwdriver (Phillips or standard, to match the screws)

- ❑ Utility knife (if you need to score the paint around the trim piece to remove it)

- ❑ Small pry bar or standard screwdriver to remove trim piece, if the screws are underneath

Ounce of Prevention

Careless painters may have painted the edge of the trim piece where it meets the door. If your door trim is paint-bound, use a utility knife to carefully score the paint around the rose so you won't mess up the surface of the door by hacking away at it with the screwdriver.

Only one step here—tighten the screws. Hold both trim pieces tight to the door with one hand as you tighten the screws with the other. Tighten the screw closest to the edge of the door first.

The house I grew up in (circa 1940), and the one I live in now ("renovated" in the 1870s), have old-style doorknobs. You may have them, too. Instead of two screws passing through the lock cylinder to the other side of the door, there is a square metal spindle with threads on both ends that passes through the rose. The spindles are covered on both sides of the door with little metal shanks; the knobs screw (usually) onto the spindle at each threaded end. All of this is held in place by means of a single set screw in each of the two shanks. The screw threads through the shank and tightens against the spindle on one of its four flat surfaces.

Old-style doorknob.

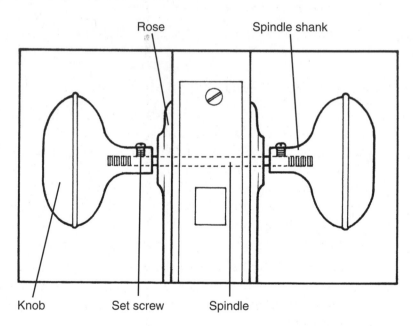

Wobbles happen when the set screw gets loose, or disappears. You may have to hunt for a replacement screw (see Appendix B for a dealer in old hardware), but these antique knobs are often beautiful, made of glass, bronze, chrome (1930s), or nicely aged and worn wood. They're worth saving—or selling to someone who likes them!

You'll need the following:

- ❏ Standard screwdriver—make sure it's the right size or you may deform the set screw head; some late-model (1940s and after) set screws may unscrew with a hex head (Allen wrench)

- ❏ Lubricating oil (penetrating oil, such as WD-40)

1. Loosen the set screw in the shank of the loose knob. If the screw is tight, don't force it! Lubricate the screw with a drop of lubricating oil, and then try to unscrew it.

2. Examine the screw. If the base (the opposite end from the head) looks deformed, it should be replaced. You can finish the repair once you have a new set screw.

3. If the screw is intact, check the set screw that holds the knob in place on the other side of the door. If it's tight, proceed.

4. Press the knob that still has its set screw in place tightly against the rose on the other side of the door. Turn the knob until one of the flat sides of the spindle is facing up through the set screw hole. Replace the set screw, tightening it firmly against the flat side of the spindle.

5. Operate the knob; you should be able to turn it freely.

Replacing a Passage, Privacy, or Keyed Entry Lockset

It's fairly easy to replace a set of doorknobs and latch with a modern doorknob—the kind that attaches both knobs and engages the latch with two long screws. Remove the screws, and then the knobs and trim will pull out easily. Then take the old set to the store and purchase a new one by the same maker. The new set will install in the reverse order that you removed the old set. All it takes is the right screwdriver; on modern doorknob sets, usually a Phillips head. If the trim piece conceals the long screws, you'll need a standard (flat head) screwdriver or small pry bar to pry off the trim piece.

If you've got the old-style doorknobs in your house, replacement is more problematic, as these are not so standard. Refer to Appendix B for an old house parts supplier; they may have the parts or replacements to do the job, and they work by fax or e-mail to assist customers.

Screen and Storm Doors

Having an extra door can be helpful. In winter, a glass-windowed storm door adds an extra layer of insulation to the door. Usually these doors have interchangeable storm and screen panels. In summer, when you change to screens, you can get a nice breeze going through your house when the entry doors are open and the screen doors are closed. One problem with these extra doors is that the screens can get torn or loose and need replacement. See Chapter 8 for instructions on repairing and replacing screens.

Adjusting the Door Closer

The other problem with storm/screen doors is that they usually operate with a mechanical closer that may be too fast or too slow—either slapping into your ankles or letting in flies along with the person who's coming or going. The good news is that this problem is incredibly easy to fix.

Let's take a look at the most common mechanical closer, the *pneumatic* variety. It looks a lot like a bicycle pump.

def•i•ni•tion

Pneumatic refers to a tool or machine that is operated by compressed air.

This device is attached to the hinge jamb and (usually) the top rail of the door. When you need to hold the door open, you can adjust the little washer shown in the illustration to keep the door in place; move the washer next to the tube when you want the door to close as usual.

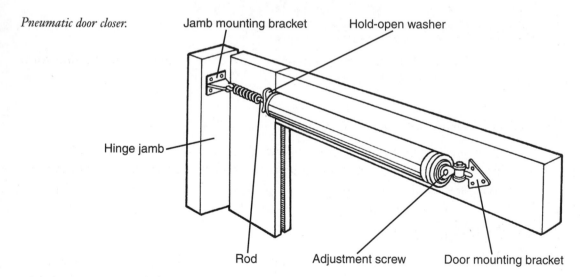

Pneumatic door closer.

Jamb mounting bracket   Hold-open washer

Hinge jamb

Rod   Adjustment screw   Door mounting bracket

To slow down or speed up the closing action, you'll need to use a Phillips or standard head screwdriver to turn the adjustment screw, usually located in the same position on the closer as the one shown in the illustration. To slow the closing action, turn the screw clockwise (righty, tighty). To speed up the door, turn the screw counterclockwise (lefty, loosey).

If You Need a New Closer

These door closers have a long life span. But they eventually wear out, and installing a new one is very easy. If you can find a duplicate model, you can even use the same screw holes for the brackets. If you have to drill new holes, follow the closer package instructions, use a torpedo level to make sure the installation is level, and wear safety goggles when you drill the bracket holes.

Just be sure to put a stop or bit of masking tape on your drill bit at a length less than the door's thickness, so that you don't drill *through* the door!

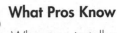 **What Pros Know**

When you install a door closer, you can position it anywhere on the screen door, as long as the jamb bracket is unobstructed by other hardware; however, it's generally attached along the top rail of the door, so it doesn't interfere or get tangled with people and things passing by.

Lock and Key Dilemmas

Usually, your key fits in its corresponding lock, the door opens, no problem. But when glitches happen, here's what to do.

Key Sticks in the Lock

If the key does not go smoothly into and out of the keyhole, you can put a little graphite on the key, and work it into the lock, or squeeze a little graphite into the keyhole, and do the same.

Key Breaks Off in the Lock

This happens, but don't panic. Before you call the locksmith, try to grab whatever is still sticking out of the lock with locking or needlenose pliers. Pull *straight out*. If the key fragment won't budge, try squirting a little lubricant into the lock, and try again with the pliers. If this doesn't do it, or if you can't grip the key fragment that remains in the lock, you'll have to call the pro.

Lock Is Frozen

This occasionally happens when there's been a lot of wet weather followed by bitter cold; the moisture freezes and can find its way into keyholes, too. Keep a small container of spray de-icer in your purse or other easily accessible place in the wintertime. Spray a little on the keyhole, and it should break the ice in seconds. I've also heard of people warming up the key with a hair dryer, but this isn't going to work if you're locked outside the house!

Locked in (Privacy Lock)

If you have small children or live with elderly family members, the kids or seniors may occasionally lock themselves into a room that is accessed with a privacy doorknob set; that is, there's a locking mechanism on the inside of the door. They lock themselves in, and can't get themselves out. And there's no key on the exterior doorknob for you to unlock.

You can first try to coax your elderly relative or child to turn the little locking mechanism on the inside of the door to the "unlock" position. If that doesn't work, try the following fix. Assuming you have modern doorknobs, you can release them if you can locate a slot or hole on the exterior doorknob, or on the rose (trim piece) of the exterior doorknob. Use the tip of a metal nail file, or the point of a straightened paper clip to push straight into the hole or slot. This will probably open the door. If it doesn't, you'll have to call a locksmith.

While children are small, or seniors are living with you, consider changing from privacy to passage locks. My daughter locked herself in the bathroom when she was little, and the experience scared her enough that she didn't repeat it. However, kids and elders alone in the bathroom are always at risk for an accident while they're stuck.

Installing a Peephole

If there is no way to see who's on the other side of your exterior door, it's a good idea to install a peephole. You should never open the door if you don't know the person who's there, or if the person will not identify himself/herself. You can buy peepholes in the section of the hardware or home center where locks, keys, and other door security equipment is sold. Look for one that has a vision field of 190°, which will permit the widest view of who's standing outside your door.

To install a peephole, you'll need a good-sized bit to drill a hole of sufficient diameter to accommodate this device. (This fix presumes your door is wood, not metal or metal-clad. If you have the latter type, ask your hardware salesperson to recommend the right drill bit for the job.)

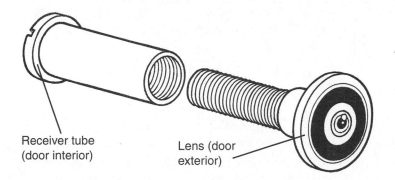

Door peephole.

Receiver tube
(door interior)

Lens (door
exterior)

You'll need the following:

❑ Pencil or awl

❑ Measuring tape

❑ Electric drill

❑ $9/_{16}$" spade bit (for peephole shown; check package)

❑ Old toothbrush

The spade bit is designed for drilling large holes at slow speed.

1. Mark a point on the inside of the door with the pencil that is at eye level with the shortest adult in your house (children shouldn't answer the door to unknown people!).

2. Measure the center point of the door from left to right at eye level and mark it with a pencil or tip of an awl.

3. Close and lock the door. You may want to position someone on the other side of the door for Step 4.

4. Attach the spade bit to your drill, and put on the safety goggles. Using the awl or pencil center mark as a guide, position the tip of the drill on the mark, and drill straight through the door. It is important that you hold the drill steady

and straight. When you feel the center point of the spade bit touch the surface on the other side of the door (or your friend sees it), stop drilling forward and remove the bit straight out from the hole you've drilled. (Don't stop the movement of the bit as you remove it.)

5. Go around to the other side of the door; close and lock it, and, using the bit mark as your center point, drill through the door from the outside. Brush any wood splinters or sawdust out of the hole with the old toothbrush.

6. Insert the receiver tube through the hole from the inside of the door; then thread the lens end into the receiver tube from the outside of the door.

Sliding Door Fixes

Sliding doors make for an easy transition from indoors to outside; their big glass panes provide a nice view. But the problem with sliders is that they are heavy, and when they don't slide smoothly, they're annoying to use.

There are two ways that sliding doors may not measure up:

♦ They don't slide smoothly.

♦ They are a security risk.

Let's address the first problem.

Wobbly Tracks

You'll need a screwdriver to tighten the screws in the sliding door tracks (usually Phillips). If the screws seem not to want to stay put—they spin uselessly in their screw holes—it means that the screws are stripped, and not engaging with the wood sill that should anchor the door below its metal frame. Replace the screws with longer ones, to better hold them down. Make sure the doors are aligned in the tracks before you tighten the new screws.

Dirty Tracks

Dirt, grease, leaves, gunk—all of these can make a sliding door bump and balk. Clean out the tracks and lubricate them; some people like to rub paraffin in the lower track to assist door movement.

Bent Track

If the slider track is only slightly bent, you can bend it back into shape by putting a wood block on either side of the bend (room side and track side) and hammering the block on the room side of the bend to iron out the bend.

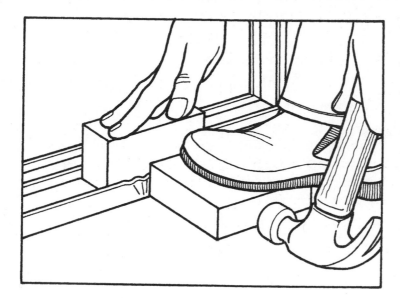

Straighten bent sliding door track.

Now, for the second problem.

Securing a Sliding Door

The simple latch on a sliding door is easy for any burglar to foil. Because they usually open to back yards and other property areas not visible from the street, many burglars attempt entry through a slider.

Many people stop unwanted entries by wedging a broomstick or 1"×2" piece of lumber cut to length between the edge of the slider and the door frame. This would jam the door if someone were to try to pry it open.

You can also buy locking devices that are more secure. You will need an electric drill, a drill bit for drilling through metal, and mounting screws, to install either a "Charley bar"—a locking metal bar that serves the same purpose as the stick—or a foot-operated lock that prevents the slider from opening. Follow the manufacturer's instructions for installing these.

The Least You Need to Know

♦ Don't attempt a dramatic fix when simple will serve you. Sometimes doors that stick simply need the hinges or strike plate tightened to the jamb.

♦ You can fill a loose hinge or strike screw hole with glued up matchsticks for a tighter fit, or use a longer screw.

♦ The adjustment for a storm/screen door closer is usually the turn of a single screw.

♦ When creating a security peephole for an outer door, drill straight through the door; a spade bit works well for this large-sized hole.

Part 3

The Circulatory System: Plumbing and Fixtures

The idea of water running through pipes from underground, to provide for drinking, cooking, and cleaning, would have been considered miraculous to the original owners of my New York house. They had a nearby pond and a two-hole privy to take care of water and waste disposal. Fortunately for us, subsequent owners updated the place, and we've got all the conveniences, including a bathroom on every floor. Modern plumbing has solved the problems of maintaining a running water supply—where and when we need it—and disposing of waste with near-invisible efficiency. Our system of pipes and fixtures is practically infallible.

But like the veins and arteries of our own circulatory system, the pipes that bring us water and take away waste can sometimes clog or leak, causing a small breakdown that can get much worse if it's not addressed promptly. And the plumbing system's "organs"—the tubs, toilets, sinks and showers—can also wreak havoc on a house when they're not doing their jobs, letting water travel where it shouldn't. Part 3 helps you take care of this vital home system, keeping the water flowing, and in its place!

"Oh, darling! I looove it!"

Chapter 10

Solving Pipe Problems

In This Chapter

- ◆ Quickly stopping a pipe leak until the plumber shows up
- ◆ Defrosting a frozen pipe, and preventing it from happening in the future
- ◆ Winterizing an outside faucet
- ◆ Quieting noisy pipes
- ◆ Keeping drain pipes free from obstructions
- ◆ How to rescue what falls in the sink trap

Problems with your home's system of water delivery and waste disposal fall into two general categories: supply flow and drainage. If clean water's not flowing properly, or waste water's not discharging, sooner or later you'll have water or waste (yuck) where it's not supposed to be.

This chapter will help you tackle the minor disruptions to flow and disposal, and also provide some guidance for maintenance to keep things moving along as they should.

Small Leaks: Emergency Fix

Copper—the most common material used for supply lines—and other metal pipes last many years, but occasionally, one of your pipes will spring a leak. You'll have to stop the spray until the plumber shows up. The kind of repair described next—using a clamp and gasket material—will often hold for quite a while, but don't be overconfident. Call in the plumber as soon as you can to replace the leaking section of pipe.

Where the leak happens will determine how you first shut off the water, and then do a temporary fix on the leak. If the pipe is leaking between a supply stop and an appliance, simply shut off the water at the supply stop. Of course, you won't be able to use that appliance until you've done the repair.

If the leak is in one of the supply lines running from the main shutoff to somewhere else in the house, and there is no interim supply stop between the leak and the main valve, you'll need to shut the water off at the main. (See Chapter 4 for locating/ shutting off directions.)

If you've stocked your supply closet with emergency supplies as discussed in Chapter 3, you'll be glad you have them now!

To stop a small leak, you'll need the following:

- ❑ Scissors
- ❑ Rubber gasket material
- ❑ Hose clamp
- ❑ Screwdriver
- ❑ Bucket
- ❑ Mop or sponge

1. Shut off the water supply at the closest supply stop, or at the main.

2. Wearing safety goggles, cut out a small piece of rubber gasket material, of sufficient size to wrap the pipe, cover the leak and provide about $1/2$" of material on either side of the leaking spot. Wrap it around the pipe at the site of the leak.

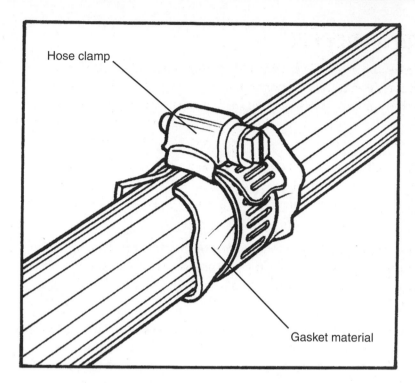

Emergency leak repair.

3. Unstrap the hose clamp, wrap it around the gasket material at the leak site, and thread the strap end through the end that has the screw mounted on it. Make the strap fit snugly around the gasket repair.

4. Tighten the clamp screw with the screwdriver.

5. Clean up the area around the leak with the bucket and mop (if it was leaking for awhile), or sponge (if you caught it quickly).

6. Turn on the water supply. Sometimes the repaired area will drip briefly; if the dripping continues, you can tighten the clamp/gasket. And call the plumber! Even a really good repair won't hold indefinitely.

What Pros Know

Small ruptures or splits in supply pipe are rare, but they happen. To make an emergency fix, you'll need a different kind of metal clamp, called a sleeve clamp. This does what it says: wraps around the pipe and gasket material like a tight metal sleeve. Like the hose clamp, it closes with screws. You can make the repair as above, with this exception: use a metal file to smooth any roughness or sharpness around the pipe rupture, so that the leaky spot doesn't cut the gasket material.

Thawing Frozen Pipes

You know there's a frozen pipe when you turn on a faucet and no water comes out, or if it barely drips, and the weather's been very cold.

One bitter January evening, we had our first pipe freeze-up at the kitchen sink of our New York house. It was some kind of a record cold snap, -15°F. outside, and we'd just gotten home from work in the city to discover that the water wasn't moving. Of course, we hadn't made dinner yet, so we were hungry, too!

Fortunately, the freeze-up wasn't significant. We got the water moving again with a hair dryer aimed at the supply pipes under the sink. We kept the under-sink cabinet doors open on all subzero nights after that, and, just to be safe, let the water drip all night whenever a deep freeze was predicted. It sounds wasteful, but a little drip will waste far less water than a burst, spurting supply pipe! And it certainly won't damage the house the way a burst pipe can.

We had neighbors in Maine who had a four-season house that they used occasionally throughout the year. They didn't have a caretaker, though. One miserable winter, when they didn't visit, and the temperature dipped below zero for more than two weeks, the neighbors' pipes froze. When the thaw finally arrived, a pipe burst in an interior wall. They hadn't shut off their water at the main, and the damage was in multiple thousands of dollars. Plus, they had to pay the water company for 30,000 gallons of water that served no other purpose than the destruction of their walls, floors, furniture, and appliances!

Moral of this story: if your house will be unoccupied in the coldest weather months, shut off the water at the main. If you don't drain the pipes, have someone check the house regularly.

Here are some basic rules for thawing pipes:

- Shut off the water supply at the main. This will ease the pressure at the freeze site (remember, water expands when it freezes).

- Open (turn on) the faucet closest to the freeze site. Once the water starts moving, it needs somewhere to go!

- In case there's a leak or a burst of water when the pipe thaws, cover the surrounding area with plastic drop cloths, or position a bucket or two underneath the freeze site.

- Work from the open faucet toward the area of the freeze.

Hot Water Thaw

To thaw frozen pipes, try this simple method first. You'll need the following:

❑ Rags or old towels

❑ Bucket

❑ String or masking tape

1. Boil some water in a teakettle.

2. Wrap the frozen pipe in rags; secure the rags at each end with string or tape. Put the bucket under the pipe to catch the poured water.

3. Slowly and carefully pour the hot water over the rags.

Applied Heat Thaw: Beware!

You can try using a hair dryer to blow warm air on the frozen pipe; you can also wrap the pipe with heating tape plugged into a nearby outlet. However, remember that water and electricity do not mix! If the electric receptacle for the hair dryer or tape is not equipped with a *ground fault circuit interrupter* (GFCI), you risk electrical shock if the appliance or heat tape comes into contact with water (for example, if the pipe bursts while you're using the electrical device). You must be very careful.

def•i•ni•tion

A ground fault circuit interrupter (GFCI) is a device used in code-compliant electrical receptacles near water sources. The GFCI almost instantly cuts power to a circuit if it detects a leakage of electric current.

Preventing Frozen Pipes

To prevent pipes from freezing next time, remember these strategies:

◆ On very cold nights, open hot and cold faucets to a constant trickle.

◆ To allow warm air to circulate around pipes, open kitchen and bathroom sink cabinet doors in freezing weather; the ambient room temperature will keep them warmer.

◆ *Before* cold weather sets in, wrap insulating foam tubing around uninsulated pipes that run close or adjacent to exterior walls, under sinks, or anywhere the pipes are likely to freeze. This will also prevent the pipes from "sweating" in hot, humid summer weather, and keep the hot water in hot water supply pipes warmer, longer—an energy saver.

Another Cold Subject: Winterizing an Outside Faucet

If you have exterior faucets for the garden hose on the exterior walls of your house, and you live in a freeze-prone zone of the country, you'll want to shut off and bleed these faucets before the first frost.

Most exterior faucets have an inside supply stop, usually a ball-valve (turns off with a quarter-turn) or a gate valve (wheel-shaped, shuts off clockwise—for illustrations see Chapter 4).

This cutaway drawing shows the usual location of the inside shutoff for an exterior faucet, which is also referred to as a hose bib.

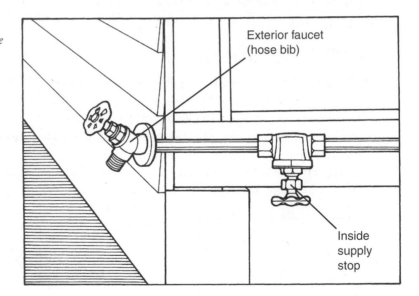

Exterior faucet (hose bib)

Inside supply stop

1. Turn off the water supply at the inside stops.

2. Go outside and turn on the faucet until the remaining water in the pipe drains out.

3. When the water drains out, turn off (close) the faucet.

You can buy foam faucet covers for exterior faucets; they provide an extra layer of protection from the freeze-burst scenario.

Pipe Down! Quieting Noisy Pipes

Pipes that bang and squeak are annoying. Usually, pipes are anchored every few feet along long horizontal and vertical runs. The vibration caused by water moving through the pipes can make them noisy, when they bang against a joist or wall. Tightening the straps, insulating the pipe, or installing more pipe straps should settle them down.

You'll need a flashlight to do the detective work. Once you locate the source of the bangs or squeaks (squeaks come from hot water pipes, which expand from the hot water moving inside them), you can insulate between the pipe and strap with rubber gasket material, tighten loose strap screws, or install additional straps.

To insulate a noisy pipe, you'll need the following:

- ❑ Scissors
- ❑ Rubber gasket material
- ❑ Screwdriver (standard or Phillips, depending on strap screws)

You can cushion a noisy pipe (or squeaky hot water pipe) with the same gasket material that you use to stop a leak in an emergency. Just cut the right amount of gasket to fit around the pipe between the pipe and the strap, as shown in the following illustration. Then loosen the straps with the screwdriver, wrap the pipe with the gasket material, and tighten the straps.

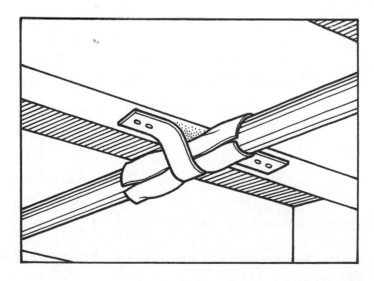

Insulate a noisy pipe with rubber gasket material.

Preventing Drainage Disasters

Clogged sinks, showers, and toilets are usually the unpleasant consequence of inappropriate items finding their way into your waste disposal (sewage) system. When my daughter lost the top to a bottle of shampoo down the toilet, our septic system balked. Within a couple of days, the system was backflowing into the lowest drain in the house—the first floor bathroom shower. It was a stinky mess, and no job for the DIY 101-er. I called our septic system guy, who repaired the problem in a couple of hours.

The following rules really help keep your drainage system intact if you follow them:

◆ Once a month, boil water and pour a kettleful down each drain in your house: sinks, tubs, shower. This is the most carefree way to keep them flowing. Of course, be careful when you're carrying/pouring the boiling water. You don't want to scald yourself.

◆ Keep the stopper in the sink when you are brushing your hair/shaving/ applying makeup/giving yourself a facial, even if you're not using the water. Dropped stuff and drain pluggers like hair, bottle tops, and makeup brushes will stay in the sink bowl. You can politely remove them/wipe out the bowl when you're finished with grooming activities.

◆ Keep the toilet lid closed when you're not using this fixture. If men live in your house, you know already that this will never happen. But you can try; tell them my septic repair bill for the shampoo cap was $400; maybe that will be an effective deterrent. Maybe not.

◆ I know it's not the most pleasant task, but take a moment to remove hair from the drain right after you shower. Hair and ordinary gunk that goes down the drain will create a nearly impenetrable clog in a pretty short time if you neglect to remove the hair after every shower.

◆ Do *not* throw anything more fibrous than a few sheets of toilet or facial tissue in the toilet and try to flush it away. Contrary to urban legend, household drain pipes will not accommodate full-grown alligators. I am always amazed at what people think will flow away to the municipal sewage system or the septic field: disposable diapers, huge wads of paper towels, even rags. Don't make this expensive mistake.

◆ Grease is the enemy of kitchen drains; letting grease ooze down the sink drain is the equivalent of pouring glue into the pipes. Everything will stick to the grease, and soon you'll have a nasty old clog. Pour leftover cooking oil, bacon grease, and other slimy stuff in a coffee can and dispose of it in the trash.

Unclogging a Sink

What's done is done. The water in the sink won't drain. You can first try pouring a kettle of boiling water into the drain. But if the water doesn't start to move, you'll need stronger measures.

Chemical Reactions

Using commercial liquid or powdered drain openers in a drain that's already clogged can be a problem. The chemicals are highly caustic and toxic, and if water is already backing into the sink, you may splash the chemicals on yourself if you later have to plunge the drain. Many of these concoctions are also toxic to the bacteria that keep your septic system (if you have one) flowing. If you must use a commercial drain de-clogger, follow the package directions to the letter.

If you want to try to create a harmless chemical reaction that just might work, use this nontoxic household remedy. It reminds me of my childhood days making "volca-noes." Pour a half-cup of vinegar and a half-cup of baking soda down the drain; stuff a rag in the stopper opening. The chemical reaction may be enough to loosen the clog's grip on your pipes. If not, try mechanical means.

Ounce of Prevention

Keep commercial drain decloggers out of reach of children or pets—they're deadly!

Taking the Plunge

There are two kinds of plungers. Plungers used for clearing toilets usually have a second, ball-shaped cup inside the outside cup. The plunger used for sink, shower, and tub drains is the single-cup model shown in Chapter 3.

You'll need the following:

❑ Plunger (the plunger cup should be large enough to fully cover the drain opening)

❑ Rag

1. Remove the sink stopper. If you're working on a bathroom sink, find the overflow hole and stuff the rag into it; the overflow hole is usually positioned high up on the basin on the side of the bowl opposite the faucets. Feel under the lip of the sink if you can't find it.

If you're working on a kitchen sink, there will be no overflow hole. However, if your kitchen sink has two basins, you'll need to plug one of them with a rag. Otherwise, you'll divert the drain water into the second sink, rather than clearing the clog.

2. Fill the sink with enough water to nearly submerge the plunger cup; this will provide added pressure as you plunge.

3. Position the plunger cup over the drain hole so that the drain is completely covered.

4. Holding the plunger upright, pump the handle up and down forcefully, fifteen to twenty times; make sure the plunger cup is sealed over the drain. Then check to see if the water drains. If not, try again. Try plunging for three or four rounds of fifteen to twenty strokes each before you give up. (Most people quit too soon.)

Plunge a sink.

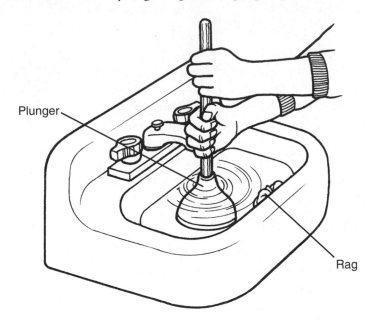

If plunging doesn't work, it's time to meet the trap.

Meet the Sink Trap

The trap—a piece of bent pipe in the shape of a "P" resting on its side—was invented about 150 years ago, and made the wonders of indoor plumbing possible. Because of its shape, it always holds some water, which effectively seals off the waste line and prevents noxious gases from leaking up into the house. Its use as a clog-maker and holder of valuable objects is only a side benefit.

Back to your clog. The trap's shape also makes it a great place for grease and gunk to collect. A big enough build-up has gotten you to the point where the waste water has no escape and is backing into the sink. Plunging hasn't improved things, so now you've got to move to the trap.

Clearing the Trap

This is easy to do; the gunk and the gunk's odor make it somewhat unpleasant.

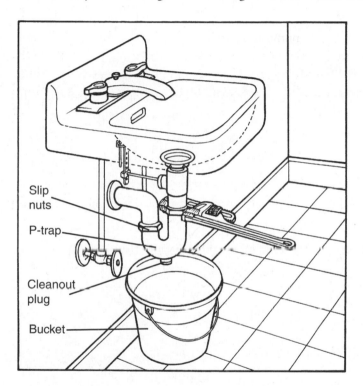

Clear the trap.

Slip nuts

P-trap

Cleanout plug

Bucket

You'll need the following:

❑ Pipe wrench or slip-jointed pliers

❑ Painter's or masking tape

❑ Bucket

❑ Lubricating spray

A pipe wrench or slip-jointed pliers have jaws large enough to get a grip on plumbing pipes.

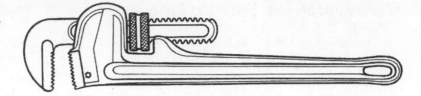

1. Turn off the faucets; don't run any water.

2. Tape the jaws of your pipe wrench or slip-jointed pliers with painter's or masking tape so they don't mar the nuts you'll be loosening or scratch the pipe's metal finish.

3. Position the bucket under the trap.

4. If the trap under your sink has a cleanout plug (like the one in the earlier illustration; not all traps do), loosen the plug and let the water/debris fall into the bucket. If there's no cleanout plug, go to Step 5.

5. Using the wrench/pliers, give each slip nut a half-turn counterclockwise, then loosen them the rest of the way by hand.

6. Remove the trap pipe. Don't lose track of the slip nuts and washers. Use lubricating spray if the nuts are stubborn.

7. Wearing rubber gloves, empty any debris inside the trap into the bucket.

8. Examine the trap pipe, the slip nuts, and washers. If any of these parts look worn, now is the time to take them to the hardware and purchase an exact replacement.

9. Using a flashlight, examine the pipe beyond the trap piece where the sink drain leads out to the larger drain system. Clear any obvious blockages you can see.

10. Replace the cleaned (or the replacement) pipe and washers, and tighten the nuts. Don't forget to replace the cleanout plug, if there is one. Turn the water supply back on with the supply stops. If the water runs freely down the drain and there's no leak at the trap, you're done. Remove and clean out the bucket. Put the gunk in the trash, not back in the drain!

When Valuables Go Down the Drain

If a piece of jewelry or other valuable object goes down the drain, *immediately* turn off the water and plug the drain hole with the sink stopper. Then, using the same tools and materials as in previous directions, follow Steps 2–7. Go through all the gunk that falls into the bucket. If your valuable isn't there, there is still a chance it may be in the pipe between the drain hole in the sink and the trap. Leave the bucket under the open trap and run the water briefly. Examine the pipe section with the flashlight and check the debris. If the jewelry or valuable isn't there, it's gone. But you did your best.

Replace the trap as in Step 10 above.

The Least You Need to Know

◆ A hose clamp and gasket material can stop a small leak; it's an easy repair, so keep these supplies around.

◆ Insulate pipes that are vulnerable to freezing—near exterior walls, in unheated parts of the house—with foam sleeves. When you insulate the hot water pipes, the sleeves will also save on water heating costs.

◆ Putting masking/painter's tape around the jaws of your pipe wrench or pliers will prevent the tools from marring your metal pipe and parts.

◆ Quick action is necessary if something valuable goes down the drain; turn off the water immediately.

Controlling the Flow: Faucets, Sprays, and Showerheads

In This Chapter

- ◆ How faucets come apart and go together again
- ◆ Maintaining your sink sprayer
- ◆ Replacing a showerhead
- ◆ Adjusting a bathroom sink stopper so it opens and closes easily

Leaky hardware wastes a lot of water, and you don't usually have to be a pro to make good fixes on your faucets, sprayers, and showerheads. And that drain stopper in the bathroom that won't pop up—or go down? It's easier to adjust than you think.

Faucet Facts

The drip, drip, drip of a leaky faucet is annoying, and getting to the cause of the problem may seem complicated. But the fix is usually the replacement of a small and inexpensive part. It just requires patience to get there and back!

If you have very old (50-plus years) faucets, the biggest problem with fixing them may be finding replacement washers and nuts. Follow the directions for fixing compression faucets, as old stem faucets are put together in much the same way. But most of the old stuff wore out long ago, so chances are you've got faucets that can be repaired with parts or kits that are easily obtainable to replace worn or broken components.

Modern faucets are a little more complicated than the old-fashioned kind. Some have lots of little pieces! Be methodical when you repair a multi-part gizmo like a faucet. Careful work is always more effective than a hurried job.

If you don't know the brand and model number of your faucet, or it's very old, you'll need to remove it and bring it with you to find the correct size replacement parts and fittings.

Ounce of Prevention

If you're going to take apart a faucet, clear an area where you can line up the pieces in the order you remove them. If you need to take parts to the store to find replacements, make a list of the parts and the order, so you can put things back the way you took them out. It's always so frustrating to put something back together and have one piece left over!

Faucet Fix Prep List

Before you begin fixing any type of faucet, you'll need to do four things:

1. Shut off the water at the supply stops under the sink; if you don't have supply stops, shut off the water at the main. Drain whatever water remains in the faucet.

2. Close the sink drain with its stopper and cover it with a towel or rag—preferably white or light-colored. That way, if little faucet parts (some are tiny!) should fall in the sink, they won't go down the drain. Lining the sink with a towel or cloth will also protect the finish if you drop your tools.

3. Tape the jaws of whatever pliers or wrenches you are using with masking or painter's tape, so the tool doesn't scratch the fixture.

4. Figure out where you'll lay out your parts in order.

Basically, there are four types of faucets. The *compression* faucet has two handles. Opening or closing the handles, which in turn loosens or compresses the rubber washers at the base of the stem beneath each handle, controls the water flow (see the illustration in the next section). Because the key controller is made of rubber, which wears out more quickly than plastic, metal, or ceramic, this type of faucet needs repair more frequently than other types.

The other types of faucets are often called *washerless* faucets. *Ball-type*, *cartridge*, and *ceramic disk* faucets are appreciated for their sturdiness, but they also have small rubber and plastic seals and O-rings that are part of flow control and can wear out.

Balls, cartridges, and ceramic discs—the "works" of these other types of faucets—occasionally need replacement, but you can purchase the entire set of parts—the assembly—for much less than the cost of a new faucet. (You're not buying the handle(s) and spout, just the innards.)

Every manufacturer makes many variations of each type of faucet, so it's impossible to illustrate every detail of all of them. Use the illustrations shown as a general guide.

> **What Pros Know**
>
> If you get a printed diagram when you purchase parts or a faucet assembly, save it and put it in your home workbook (see Chapter 4). It'll make the next repair easier.

Fixing a Leaky Compression Faucet

Generally, leaks from the spout indicate a worn washer; leaks from the handle are caused by a worn O-ring. Once you get the faucet apart, examining all the parts for wear and corrosion is a good idea. You can fix what's broken *and* replace a worn part at the same time. Be sure to bring the defective part(s) with you to the store. O-rings and washers come in so many sizes, you need to know what will exactly replace the worn, damaged, or broken part.

Compression faucet.

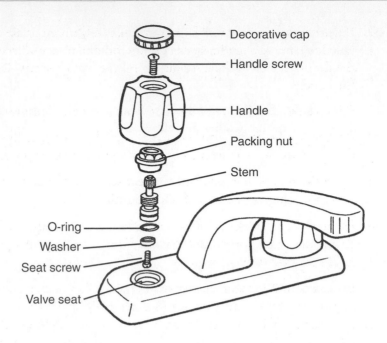

Decorative cap

Handle screw

Handle

Packing nut

Stem

O-ring

Washer

Seat screw

Valve seat

You'll need the following:

❏ Adjustable wrench

❏ Screwdrivers (Phillips and standard)

❏ Penetrating oil or other lubricant

❏ Fine steel wool

What Pros Know _____

When you buy replacement washers and O-rings for a compression faucet, always buy several—they're cheap—label the leftovers, and keep them in your supply closet. That way you won't have to disassemble the faucet and bring the works to the hardware store to find replacement washers, rings, and the like, next time.

❏ Rag or towel

❏ Heatproof plumber's grease

❏ Replacement parts: washers, O-rings, or packing

1. Do all the steps in the "Faucet Fix Prep List" earlier in this chapter.

2. If the handle screw is visible, unscrew it and lift the handle straight up and off. If you don't see the handle screw, use the tip of the screwdriver to carefully lift off the decorative cap, which should reveal the handle screw. Unscrew it and remove the handle.

3. Remove the packing nut with your taped wrench or pliers.

4. Put the handle back on the stem and turn the handle to loosen the stem. If this doesn't work, use the wrench or pliers to loosen the stem. Lift it out.

5. Once the stem is out, unscrew the seat screw and remove the washer. If it's tough to remove the screw, use a little penetrating oil.

6. Using the tip of the standard screwdriver, gently guide the O-ring out of its little groove and remove it from the stem. Don't break or cut it; you need the original to buy its exact replacement.

   Instead of an O-ring, you may have found a soft washer-like part made of wound string at the top of the stem—this is called *packing*—and is sometimes found in older compression faucets between the stem and the cap. If your faucet has packing, you'll need to bring this stuff to the hardware store, buy replacement packing, and rewind it on the top of the stem.

7. Once you've got your replacement parts, clean up the screws and stem by buffing them with steel wool. Clean and wipe everything off so there's no steel wool or other residue that may wear the new parts.

Ounce of Prevention

A lot of plumbers will take this interim step before they reassemble a faucet. After removing the towel and any tools or parts from the sink, they'll cover the faucet hole with a rag, open the supply stops a little to let water flush out any residue from the repair that remains. Little bits of rubber, metal, or steel wool can mess up their work! Then they turn off the water and reassemble the faucet.

8. After coating them with heatproof plumber's grease, install the new washer and/ or O-ring (if one is worn, it's good to do both) and reinstall the faucet. Open the supply stops and try it. If you hear a funny noise or the spout still leaks, you'll have to disassemble and tighten the screw (the one that holds the washer to the stem) another quarter turn. Don't tighten too hard or you'll deform the washer.

Still Dripping?

Don't despair. There's one more thing you can try: you may need a new valve seat (if it's removable, you'll need an Allen wrench or a seat wrench to get it out), or you may need to grind the existing valve seat with a seat-grinding tool. If you grind the old seat, this will create some debris. Be sure to flush the seat out with water (see the previous sidebar) before you reinstall the faucet.

Fixing a Leaky Rotary Ball Faucet

About 30 percent of all kitchen faucets are this type. Most DIY-ers find rotary ball faucets the most annoying to fix: they have more parts than any of the other types!

Once you disassemble this faucet, bring the works to the hardware and buy a kit with all-new parts. The kits are cheap and it's hard to tell what's causing the leak in a ball faucet. Unless you really love taking this faucet apart repeatedly, it's much easier to just replace everything. Your parts kit should come with a schematic drawing of the faucet and its parts. You can use this as a guide to get everything back together in the proper order.

Rotary ball faucet.

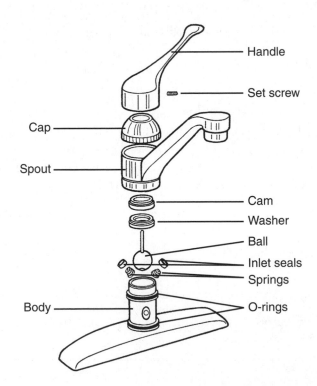

You'll need the following:

- ❏ Allen wrench set
- ❏ Adjustable wrench or pliers
- ❏ Tweezers (for removing/setting the seals and springs; they are minis!)
- ❏ Standard screwdriver
- ❏ Rag or towel
- ❏ Heatproof plumber's grease
- ❏ Replacement parts kit for your faucet

1. Do all the steps in the "Faucet Fix Prep List" earlier in this chapter.

2. Turn the handle so the lever faces you. Lift it, and remove the set screw that holds it in place with the Allen wrench. Lift off the handle. (Tape the set screw to the handle so you don't lose it!)

3. Use the tape-wrapped wrench or pliers to remove the cap; then lift off the spout.

4. Carefully remove the cam and washer, then lift out the metal or plastic ball.

5. With the tweezers, lift out the seats and springs. Lay them on a piece of tape and mark how they are inserted so you can put the new ones back the same way.

6. Peel off the O-rings. Use the tip of the standard screwdriver to ease them off; don't cut them.

7. Once you've gotten your replacement parts kit, reassemble the faucet. Coat the O-rings with plumber's grease to make it easier to slide them into their grooves. Pay very careful attention to the instructions that come with the kit, especially the order and positions of the little springs and seats.

8. When the faucet is reassembled, open the supply stops and turn on the faucet.

What Pros Know

The ball and seats of a rotary ball faucet are prone to clogging—the little inlets are quite small. Now that you know how to take this one apart, you know how to get to the ball and seats to clean them out if the water flow seems to be restricted and the problem's not the spout's aerator (see "Cleaning a Clogged Aerator" later in this chapter).

Repairing a Cartridge Faucet

As you may have noticed from the other faucet repair instructions, each type of faucet has its own assets and drawbacks. The main difficulty with cartridge models is that there are so many kinds of cartridges—you really must bring in the old one to find its exact match.

While the cartridge faucet will work just fine once you replace the faulty cartridge, you need to be careful when trying to remove it. The cartridge is secured by a small clip on an interior ring below the cartridge, or a little clip that you may be able to feel below the handle; if you feel it below the handle, then pull it out with a pair of pliers or screwdriver; then you can remove the handle, unscrew the retaining cap below the cartridge, and lift out the cartridge.

Cartridge faucet.

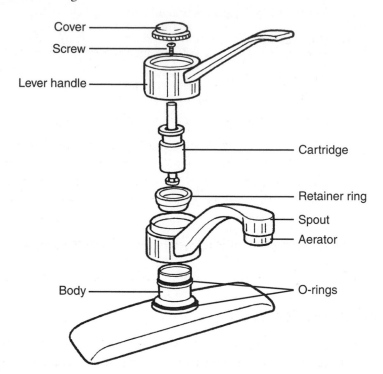

You'll need the following:

❑ Adjustable wrench or pliers

❑ Needlenose pliers (to remove retainer clip)

❏ Screwdrivers, standard and Phillips

❏ Allen wrench set

❏ Rag or towel

❏ Heatproof plumber's grease

❏ Replacement cartridge and O-rings

1. Do all the steps in the "Faucet Fix Prep List" earlier in this chapter.

2. Pry off the decorative cap on the handle. Remove the screw. Then tilt the handle back and pull it up and off.

3. If there's a retainer clip holding the cartridge, use the needlenose pliers to remove it. Pull the cartridge straight up and off.

4. Remove the spout and then pry off the O-rings.

5. When you have the replacement cartridge and O-rings, coat the new O-rings with plumber's grease and slip them onto the body and into the grooves. Replace the spout, the retainer ring, and the cartridge. Insert the retainer clip in the same location from which you removed it. Replace the handle, the screw and the decorative cap.

6. When the faucet is fully reassembled, open the water supply stops. It's ready to use.

Ounce of Prevention

Whenever you're replacing a major faucet part, go ahead and replace the O-rings. It beats having to disassemble the faucet once again!

Ceramic Disk Faucet Fix

This type of faucet is expensive and usually quite sturdy. Check the manufacturer's website or call the manufacturer; ceramic disk faucets often have a long or lifetime warranty, and you may be able to get free parts and directions if you contact the maker of your faucet.

Ceramic disk faucet.

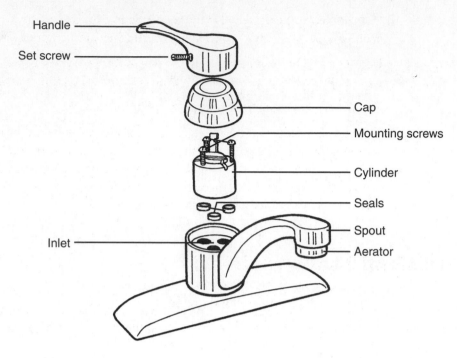

You'll need the following:

❑ Adjustable wrench or pliers

❑ Allen wrench set

❑ Screwdrivers, standard and Phillips (to loosen disk mounting screws and lift seals on the disk)

❑ White vinegar

❑ Old toothbrush or nonscratch abrasive pad (blue)

1. Do all the steps in the "Faucet Fix Prep List" earlier in this chapter.

2. Push back the faucet handle to reveal the set screw; remove the set screw with the right size Allen wrench and lift the handle off. Remove the cap and any other parts above the ceramic disk; use the taped wrench or pliers when necessary.

3. Unscrew the disk cylinder's mounting screws with the Phillips screwdriver and lift out the cylinder.

4. Use the flat tip of the standard screwdriver to lift off the seals from the bottom of the disk. If they are worn, replace them (they are very inexpensive).

5. If it's not broken or cracked, clean the cylinder with vinegar and the toothbrush or soft abrasive pad. If it's broken, replace it with the exact matching part.

6. Replace the seals and disk, and reassemble the faucet.

7. Ceramic disk faucets can be susceptible to damage when you reopen them, so you must be careful turning on the water! Open the faucet in the center position before you open the supply stops. Then open the supply stops very gradually and slowly. Air forcing its way through the pipes ahead of the water can crack the disk, so you need to proceed with caution.

Cleaning a Clogged Aerator

If the water pressure at one of your faucet spouts is weak, or if the water is coming out irregularly— spitting or splashing out of the sink, for example—the problem is probably a dirty or faulty aerator in the spout (see the following illustration).

You'll need the following:

- ❏ Rag or towel
- ❏ Adjustable wrench or pliers
- ❏ White vinegar
- ❏ Wire brush
- ❏ Old toothbrush

You don't need to turn off the water at the supply stops for this repair; just turn off the water at the faucet. Put a towel or rag over the drain so you don't lose a part.

What Pros Know

Weak water pressure throughout the house may be an indication of some problem with the main coming into the house (a leak, perhaps), or with your well or pump, if you have private water. Call your water company or well service company for professional help.

1. To remove the aerator from the spout, turn it by hand in a counterclockwise direction (remember: lefty, loosey). If it won't budge, gently loosen it with the tape-wrapped wrench or pliers.

2. Once you remove it, you'll notice that the aerator may have several parts; set them out on a flat surface in the correct order. Rinse the pieces in water to

remove debris. If they still look clogged, soak them in white vinegar for a few minutes and scrub them with the wire brush (metal screen) or old toothbrush (plastic parts).

Cleaning the aerator screen.

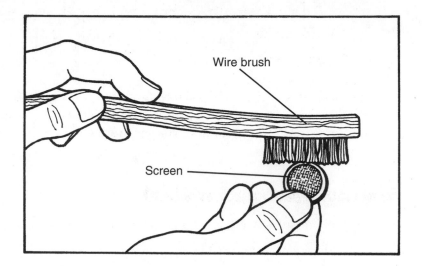

3. If any of the parts are damaged, bring them to the hardware store and find replacements.

4. Put the aerator parts back together in the right sequence. Reinstall the aerator on the faucet spout by hand-turning it clockwise. Try the faucet; the cleaned/replaced aerator should correct any flow/pressure problems.

Brushing Up on Showerheads

You may have an old showerhead that's begun to leak at the joint between the head and the arm, or you might simply want to remove an old model and change it for a new style with a different flow pattern. Either way, it's fairly simple to repair or change the head.

Sometimes the little holes that direct the shower spray get clogged by dirt, or by mineral deposits in the water. It's easy to clean them. White vinegar is a great cleaner for many types of plumbing fittings; it dissolves crud, and does not damage the fixtures.

Cleaning Showerhead Outlet Holes

You'll need the following:

❑ Screwdriver (standard or Phillips head)

❑ White vinegar

❑ Straight pin

The flat metal surface of the showerhead from which the water spray emerges is called the faceplate. You can detach it from the showerhead by removing the faceplate screw or screws. Soak the faceplate in vinegar overnight, and clean the water outlet holes with a straight pin.

Removing/Replacing a Showerhead

As you did with faucets, you'll need to prepare your work area and tools:

1. Shut off the water at the supply stops or the main.

2. To protect the fixture, wrap the jaws of your wrench or pliers with masking or painter's tape.

3. Close or cover the drain with a rag or towel so you don't lose any parts. If your shower is in the tub, you may want to further protect the tub by putting corrugated board on the tub bottom, or cover the whole tub with a drop cloth.

4. Clear a place to set out the showerhead parts in order. There are usually only a few parts, but you don't want any to go astray if you're putting back the same head.

You'll need the following:

❑ Locking pliers

❑ Adjustable wrench or pliers

❑ Lubricating spray

❑ Teflon tape

The showerhead and the shower arm screw together by means of a collar nut on the showerhead, which threads onto the shower arm. The shower arm is wrapped with Teflon tape that provides a secure seal between nut and threads.

1. Hold the shower arm in place with the taped jaws of the locking pliers; with the taped jaws of the adjustable wrench or slip-jointed pliers loosen the collar nut of the showerhead by turning it counterclockwise. If it's stiff and won't turn, try a little lubricating spray.

2. Once the collar nut is loosened, finish loosening it by hand and remove the showerhead.

   Once the showerhead is removed, you can perform these fixes (if you're replacing the head, skip to Step 3):

   ◆ If the showerhead is leaking near the collar nut, you may have a bad washer. Unscrew the showerhead until you expose the swivel ball and washer. If the washer looks corroded, you can take it to the hardware store and get a replacement.

   ◆ If the shower has a stiff pivot, you can lubricate the swivel ball with some petroleum jelly.

3. Remove any old tape from the shower arm, and clean the arm so there's no residue remaining. Wrap the threads at the end of the shower arm with Teflon tape. Wind the tape counterclockwise, with two layers. The tape should be taut, but the threads of the shower arm should not be cutting through the tape.

4. To replace or reinstall the old showerhead, screw the head onto the tape coated arm, then tighten the collar nut with the adjustable wrench or slip-jointed pliers, while keeping the shower arm immobile with the locking pliers.

5. Uncover the drain, open the supply stops or main water control, and turn on the shower. If there are no leaks, you're done. If there's a drip, turn off the water and try turning the collar nut another quarter turn. Don't over-tighten. If the leaking persists, you'll have to remove the showerhead, unwrap the Teflon tape, wrap with new tape, and reinstall the showerhead.

When the Pop-Up Stopper Flops

Pop-up drain stoppers in bathroom sinks are a convenient invention, but fixing them requires you to crawl around under and behind the sink—tough duty if your bathroom sink is mounted in a vanity cabinet. You'll have to unload everything you've stored under the sink (be careful to put any toxic items out of the reach of children or pets), and use a flashlight to take a good look at what you're working on.

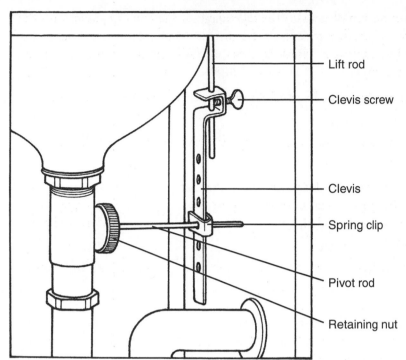

Pop-up drain assembly.

Lift rod

Clevis screw

Clevis

Spring clip

Pivot rod

Retaining nut

The mechanics of a pop-up drain stopper are really pretty simple; the handle of the lift rod sits on top of the sink between the faucets and (usually) behind the spout. When the handle is raised, the pop-up drain closes; when the handle is pushed down, the drain opens.

Underneath the sink, the lift rod attaches to a perforated metal bar called the *clevis* by means of a *clevis screw*, which is loosened or tightened by hand or by screwdriver.

Also attached to the clevis with a spring clip is a *pivot rod*, which passes through a retaining nut into the drain. Beyond the retaining nut, the rod also passes through a pivot ball, a plastic gasket, and a washer. It then passes through a small loop in the tail end of the pop-up stopper. So—the lift rod connects to the clevis, which connects to the pivot rod, which connects to the pop-up stopper. Got it?

Here's how to adjust the under-sink mechanics so your pop-up stopper will work the way it's supposed to.

If the pop-up stopper doesn't sit tight in the drain when you raise the lift rod:

1. Loosen the clevis screw (with your fingers, a screwdriver, or an adjustable wrench, depending on the type of screw).

2. Push the stopper down by hand to close the drain.

3. Tighten the clevis screw. Once you make this adjustment, the stopper should close snugly.

If the pop-up stopper doesn't stay open when you push down the lift rod:

1. Squeeze the spring clip (see the previous illustration), and release the pivot rod from the clevis.

2. Move the pivot rod to the next hole up on the clevis, holding it in place with the spring clip.

If you need to remove the pop-up stopper to clean out the drain, or for any other reason (you'll need an adjustable wrench or slip jointed pliers with taped jaws to perform this repair):

1. Loosen the retaining nut with the wrench and pull back the pivot rod, which will disengage the rod from the stopper. If you remove any parts from the pivot rod, be sure to replace them in the right order.

2. Once the rod is disengaged from the stopper, you can lift it right out.

Ounce of Prevention

Bathroom drains get gunky with all of the hair and grooming products that slide down into the pipes. To prevent clogs, and prevent the need to go through the acrobatics of working under the sink to remove the pop-up stopper, do the following preventive maintenance:

1. Keep the stopper closed when you're using grooming aids, and wipe out the basin before you let the water run.

2. Once a month, run very hot (or a pot of boiling) water down each of your bathroom drains; this will help keep them flowing.

The Least You Need to Know

- There are four basic types of faucets: compression, rotary ball, cartridge, and ceramic disk.

- Arrange faucet parts in the order you remove them; this will help you get them back in the correct order—a must for an effective repair.

- Your spitting faucet is probably a sign of a clogged or faulty aerator—an easy fix.

- Pop-up bathroom sink stoppers are controlled from behind and underneath the sink. You'll need a flashlight and some physical agility to squeeze in for the repair!

Chapter 12

Tub and Toilet Techniques

In This Chapter

- ◆ Cosmetic improvements for the tub
- ◆ How to clear tub and toilet clogs
- ◆ How to stop a running toilet in its tracks
- ◆ Toilet innards, old and new

Tubs and toilets are sturdy fixtures; most last for years without any major problems. If you have an old, porcelain enamel-coated cast iron tub, you can improve its looks by repairing chips with a kit from the home center. And you can guard against moisture problems around the tub by occasionally renewing the bond between tub and wall.

As for the toilet, there's a lot you can do to improve the way it works beyond the old "jiggle the handle" trick, which rarely fixes one of its potential problems, and then, only temporarily.

Bathtubs: The Surface Story

A century ago, after indoor bathroom fixtures became more universal, the standard tub was cast iron, coated with white porcelain. In the past couple of decades, however, coated stainless steel and molded acrylic are lighter-weight, cheaper, and easier-to-install tub alternatives.

If you've got an old tub, you can improve its appearance. New products can help you repair the surface of an old fixture.

Concealing Surface Flaws in Porcelain-Enameled Cast Iron

Cast iron tubs are very heavy. Rap your knuckles against the tub wall; iron will respond with a deep thrum (and probably hurt your knuckles). The only vulnerability of these sturdy standbys is their lovely porcelain skin. Dropping something heavy in the tub can crack or chip the porcelain enamel, sometimes exposing the iron beneath the delicate surface.

The only permanent and flawless solution to repairing the damaged "skin" of an old fixture is to have it completely resurfaced (see Appendix B). The process is somewhat expensive, but far less than the cost of removing an old cast iron tub and replacing it with a similar model.

However, improvements in epoxy products have made spot repairs more acceptable. Hardware stores and home centers now stock repair kits for filling chips and small cracks in a porcelain surface. Several companies offer the repair products in a range of colors beyond plain white (and anyone who has white fixtures knows that there is a range of whites, as well).

These repairs should be done carefully, according to product directions. There are usually three steps:

1. Sand the chipped or cracked area with very fine sandpaper (220-grit or higher) or an emery cloth, and clean the surface thoroughly.

What Pros Know

Enameled cast iron kitchen sinks can be repaired with the same type of repair kits used to spot-repair an old tub.

2. Apply a chip filler with a putty knife or tongue depressor. If the chip or gouge is deep, Steps 1 and 2 are repeated several times, allowing the filler to dry according to instructions.

3. When the repair is smooth and dry, apply a porcelain touch-up glaze and allow to dry according to directions.

If a large piece of porcelain chips off, don't discard it. Use epoxy cement (according to directions) to glue it back in place, then perform the repair just described.

Renewing a Scratched Acrylic Tub

These tubs are molded from sheets of acrylic; the surface color goes completely through the material. However, people who don't realize that acrylic is *plastic* mistakenly use an abrasive cleaner on this surface, and wind up scratching or dulling it. You can remove the dullness by using a product designed to polish plastic surfaces. (Many people swear by a liquid polish called Gel Gloss.)

Remove scratches and burns from acrylic tub surfaces with extremely fine sandpaper (1,500-grit is available at automotive supply stores); use a little water when you sand. Then finish the job with the liquid polish.

Waterproofing Around the Bathtub

Whether the walls around your tub are tile, laminate, paneling, or wallpapered drywall, there should be a waterproof seam between the top edge of the tub and the wall. This nice finish is usually accomplished by applying a line of waterproof *caulk* at the juncture between tub and wall. The caulk prevents water from the tub or the shower-in-tub from leaking behind the tub edge, and damaging the adjoining walls and the floor beneath.

Caulk does eventually dry out, but the real culprit that cracks caulk around the tub is weight. Remember, water is heavy—more than seven pounds per gallon. So every time you fill the tub, with water and yourself, you are putting some stress on that nice, straight caulk seam. Here's how to renew it.

def•i•ni•tion

Caulk is a material used to create a watertight seal between two adjoining surfaces.

To remove old caulk, you'll need the following:

- ❏ Painter's tape

- ❏ Standard screwdriver

1. You'll want to protect the wall and the tub surface when you remove the old caulk. Apply painter's tape to the edge of the wall above the caulk line, and to the edge of the tub below the caulk.

2. Using the standard screwdriver, and wearing rubber gloves if you don't want to touch the old caulk, remove the old caulk, using the tip of the screwdriver to scrape it away anywhere it sticks.

3. Clean any dirt or mildew from around the seam location. New caulking will not adhere properly to a dirty surface. Let the open joint dry. If the painter's tape has lifted, reapply it so you have a nice clean guideline for installing the new caulk.

To install new caulk, you'll need the following:

❑ Painter's tape

❑ Waterproof caulk (silicon or other product recommended for tub joints)

❑ Caulking gun

1. Apply painter's tape to the edge of the wall above the caulk line, and to the edge of the tub below the caulk.

2. Puncture or cut the tip of the caulking tube and insert the tube in the caulking gun according to gun directions. (Some sealants come in a hand-held tube; use them according to package instructions.)

3. Starting from a corner or end of the tub, install a straight bead of caulk along the joint between tub and wall.

Install new caulk. The caulking gun shown is a common type, but there are many designs for this tool.

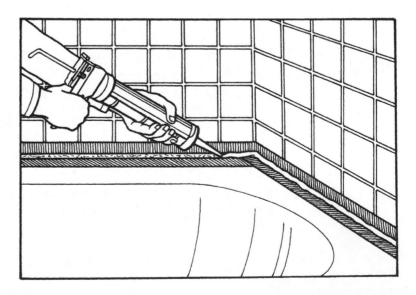

4. Allow the caulk to dry according to package directions.

5. Remove the painter's tape.

You can use the same process to install new caulk in the joint between the base of the tub and the floor.

Clearing a Tub Clog

Because the pipes that supply and drain the tub are usually behind the wall and/or under the tub, clearing a clogged tub drain is slightly different than clearing a sink drain. Some tubs have pop-up stoppers (like sinks), while others have strainer/drains. Old claw foot tubs may have a rubber plug!

Pop-Up Stopper

The overflow for a tub is located above the drain on the wall of the tub below the tub spout.

1. Open the stopper, using the lever on the overflow.

2. Turn the stopper counterclockwise, then pull it out.

3. Wearing rubber gloves, remove any accumulation of hair and other yucky stuff. Replace the stopper.

Strainer

You'll need needlenose pliers for this one.

1. Grip the strainer by inserting the two narrow jaws of the pliers into two holes in the strainer.

2. Turn the strainer counterclockwise, then lift it out.

3. Wearing rubber gloves, remove hair and other debris; replace the strainer, gripping it with the pliers as before. Turn it clockwise to set it back in place.

Take the Plunge

If the clog is stubborn, try the plunger. You'll need the following:

- ❏ Screwdriver (standard or Phillips) to remove the overflow cover
- ❏ Rag
- ❏ Plunger

What Pros Know

Address slow bathtub drains *before* you have standing water—an indication that the problem has become a difficult one. To avoid future clogs, pour a kettle full of boiling water down each of your tub drains once a month. Remove hair from the drain stopper regularly—whenever you use the tub.

1. Unscrew the metal cover on the overflow and stuff the rag in the hole.

2. If there's sufficient standing water in the tub to cover the plunger cup, proceed to the next step. If not, add water so it covers the plunger cup.

3. Maintaining the seal of the cup over the drain, plunge straight up and down a dozen times; see if the water starts to flow down the drain. Repeat this process at least three or four times before you give up! It usually works.

The Worst Case: Toilet Clogs

Warning! When the flush handle on your toilet fails to move the water and waste out of the toilet and down the drain, *ignore* your impulse to flush again. You'll probably succeed only in making the water (and everything else!) wind up on the floor.

An excess of paper (usually big wads of toilet paper) is often the culprit in a clog. Before you try any muscular solutions, try the following fix.

Low-Tech De-Clogging

When my kids were little, they often used toilet paper *enthusiastically*, and the toilet would clog. My husband was the pro in this case. He'd ignore my bleats of dismay and go to his closet for a wire coat hanger. He'd untwist the hanger and maneuver one end into the drain portion of the toilet until the hanger hooked into the paper dam that one or the other child had created. Then he'd ease the paper back up into the bowl, with instructions to leave the mess alone for a while. If it was a really huge mass of paper, he'd remove some and dispose of it in another toilet. An hour or two later, the remains of the original offending wad would have disintegrated a bit, and usually flushed right down.

You can try it, especially if your little ones are extravagant users of toilet paper!

Ounce of Prevention

Other toilet cloggers are dental floss, napkins, paper towels, and nonflushable feminine sanitary products. *None* of these should be discarded in the toilet! These items are also fatal, or nearly so, to septic waste systems.

The Toilet Plunge

For a basic toilet plunge you'll need a plunger and a bucket.

1. Turn off the water at the supply stop underneath the toilet. If there is no supply stop, turn off the main water supply valve.

2. If the toilet bowl is less than half full, add enough water to cover the plunger cup, once you place the plunger in the toilet over the drain hole. If the toilet is quite full, get a cup and bail some water from the bowl into the bucket. Otherwise you'll splash water all over the place when you plunge.

3. Pump the plunger up and down at least a dozen times. If the water doesn't start to drain, plunge again. Try this routine a couple of times. Be patient, and don't pump violently; push the handle down gently, then pull it up. If you shake the bowl too much you could unseal the ring-shaped wax gasket that seams the base of the toilet (called the *horn* in plumbing lingo) to the waste pipe. (The only solution to a broken wax seal—which can cause a leak—is removing the toilet and replacing the gasket, a job for a pro.)

4. Once the obstruction clears, turn on the water supply at the supply stop or main valve.

If you cannot clear the obstruction, you'll need to call a pro.

Plunge the toilet.

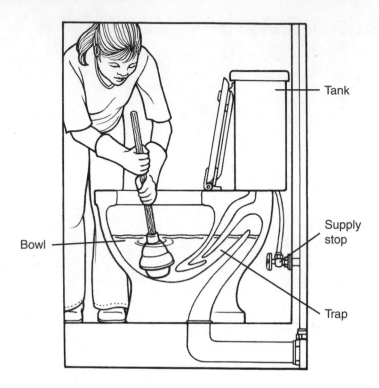

Tank

Bowl

Supply stop

Trap

Other Toilet Trouble

Q: Is your toilet running?

A: Yes.

Well, go catch it!

Five-year-olds love this joke, but for the adults in the house, a running toilet isn't funny. It's annoying and it wastes a lot of water.

In addition to running when they shouldn't, toilets can sweat, leak, and (believe it or not) rock. Here's how to handle some of these problems (and which ones to leave for the pros).

What Pros Know

Old toilets of pre-1990s vintage should be replaced whenever your budget will allow. Most older toilets flush with about 7 gallons of water; new models flush with 1.6 gallons! If you live in a drought-prone area, or pay a water company for your water, the new fixture will soon pay for itself.

Inside the Tank: A Toilet's Vital Organs

First, let's take a look at two common configurations you're likely to see inside the toilet when you lift the tank lid.

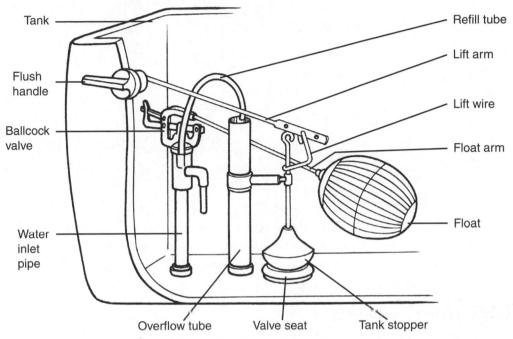

Toilet with ballcock valve assembly.

Yes, there are a lot of named parts in this setup. But if you look at the drawing, you'll see that the way it works is rather simple.

When you depress the *flush handle* to flush the toilet, the *lift arm* raises the *lift wire*, which raises the *tank stopper* (also called a *flapper*) out of the *valve seat*, so that water can move from the tank to the bowl, creating the flush action that siphons waste into the drain.

Because the water level is going down, the *float* (in this configuration, a big rubber ball) begins to drop down in the tank, also lowering the *float arm*. The lowering float and arm pull open the *ballcock valve*, which allows fresh water to enter the tank through the *refill tube*. As the water rises, so does the float, gradually closing the ballcock valve. When the tank is full, the water should stop flowing.

Float cup fill valve assembly.

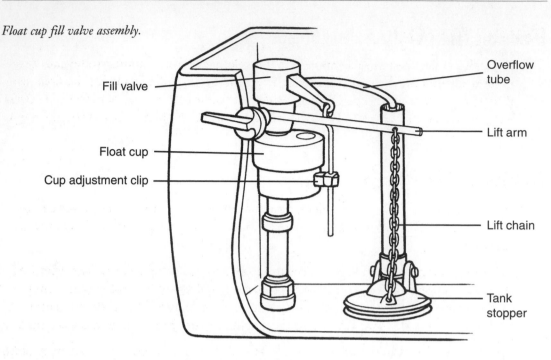

Fill valve

Float cup

Cup adjustment clip

Overflow tube

Lift arm

Lift chain

Tank stopper

In this more modern setup, the *float cup* takes the place of the float (the rubber ball) in the older version. The cup can be raised or lowered to adjust the water level in the tank.

Stopping a Running Toilet

If the water runs and runs after you flush, you'll need to take a look inside the tank. So remove the lid and observe the following.

Worn-Out Float Ball

If you've got a float ball in your tank and it's partially submerged, or has water inside it, you need to replace it. Shut off the water supply at the supply stop (or the main, if there is no supply stop), and flush the toilet. Unscrew the float from the float arm (turn counterclockwise), take it to the hardware store and buy a replacement. Attach the new float (turn clockwise), and turn on the supply stop.

Float Ball Won't Rise

If the float won't rise sufficiently to stop the inlet valve from running water into the tank, then the water will keep running. To adjust the float, manually lift the float arm; if that stops the water from running, bend the float arm down, or away from the tank wall. To adjust the float cup, press the clip that adjusts the float cup and try moving it up to raise the water level.

Tank Stopper Won't Close

If the water level is not the problem, a running toilet is often caused by a poor seal between the tank stopper and the valve seat. Or, the stopper is worn and needs to be replaced.

With the tank lid open, if you observe the flush and notice that the tank stopper (see the earlier illustration of a toilet with ballcock valve assembly) is not closing firmly over the toilet valve seat, the water will continue to run out of the tank, no matter how much water flows in. You want the stopper to drop directly over the valve seat.

Try changing the position of the lift rod (or chain) on the lift arm. You can try making the chain longer or shorter. If that doesn't help the stopper seal over the valve seat, you can try two other fixes.

To clean the stopper and valve seat, you'll need a sponge and a pad of fine steel wool.

1. Turn off the water and flush the tank to empty it.

2. Lift the stopper. Clean it with the sponge.

3. Examine and feel the edge of the valve seat. It may have corroded a bit and feel rough. Smooth and clean it with the steel wool.

4. Replace the stopper. Turn the water back on, and leaving the tank lid open, watch the stopper as you flush. If the stopper seals and the water stops running, you're done.

If not, here's how to replace the stopper.

1. Turn off the water and flush the tank to empty it.

2. Remove the stopper from the lift rod or chain (it will unscrew or unhook), and bring it to the hardware store or home center for a replacement.

3. Install the new stopper.

The Flush Is Weak

You'll need to remove the tank lid to watch the flush action.

If the screw that connects the flush handle to the lift arm is loose, tighten this connection.

Or the stopper may close before the tank empties; in that case, adjust the lift rod or chain. If this is the cause, usually the rod or chain needs to be lengthened a bit to give the water a tiny bit more time to drain out.

Leak or Sweat?

Water dripping in various locations on the outside of the tank or bowl can mean a leak—which can be serious. Or the water can be a result of condensation ("sweat"), which can be cured by insulating the inside of the tank.

To detect a leak, you'll need the following:

❑ Old clean towels or rags

❑ Food coloring (red or green)

❑ Paper towels

1. Flush the toilet, then use the towels to dry all the exterior surfaces: tank, seat, bowl, bolts, everything.

2. Open the tank lid and pour a little (half a teaspoon) of the food coloring into the water. Cover the tank, and wait an hour or so.

3. Wipe a paper towel under the tank where it connects to the bowl. If the towel shows food coloring, you've found your leak.

4. If not, run the paper towel around the base of the toilet. If the towel is the color of the food coloring, you've probably got a leak at the wax gasket connection.

With either of these problems, the toilet needs to be taken apart. It's best to call a plumber. However, if there is no leak, you've probably got a condensation problem. This often happens in the summer, when humid conditions create the ideal environment for sweaty toilets. You can live with the problem in hot weather, wiping down the fixture when it gets sweaty, or you can be industrious and insulate the tank.

Personally, I just use a towel in hot weather when one or more of our toilets sweat. But if you want, you can insulate the tank with $1/4$" sheets of polystyrene foam cut to match the dimensions of the sides, front and back of the tank.

To do this, you need to turn off the water supply, flush the toilet until the tank is empty, wipe it down, and create paper templates for all four inside walls of the toilet tank. Trace the dimensions of the templates onto the polystyrene sheets, cut them out, and then fit them in the tank. Glue the polystyrene to the walls of the tank with waterproof mastic. Be careful that the insulation does not block or impede any of the toilet's inner workings.

If this sounds like too much work, when your toilet starts to sweat, just grab a clean old towel and do the daily wipe down!

When the Toilet Rocks

A rocking toilet is not a good thing. When you sit on the toilet and it seems to rock, it most likely means that the wax ring seal is broken. This can cause a leak that can ruin your floor (and the ceiling below it). Call a plumber right away.

The Least You Need to Know

- It's possible to spot repair the finish on an old enameled cast iron tub.
- Keep tub drains flowing by removing hair after every use, and pouring a kettle of boiling water down each one, every month.
- Toilet tanks seem to have a lot of stuff in them, but the mechanics are simple.
- Leaks from the tank, the base, or a rocking toilet bowl require professional attention.

Part 4

Mission Control: Wiring, Appliances, Heating, and Cooling

Now we come to the brains of your home: its system of wiring and conveniences that make daily life run smoothly.

I often look around my house and try to imagine how its original owners managed with just a couple of candles and the heat from their fireplaces. Winters must really have been dark, chilly, and unrelenting.

Lights, central heating, automatic washing machines, refrigerators—how could we live without them? When one of these things doesn't work, we're up in arms in a matter of hours. Part 4 won't keep you free from power outages—they're beyond your control—but it will help you keep things humming along smoothly otherwise.

"June, I can do this wiring myself. Trust me.
It's not a fire hazard, and we're not going to get electrocuted."

In the Loop: Understanding Your Wiring

In This Chapter

- ◆ A look at electrical terms
- ◆ Mapping your home's electrical system
- ◆ Understanding circuitry
- ◆ Really receptive receptacles
- ◆ GFCI: four initials you need to know
- ◆ Removing a broken bulb from a light socket

The NEC (National Electrical Code) Handbook is nearly 800 pages long; a new edition is published every three years. That's a lot of reading just to learn the standards for electrical systems.

Then you have to learn to *do* this stuff. An apprenticed electrician studies for two years and spends 8,000 hours on the job (about four years), just to earn the designation of Journeyman for his trade.

Why am I telling you all this? Because working safely with electricity requires knowledge and skill. There's a lot to learn. And mistakes can be dangerous to your health. So my advice to you as you learn about your electrical system can be summed up in three words: proceed with care. If you are unsure or confused about anything described in this chapter, don't hesitate. Call a licensed electrician to help with your wiring problem.

Time to Call a Pro?

In this chapter, you'll find a lot of information about household electrical systems, but only a couple of things to do yourself. Some houses have up-to-date electrical systems, and others are deplorably out of date. If yours is of the latter variety, I advise you not to work on it yourself. And even if you have a modern system, there are as many "exceptions to the rules" in wiring as there are conforming setups. To become well versed in wiring takes more space than there is available in this chapter.

Ounce of Prevention

If you need an electrician, beware of using a friend of a friend who "works with wiring." You want a *licensed* electrician. Ask: "Are you licensed?" The genuine article will be happy to give you his or her license number. It's a credential that's earned with a lot of hard work.

I can't see what's in your house and behind your walls. If your equipment is thoroughly up to date, you can do a few things yourself, like change a light fixture or install a dimmer. Refer to the equipment instructions for those projects. But for more complicated projects, study a book that's strictly devoted to household electrical systems. And don't attempt things you don't understand and are not comfortable with; call a pro.

Your Electricity Dictionary

Volts, amps, watts ... aren't they all the same thing? If you think so, you may be in a bit of trouble around an electrical panel. Let's start by defining our terms.

Electricity is the flow of electrons through a *conductor*. In the case of your electrical system, the conductor is wire, which for safety is encased in a nonconductive sheath. The force with which the electrons move is measured in *volts*. The speed with which electrons move is measured in *amperes* (commonly known as *amps*). Output of electricity is measured in *watts*.

The electrical service that enters your home from the utility meter, and connects to the electrical panel, consists of two 120-volt "hot" (live) wires and one neutral. An old electrical system will have only one 120-volt wire plus the neutral, and is usually insufficient for most large, modern appliances. If you have the latter, it's time for an upgrade.

In Chapter 4, I covered your home's electrical power source—the electrical service panel. From this control center, the power coming into the panel is divided into branches of electrical current, which travel around your house along loops of wire, called *circuits*, that begin and end at the panel. Circuits are controlled by means of individual circuit breakers or fuses. Each breaker or fuse has a number—15, 20, 30— which represents the number of amps that a circuit can conduct. Large equipment such as clothes dryers, electric ranges, or air conditioners usually requires a large-capacity (= large number of amps) circuit to run, so each of these appliances usually has a circuit dedicated solely to its operation.

When a particular circuit breaker keeps flipping to "off," or a fuse keeps blowing, sometimes the cause is too great a demand for electric current along a particular circuit. You will have to unplug some power-using devices (lights or appliances) to lighten the demand (also known as the *load*) on that circuit. If there's another circuit nearby where you can safely plug in the additional items, your problem is solved. If you can't solve the overload problem, or if that does not seem to be the cause of the blown fuse or tripped circuit breaker, you'll need the assistance of a licensed electrician.

When you create a map of the circuits on your panel, which is the layout of your home's electrical system, you will be able to see if the capacity of your electrical service is equal to or greater than the load. It's good knowledge to have, and reassuring when you know you've got plenty of power. If your home is underpowered for all the equipment and appliances you want to use, you should make an electrical upgrade as soon as you can manage it. An underpowered system is dangerous.

Mapping Your Electrical System

First, look at your electrical panel; on most panels, each circuit breaker or fuse is numbered on the face of the panel. If yours are not numbered, you can do this yourself with a fine-tipped permanent marker. Starting with number 1 at the top left, put a number on the panel next to each breaker or fuse, sequentially.

You may notice that in some cases, two circuit breakers seem to be toggled together. These are the large capacity breakers for major appliances and systems. Their amperage (30, 40, etc.) is marked on the toggle.

This is a 20-amp—see its markings—circuit breaker, which has been flipped off.

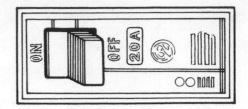

If your electrical panel is equipped with circuit breakers, you will need to flip the breaker to the "off" position to shut off power to any location that is serviced by the circuit it controls.

To return power to the circuit, you'll need to flip it back to the "on" position.

Remember, use *one hand* when you work at the panel. The other hand should be at your side. You want to avoid becoming an open circuit for any loose current!

When a fuse has blown, its center may look black (like the illustration below on the right) or the little lead strip in the center may look broken or melted. Either way, it must be replaced. Again, use one hand to remove/replace the blown fuse, with your other hand at your side.

A fresh, 20-amp fuse is shown on the left; a fuse that has blown is on the right.

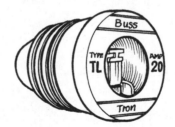 

The fuses shown can be removed and replaced with a fuse of *the same amperage*. This is important. One of the reasons that circuit breaker panels have pretty much replaced fuse panels is that many accidents and fires have been caused by the replacement of one fuse with another of a different, and thus incompatible, size. Circuit breakers are not necessarily safer than fuses. But the problem with fuses is that you need to have a supply of them, in all the right sizes, at all times.

Ounce of Prevention

Ordinary fuses (Type T, shown in the previous illustration) can be replaced by equipping the fuse receptacles in an electrical panel with Type S fuse adapters, which use only Type S fuses of the correct amperage. This will prevent anyone from replacing a fuse with anything except a fuse with the right number of amps.

Now, let's get to mapping. You'll need the following:

❑ Clipboard, pencil, and paper

❑ Plug-in radio or lamp, or a voltage tester, for testing circuit locations

Voltage tester. When turned to "on," this simple, battery-operated tool will light and beep when its point is inserted into the "hot" (live current) side of an electric receptacle.

1. Begin by turning on any light fixtures or receptacles that are controlled by wall switches. If a receptacle is controlled by a wall switch, plug in the lamp or radio, or test the receptacle with the voltage tester, to make sure the receptacle is on.

2. In a room with no overhead light, plug in and turn on a lamp in that room. This will help you to identify the general location when a circuit is turned off, because the lamp will go out.

3. Once you know the power is on throughout your house, start with the circuit breaker or fuse in the location labeled 1. Next to number 1 on your paper, write down the amperage of the circuit; this will help you later (for example, if it's a 15-amp circuit breaker or fuse, make a notation that reads: #1–15 amp). Flip the circuit breaker off, or remove the fuse.

4. You or a friend need to identify which fixtures and receptacles the circuit controls by locating which lights and receptacles are now off. Write down the location of all the fixtures and receptacles controlled by breaker/fuse #1.

5. Continue turning off circuits and identifying fixtures and receptacles on each circuit until you have a complete map of your electrical service panel. Tape a copy of the map on the door of your service panel; make a photocopy and put it in your home workbook (see Chapter 4).

Once all of the circuits in your house are identified, it will be safer and easier to work with your home's electrical system.

> **What Pros Know** _____
>
> Pros know, and you should, too, that some houses were wired by amateurs. If you're using a voltage tester to check for power, test both straight slots of an electrical receptacle before you determine it's off. It may have been wired backward. Most receptacles are duplex (for two plugs); some receptacles have space for four plugs; to make certain the power is off, test all the straight slots in a receptacle. (There's more on receptacles later in this chapter.)

Calculating the Load on Your System

To find out whether your circuits are sufficient for what's plugged in or wired to them, you can calculate the electrical load for each circuit. You'll need the following:

❏ Paper and pencil

❏ Calculator

Take your electrical circuit map, and on a separate piece of paper note the number of watts for everything that's on a particular circuit. The wattage of light fixtures is the total wattage of the light bulbs in the fixture; three 100-watt bulbs have a load of 300 watts. Appliance wattage is often listed on the back or underside of the unit.

The formula for determining the maximum load is:

Total watts ÷ 120 (volts) = amps required

Or look at it another way:

Amps × 120 = maximum watts

So, if 15-amp circuit #1 has four 100-watt bulb fixtures and a radio (15 watts) for a total of 415 watts, divide that by 120 (= 3.4 amps) and you know there's room on that circuit for a few more light bulbs and probably a television set.

But if you've got a toaster oven (1,400 watts) plugged into circuit #1, you're getting very close to the limit of the 15-amp circuit's capacity (1,800 watts). That circuit is near full, and so should not have other things plugged into it.

The proper load for any circuit is about 80 percent of its capacity. So, if you've got a 15-amp circuit, a load of about 1,400 watts is just right.

By doing these calculations for your system and what's plugged into it, you'll know whether or not your home is adequately powered.

If a licensed electrician has not checked out your electrical system in ten years, or you have just moved in, you might want the pro to have a look. He or she can tell you whether your electrical service is properly sized for the amount of electricity you are using, or plan to use. In the case of an old house, you may find that your house has aluminum wiring (you do **not** want to do it yourself with aluminum wires), or that the system is not properly *grounded*. Before you go beyond your mapping project, it's good to know as much as you can about your system.

def•i•ni•tion

Grounding means just what it says. When the electrician grounds your electrical system, he or she has connected it to the earth. Grounding provides a safe path for any loose current—from a defective fixture or appliance, or exposed wire touching metal somewhere in the system.

Receptacle ID

You might call them plugs (they're not), or outlets (not quite right). The correct term for the little face-like electrical devices in your walls, where you plug in lamps and appliances, is receptacle. There are three basic types you should be able to identify:

♦ Two-pole, nonpolarized receptacle

♦ Two-pole, polarized receptacle

♦ Two-pole, three-wire grounding receptacle

A receptacle with two slots of equal size is nonpolarized. This type of receptacle is often found in old houses where the wiring has not been upgraded or grounded. If you have this type of receptacle throughout your house, you need to consult an electrician.

Polarization helps reduce the potential for shock. Most electrical devices and appliances have polarized plugs—one blade is wider than the other. Nonpolarized receptacles do not accept polarized plugs; these receptacles are outdated and should be replaced.

Two-pole, nonpolarized receptacle.

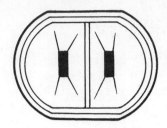

Ounce of Prevention

If you have two-prong, nonpolarized receptacles and have been chopping off the grounding (half-round) prong on an appliance plug to fit your old receptacles, I am amazed you're still alive. Never cut the half-round grounding prong off a plug.

A two-pole, polarized receptacle's slots are unequal in length; one is longer than the other. When a polarized plug is inserted in this receptacle (if it's wired correctly), the wires in the cord connect to the corresponding wires in the circuit; the short slot is the "hot" side, the long slot is neutral. This receptacle accepts polarized plugs, but does not have a half round hole for a grounding prong. These receptacles are safer than nonpolarized receptacles, but not as safe as a grounded system.

Two-pole, polarized receptacle.

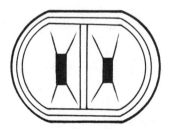

A two-pole, three-wire grounding receptacle has all the right stuff, and accepts plugs for all modern electric devices except the special plugs used for large electrical equipment and appliances (ranges, dryers), which have matching receptacles for their large-capacity circuits.

Two-pole, three-wire grounding receptacle.

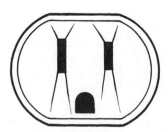

But Is It Grounded?

If you have two-pole, three-wire grounding receptacles in your home, your system appears to be up to date. One way to check that the receptacles are grounded (other than calling the electrician) is to check them with a handy, inexpensive (around $3) device called a receptacle analyzer. This device will tell you at a glance if your receptacle is properly wired and grounded. The sequence of lights will alert you to any problems.

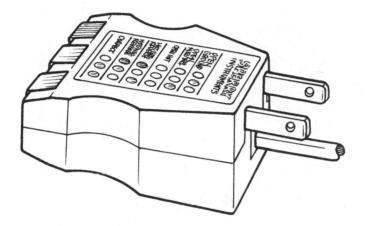

Receptacle analyzer.

Amazing, but this little plug-in will tell you a lot about the wiring of any receptacle. Besides telling you that the receptacle is grounded and all the wires are attached correctly, it will alert you if ...

- There's an open ground, meaning that the ground wire is not connected.

- There's an open neutral, which means the neutral wire is not connected.

- There's an open hot, which means the hot wire is not connected. None of the analyzer's lights go on. But remember, this indicator can also mean that the circuit for this receptacle is turned off by a removed fuse or flipped-off breaker. Check before you panic.

The receptacle analyzer will also tell you if the wires are not connected properly.

GFCI: Initials You Need to Know

In the bathroom, near the kitchen sink, outdoors, and in other spots where water may come close to electric power, the electrical code demands that GFCIs (ground fault circuit interrupters) be installed, instead of ordinary three-wire grounded receptacles. These receptacles, invented about thirty years ago, will shut down if the current level in the circuit changes even a tiny bit. This is important near water; if an appliance that's turned on should fall into water or become wet and you touch it, the result can be a lethal shock.

GFCI receptacle.

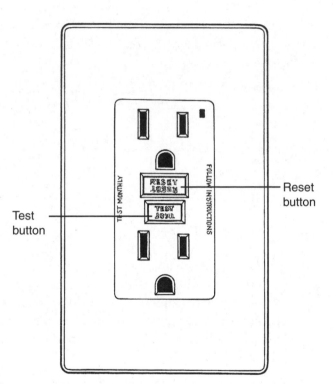

Test button

Reset button

GFCIs are useless unless they work properly, and they do wear out over time. Here how to test one; you should test every GFCI in your home every month. To do this you'll need a lamp, plug-in radio, or voltage tester.

1. Press the button on the GFCI marked "TEST." If the receptacle is operating properly, this button will shut off the current. Test that the GFCI is off by inserting the voltage tester into the short (hot) slots of the receptacle, or plugging in a radio or lamp and trying to turn them on.

2. To restart the current, press the button marked "RESET." The current should return to the receptacle: the lamp or radio will turn on, and the voltage tester will light and beep when inserted in the hot slots of the receptacle.

If a GFCI does not operate properly, it needs to be replaced.

Shattered! Replacing a Bulb That Breaks in Its Fixture

Every so often, a light bulb will shatter, and you've got a very sharp problem on your hands. If the bulb is in a lamp, unplug the lamp before you do anything else. If the bulb is in an overhead fixture, you'll need to turn off the switch that controls the bulb, and also, turn off the circuit breaker (or remove the fuse) that controls the fixture. Then you can proceed.

First, get out your work gloves; those shards of broken bulbs are extremely sharp. If you're working above your head on a ceiling fixture, you'll want to wear safety goggles, too.

You'll need the following:

❏ Voltage tester

❏ Broom handle

❏ Needlenose pliers

1. By placing the voltage tester next to the bulb socket on your overhead fixture, you can check whether there is still current at the socket. Do *not* touch the socket with your hands! If there is still power, go back and turn off the circuit breaker for that fixture. Test that the power is off before you try to remove the bulb. (If the broken bulb is in a lamp, the lamp needs to be unplugged. Then follow Step 4.)

2. Remove any loose bits of glass from the bulb base before you start working on it.

3. The right-sized broom handle can help you get a grip on the bulb base, and turn it counterclockwise (remember: lefty, loosey) to remove it from the socket.

4. If the bulb base won't move by turning the broom handle, you'll have to work on the bulb base with needlenose pliers.

Remove a broken bulb from a light socket.

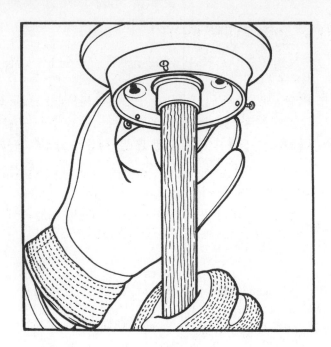

After removing as many sharp shard of glass from the bulb base with your gloved hands as you can, grip the bulb base with the ends of the pliers and try to work the bulb base out of the socket as you carefully turn it counterclockwise. This may take some deliberate, careful work; take your time and don't try to force the base. If you can't get the bulb base out, you'll need to replace the fixture.

Ounce of Prevention

When you screw in a light bulb, screw it in just far enough so it's secure in the socket, but not tight. A bulb that's screwed too tightly is the one that will break in the socket!

Many people have told me that you can use a half of a raw potato to remove a broken bulb; just stick the flat end of the potato onto the broken-off end of the bulb, and turn counterclockwise (after turning off the power, of course!). However, I've only been told this. I've never met someone who's removed a broken bulb with a potato. When I do, I can confirm the effectiveness of this method.

The Least You Need to Know

◆ If it's been a long time, or if you've just moved in, have a licensed professional check out your electrical system.

◆ The load—the power required by the various electrical fixtures and devices in your home—can be managed if you understand each circuit's capacity.

◆ A grounded system is the safest system; check your receptacles.

◆ Power near water should be protected with GFCI (ground fault circuit interrupter) receptacles.

◆ A bulb that's broken in its socket can be removed by following safe procedures, and being careful of the broken glass.

Smooth Transitions: Cleaning and Replacing Filters and Hoses

In This Chapter

- ◆ Dryer filters and hoses
- ◆ Moving water safely
- ◆ Keeping room air conditioners chillin'
- ◆ Furnaces aren't just full of hot air!
- ◆ Cleaning the filter on your range hood

The intake, flow, and exhaust of liquids and gases are factors in the everyday operation of a house. But too often, we so take for granted that everything will move smoothly that one day things take a very bad turn.

My kids went to nursery school in a neighboring town, a couple of miles from where we live. I didn't mind the commute; driving them to school, we'd pass some very beautiful houses. And since I love houses, it was a fun drive for me.

One day, while on the way to preschool, I was shocked to see that one of my favorite old farmhouses was in ruins. Except for the fireplace and chimney, the place was gone—burned to the ground. Later that week, I found out why. The newspaper reported that the fire had started in the clothes dryer when lint ignited. Fortunately, no one was hurt, but it was several years before that beautiful home was finally rebuilt.

I don't mean to scare you, but you must take care of all the filters and hoses that your systems and appliances use. Neglecting them can have negative consequences; keeping them in shape is an essential chore.

De-Linting the Clothes Dryer

The house fire caused by a dryer put me on a campaign to keep my own appliance free from fluff. If you ever hang around when the dryer is doing its work, you'll notice that the heating element gets bright red as the clothes turn in the drying drum. You want to keep the hose that vents the damp air to the outside, and the cavity where the lint trap captures other fibers, very clean. Lint is highly flammable, so clean the filter faithfully every time you use the dryer, and follow these instructions for cleaning the hose—every month, if you do a lot of laundry.

You'll need the following:

❏ Standard screwdriver

❏ Vacuum cleaner with long attachment, crevice tool, or brush

1. Before you disconnect the dryer hose, turn off the power at the circuit breaker, and unplug the dryer. If you have a gas dryer, turn off the gas at the gas supply stop (remember, "on" is parallel to the pipe; "off" is perpendicular).

2. Move the dryer away from the wall and disconnect the hose at the back of the dryer; you may have to twist off the hose, or unscrew the hose clamp that attaches it, depending upon how it is connected. Disconnect the other end of the hose from the dryer vent.

3. Using the long attachment and the brush or crevice tool, vacuum the lint from inside the hose.

4. Use your crevice tool or the lint brush to clean out the cavity underneath the lint trap. Often, lots of the fluffy stuff doesn't make it all the way to the trap. Your goal is to keep the dryer as lint-free as possible.

5. Once you've cleaned the hose and filter cavity, replace the hose and turn the electricity or the gas back on.

Clothes Washer Hoses and Filters

A couple of years ago, I came home from running an errand and heard the sound of rushing water (like a waterfall!) coming from my basement. I tore down the stairs and saw what looked like the Old Faithful geyser spewing water from behind my washing machine.

I immediately cut off the water at the supply stop behind the washer, but there was quite a pool on the floor. I cut the power to the washing machine (at the electrical panel), then unplugged it and moved the appliance back from the wall.

The washer was about 15 years old, and so were the hoses that ran from the supply valve to the machine. Made of rubber, they had grown brittle and corroded with minerals from our well water over the years. One of them finally split; that's what caused the gusher. I'd never given them a thought before the split.

Ounce of Prevention

Get in the habit of shutting off the water for the washing machine at the supply stops, whenever you finish doing the laundry. Lots of people neglect this step, but just an hour's worth of water running freely from a split hose can unleash *hundreds* of gallons of water and do thousands of dollars of damage.

If you've had your washing machine for eight years or more, it might be wise to replace the supply hoses *now*, before they do to you what mine did to me! Insurance companies—who often wind up paying out for the damage done by burst hoses—advise homeowners to replace supply hoses every 3 to 5 years.

Replacing Washing Machine Supply Hoses

You'll need the following:

- ❑ Measuring tape
- ❑ Bucket
- ❑ Adjustable or pipe wrench
- ❑ Lubricating spray
- ❑ Replacement hose
- ❑ Bristle paintbrush

1. Shut off the water at the supply stops. Then turn on the washing machine so the water that's already in the hoses empties into your machine; this will only take a few seconds before the water stops running in. Then turn off the appliance.

2. Unplug the appliance and turn off the circuit breaker that controls its receptacle. Move the machine away from the wall. Remove the drain hose from the drain; if it's cracked, replace it, too.

3. Measure the length of the supply hose so that you can buy replacements. If you're replacing a hose that has already split, don't replace just one; replace both the hot and cold water hoses. You can buy single replacements, but you really don't want another catastrophe when the other old hose gives up the ghost.

Washing machine hose gets corroded over time; insurance companies wish you'd replace it every 3–5 years.

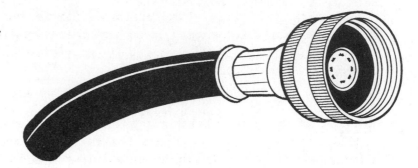

4. Put the bucket underneath the hose connections at the supply side, and remove the hoses. If they've been screwed on for years, they probably won't unscrew easily. You might need to use a bit of lubricating spray, as well as the adjustable pliers or pipe wrench. Once you've loosened the first set of connections, loosen the hose at the washing machine side.

What Pros Know

It's hard to keep track of what you did and when you did it. Take a piece of waterproof tape, write the date that you replaced the supply hose, and stick it to the hose. That way you'll remember when it's time to replace it again. Washing machines can normally last three to five hose lifetimes!

5. Before you install the new hoses, take a good look at the inlets on the washing machine side of the hose connections. If they are full of debris, clean them out with the bristle brush. If you can't get them clean, go to the next repair in this chapter (cleaning/replacing washing machine inlet filters) and follow those steps to more thoroughly clean or replace the filters.

6. Hook up the new hoses to the washing machine inlets. Then hook up the other hose ends to the water supply lines. *Be sure you attach the hot water*

line to the hot water supply, the cold water line to the cold supply. Open the supply stops and check for leaks. If you've replaced the drain hose, reconnect it to the drain.

7. Now you can push the washing machine back against the wall and plug in the appliance. Be sure that you don't put a kink in the supply hose; leave a little space between the machine and the wall so the hose bends but doesn't fold up on itself. Kinked hose will wear out faster!

About Metal Mesh Household Hoses

After my washing machine supply hose burst, I was much more sensitive to the potential for this problem. We installed a stainless steel mesh hose in place of the old rubber one, because the label said it wouldn't burst. It cost about twice what an ordinary rubber supply hose costs. But I figured, "burst-proof" sounds like a fix-it-and-forget-it option to me.

No so fast.

Insurance companies note that, while these hoses have lower failure rates than ordinary rubber hose, they can still leak. Factors like the chemical content of your water, the age of the hose, and the nonmetal interiors that may deteriorate, can lead to a breakdown. Inspect them whenever you do your routine home inspection (see Chapters 18 and 19). And replace them on the same 3–5-year cycle as you would an ordinary rubber hose.

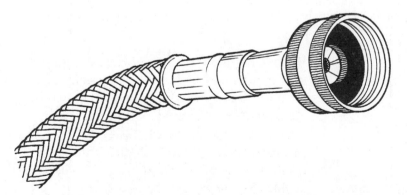

So-called burst-proof hose is made of very flexible plastic that is wrapped in a mesh of stainless steel wire—but it's not immune to leaks.

Cleaning and Replacing Washing Machine Water Inlet Filters

If your washing machine is filling slowly, or if, when replacing the water supply hoses, you notice that the little filters in the washing machine water inlets are grubby, you'll need to clean or replace them..

You'll need the following:

❑ Adjustable pliers or pipe wrench

❑ Lubricating spray

❑ Tweezers or a small standard screwdriver

❑ White vinegar

❑ Bucket

Follow Steps 1–4 for "Replacing Washing Machine Supply Hoses" described earlier.

If the inlets are not clearly marked "H" and "C" label them with pieces of masking tape before you remove the hoses, so you can properly reconnect the hoses when you're done.

1. Remove the water inlet filters with a pair of tweezers or a small screwdriver. If you damage them, you'll have to replace them, so be careful.

Washing machine water inlets.

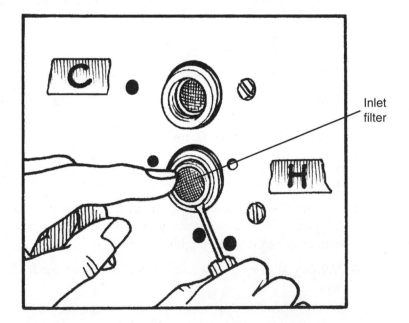

Inlet filter

2. Clean the filters by soaking them in white vinegar overnight.

3. Replace the filters with the domed side facing outward. Reattach the water supply hoses. Open the water supply stops and check for leaks.

4. Push the washing machine back against the wall, taking care not to kink the supply hose. Plug in the appliance and flip the circuit breaker to on.

Ounce of Prevention

Sometimes a too-full washing machine will leak a little water out of the tub. Also, you may want extra protection if your washer is installed on the second floor. You can buy a specially designed plastic pan (available at home supply stores) that fits underneath the washer and can catch a small leak if and when this happens. It's an extra, inexpensive layer of insurance.

Cleaning the Room Air Conditioner Filter

If you live in a section of the country with four distinct seasons, as I do, then you'll notice how your electric bill soars in the summer. The bill reflects the high cost of running air-conditioning. Room air conditioners can use even more power than a central system, especially if the filter is dirty and the appliance must work harder.

Every month during cooling season, you'll need to clean or replace the filter on every room air conditioner in your home.

You'll need the following:

❑ Replacement filter, or access to soap and water

❑ Sponge

1. Switch off the unit and unplug it.

2. Remove the front grill on the unit; if you're not sure how to do this, check your use and care manual. It usually pulls right off, but don't try to force it.

3. The filter should be right under the grill. A reusable filter looks like a thin piece of sponge. You can wash this with dishwasher soap and water, carefully wring it out, and let it dry thoroughly.

4. While you're at it, clean, rinse, and dry the air conditioner grill. It collects dust, too.

5. Reinsert the cleaned, dry filter. Usually there are a couple of clips on either side of the unit that hold it in place.

What Pros Know

Some (not many) room air conditioners have disposable filters that cannot be washed. If you've got one of these, take it to the hardware or appliance store and buy a replacement (or buy a quantity if they're cheaper that way).

Cleaning or Replacing a Forced-Air Furnace Filter

If your heating system includes a blower and ducts that deliver heat to the various rooms in your house, this forced-air system, as it is known, will have a filter to screen out dirt and debris that collect in the system. Usually the filter is located on the return-air side of the system. Refer to your owner's manual or ask your heating professional if you can't locate the filter.

There's usually a little fitting or clip that holds the filter in place. You should be able to easily remove it. You need to replace it with the same-sized filter; these are sold in supermarkets, hardware stores, even drugstores.

Change a disposable filter every month during heating season.

If the filter in your system is reusable, you still need to clean it every month in heating season. Remove it, and wash and rinse it in the tub or in your utility sink. This is easier if you have a sprayer or can attach one to your tub or sink spout. Make sure the filter is thoroughly dry before replacing it.

Cleaning a Range Hood Filter

Nearly everyone with a cooktop or a range also has some type of fan or hood to exhaust the smoke, grease particles, and steam that are byproducts of cooking.

The most common grease filters are made of wire mesh. Most can be washed in the dishwasher. Otherwise, give them a good soaking in warm water and dishwashing liquid. Carefully scrub them with a nonabrasive (blue) pad, and do this gently, so you don't crush the mesh.

Fin-type metal filters are also dishwasher safe; in fact, this is the best way to clean them. Stainless steel should not be scrubbed with abrasives of any kind—these will permanently scratch the metal. If you need to remove greasy film from the filter, use a nonabrasive (blue) plastic pad.

The Least You Need to Know

- ◆ Dryer lint can be dangerous to you and your home; lint buildup is a fire hazard. Vacuum hose, vents, and lint filter cavities every month.

- ◆ Stainless steel mesh-covered water supply hose is probably more sturdy than rubber, but is no guarantee against leaks.

- ◆ If your washing machine is filling slowly, the problem may be your water inlet filters; clean or change them.

- ◆ Dirty room air conditioner filters will drive your electric bill higher.

- ◆ During heating season, clean or replace the furnace filter (depending on the type) every month.

- ◆ Keep the range hood over your stove working effectively by washing it regularly—usually once a month.

Chapter 15

Appliance Repairs

In This Chapter

- ◆ Troubleshooting troubling appliance symptoms
- ◆ Manufacturers ' assistance
- ◆ General solutions to common appliance problems
- ◆ Service calls and replacements

What's that puddle underneath the refrigerator? Why is the garbage disposal making that noise? Why won't the burner on the stove boil water?

Modern conveniences that don't work frustrate and annoy us. But, thankfully, not everything that goes wrong requires an expensive visit from a repairperson. I learned this happy fact many years ago.

It had been a bad month for the Ostrow budget: my car needed four new tires, the old furnace needed a new motor, and record snowstorms had the plow guy working overtime on our long, hilly driveway. I didn't need another repair bill when my electric oven stopped working. So I decided to try calling the maker of my range, to see if someone at the source had a solution.

It was a revelation. Not only did the service rep who answered help me figure out what was wrong—a bad heating element—but she told me I could easily fix the problem myself. Through her I ordered the part with my credit card; two days later, with the part delivered by parcel service, I got on the line with another service rep, who talked me through the repair. In 10 minutes, I had a working oven.

While some repairs are best left to trained professionals, there are plenty of little problems you can solve yourself, with the aid of a friendly help line, Internet information, or just a bit of common sense and a few directions you find here. It will restore your faith in modern convenience!

Ailing Appliances: Diagnosis

When an appliance isn't doing its job to customary standards—the refrigerator's not keeping food cold enough, or there are troublesome small puddles where the dishwasher hose meets the sink drain—you've got to assess the problem, and figure out what's wrong before things get worse.

What's Your Model?

If you've got a use and care manual for your appliance, you're already on your way to a fix. But if you don't, you'll need to find out the model number of your appliance before you call a manufacturer for help, or to download a copy of the manual from the Internet (see Appendix B for some popular manufacturer 800 numbers and websites). The model and serial numbers are stamped or printed on a metal, plastic, or paper label affixed to the appliance.

Here's a list of the locations where the model/serial number is often found on appliances. It may vary a little from maker to maker, but it's a good place to start:

- ◆ **Clothes washer or dryer:** On front-loading models, open the door and look for the label on the left or right of the wash cavity rim. On top-loaders, look under the lid or at the back of the rim above the tub.

- ◆ **Dishwashers:** Look along the edge of the door, or along the rim of the wash cavity, left or right.

- ◆ **Range (combination unit with stovetop burners and oven):** Open the oven door and look for the label along the rim of the oven cavity. If the unit has a drawer, open the drawer and look around that rim for the label.

◆ **Wall oven:** Look along the rim of the oven cavity.

◆ **Refrigerator:** Open the door, and look for the label at eye level, left or right. In side-by-side models, look for the label on the refrigerator side.

Troubleshooting

Every use and care manual has at least one table labeled "troubleshooting," which lists common symptoms of problems and their possible causes. Using this table is always a good place to start your diagnosis. Often, manufacturers list not only the symptom and its cause, but also the cure. Reading your owner's manual is like a free repair clinic.

Always begin troubleshooting appliance problems with what my kids like to call the "duh" questions (meaning, if you don't do this first, have your brain checked):

◆ Is the appliance plugged in?

◆ Is the circuit breaker for the receptacle where it's plugged in flipped to the "on" position?

◆ If the appliance uses water and there is none (e.g., the dishwasher or the ice-maker), are the supply stops open?

It's smart to look for obvious oversights before you pursue more strenuous solutions.

I once called an electrician because I thought all the power was out in our new addition. He got to the house and showed me the circuit breaker in the main panel that controlled the sub-panel for the addition. I had flipped it off by mistake the day before when someone's hair dryer flipped a breaker on the main panel! That was an expensive error on my part—no one had labeled this controlling breaker (see Chapter 13 for directions on how to avoid this blooper).

Manufacturer Help

Because so many people now use the Internet, manufacturers' websites are equipped not only with downloadable manuals, but with their own appliance repair pages and parts stores. You can do a lot online to service your own appliances without calling a pro.

Ounce of Prevention

Many online repair sites will tell you when you can DIY, or when you really should call in the professional. In some cases, trying to tamper with the innards of the appliance may void its warranty, or be a danger to your safety. Follow the manufacturers' recommendations.

If you need the encouraging voice of a live customer service person, this is still available from several manufacturers via a toll-free call, though you may have to wait on hold for a bit. Having someone "talk me through" my first appliance repair built my confidence; it may also help yours.

Please note: appliances have different designs, and really old appliances may have different features than newer ones. If your appliance doesn't have the features referred to in the repairs below, please contact the manufacturer. These are *general* instructions that may not apply to every make and model of appliance.

Refrigerator Repairs

Refrigerators last a long time, and you can keep yours humming by paying attention to any troubling symptoms. Here are a few problems you can solve yourself.

Keeping Your Cool

The ideal temperature inside the fresh food cabinet of a refrigerator is between 36° and 38° F. For a freezer, the temperature should range between –5° and 5° F.

If you think your refrigerator and freezer are too warm or too cold, test them by putting a thermometer in the refrigerator and freezer cabinets for a couple of hours each, and check the readings. If they're high or low, try adjusting temperature controls up or down to reach the correct temperature.

If the temperature controls don't handle the problem, you need to consult a pro.

Poor Door Seal

If the seal of your refrigerator door is loose, cold air is escaping and your appliance will run more often than it should to maintain the proper temperature. Check the gasket between the door and cabinet by inserting a dollar bill and closing the door. The bill should come out, but you should feel a bit of resistance.

If the gasket isn't snug, and looks dirty or crusty, try cleaning the gasket material with warm soapy water, then rinse. You can also lubricate the gasket with a little petroleum jelly. If this improves the seal, you're done. If the gasket is hopelessly dried out and cracked, you'll need to replace it (a pro will do it right). Some people will try fixing a gasket themselves, but the gasket material isn't cheap, and you may have trouble achieving a sufficiently tight replacement seal; amateur jobs are often weak at the corners.

Cleaning Condenser Coils

Dirty condenser coils can make the appliance run overtime. You should clean them once or twice a year.

You'll need the following:

❑ Carpet scraps to put under the refrigerator feet

❑ Vacuum cleaner

The condenser coils are sometimes located on the back of the appliance; to clean these, use the brush attachment on your vacuum cleaner. You'll also need a friend to help you move the refrigerator away from the wall. Be careful, it's heavy!

1. Turn off the refrigerator. Put a couple of carpet scraps under the feet of the refrigerator so you don't scratch the floor. Move the appliance away from the wall, and unplug it.

2. Vacuum the coils using the brush attachment.

3. When you're done, plug in the refrigerator and move it back against the wall. Turn it on if you've turned it off from inside.

If the coils are not on the back of the appliance, you'll find them at the bottom of the appliance, behind the little grill panel below the door(s). For coils in this location, use the vacuum's crevice tool.

1. Turn off and unplug the appliance.

2. Remove the grill panel at the bottom front of the refrigerator.

3. Vacuum the condenser coils using the crevice tool.

Vacuum the condenser coils.

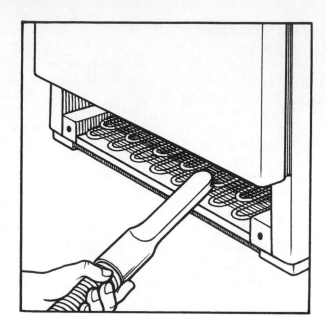

4.   Replace the grill panel, plug in and turn on the appliance.

Water in the Cabinet

If water collects in the bottom of the refrigerator cabinet, you may have a clogged drain. The drain is a little hole, usually found under the vegetable bins, that drains condensation into the drip pan under the appliance, where it evaporates. If it's not obvious where the drain is located, refer to your appliance use and care manual. (Some drains can only be serviced by a pro; if you can't find the drain, call a repairperson.)

If you see water pooling near the drain, you'll need to clear the passageway. Sometimes food or debris gets caught there and creates a clog.

You'll need the following:

❏ Piece of plastic tubing

❏ Turkey baster

Once you locate the drain hole, insert the tube down through the drain hole. Clear any debris. Fill the turkey baster with warm water and squeeze the baster tube so the water runs down the drain hole. If the drain is still clogged, call a repair pro.

Closing the Open Door

If the refrigerator is properly positioned, the front of the appliance will be just slightly higher than the back, so the door swings shut easily, by itself. If it's not positioned correctly, your door may hang open, which wastes energy and money. To correct the problem, you have to adjust the appliance's front feet.

You'll need the following:

❑ Torpedo level

❑ Screwdriver

1. Check that the appliance is level from side to side. Place the level horizontally on top of the refrigerator cabinet. If the spirit bubble is centered, it's level. If not, you'll need to adjust the front feet. If the bubble slopes to the right, you can raise the right foot slightly to level the appliance. To adjust the feet:

2. Remove the small front grill panel of the refrigerator below the door(s).

3. Each foot will have an adjusting screw. Turn the screw counterclockwise (lefty, loosey) to raise each foot.

4. Adjust the feet so the appliance is level side to side. Check your adjustment with the torpedo level. Then raise each foot just a bit more. After you make the adjustment, open the refrigerator door to make sure it closes by itself. If it doesn't, continue raising the feet a quarter-turn each time until it does.

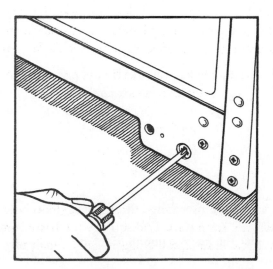

Adjust refrigerator feet.

Water Underneath the Refrigerator

Water gathering underneath the refrigerator is a troubling symptom, but often, it's not a sign of serious trouble. It could be caused by a couple of conditions.

Leaky Drip Pan

The drip pan usually sits on top of the condenser coils, under the refrigerator.

1. Remove the front grill panel. If you don't see the drip pan, shine a flashlight underneath the refrigerator, or refer to your owner's manual.

2. Remove the drip pan, put it in the sink, clean it, and fill it with warm water. If it doesn't leak, it's not the problem. If it does, get a new pan from your local appliance store or through the parts ordering service on the manufacturers' website (or via the 800 number).

Leaky Icemaker Supply Line

If you have an icemaker, the supply line may be leaking somewhere along its length.

1. Turn off the refrigerator, pull it away from the wall, and unplug it.

2. Look for the supply tubing that brings water to the icemaker. Dry it off and examine it for any drips, either along its length or where it connects to the refrigerator. If the line is leaking, you'll need to disconnect it.

3. You'll need an adjustable wrench to disconnect the line at the point where it connects to the refrigerator, and also where it connects to the supply pipe.

4. Before disconnecting the line, turn off the water at the supply stop for this line; it may be at the sink, or in the basement where the supply line joins your water line below the refrigerator. You can then disconnect the supply line and bring it to the appliance store to get an exact replacement.

5. Reconnect the new line, using the adjustable wrench.

Dishwasher Dilemmas

Most dishwashers are installed under the kitchen counter and are a major pain to repair, unless the problems are quite minor. The pro route is preferable for most problems. Here are a couple of defects you can deal with.

Leaky Drain Connection

Usually, the drain hose for the dishwasher connects to the kitchen sink drain at a junction just above the trap. Installers usually connect the flexible dishwasher drainpipe to the copper or PVC drain with a clamp. You can tighten this clamp if the connection gets drippy, or replace the clamp. It's a job just like the emergency leak repair described in Chapter 10.

Other leaks in the hose, which will require hose removal, and taking the dishwasher out from under the counter, should be left to the pros.

Dirty Dishes

Many dishwashers have built-in mini garbage disposals to handle the debris left on dishes. Others do not; they have filters that must be emptied regularly, or the dishes won't get clean and the dishwasher tub may start to smell.

Read your dishwasher use and care manual. If you have a filter in the tub, the manual will show you how to remove and clean it—an operation that usually takes less than a minute.

Ounce of Prevention

Don't overload the dishwasher soap cup. Often the problem is too much soap, not too little. Try using a little less. Sometimes an overfilled cup results in a film on your dishes, or at the very least the scent of dishwasher soap.

Washing Machines: On the Move?

Washing machines that are properly installed are usually sturdy creatures that deliver clean clothes year after year without much trouble. One of the most widely reported problems with washing machines is that the hoses leak, or they may fill slowly. You can deal with these problems when you read Chapter 14.

However, the other major complaint about this appliance is that, on occasion, it starts to move around of its own accord, usually during the turbulent spin cycle. How do you get your washer to stop "walking"?

This is another foot problem; you'll need to level the appliance. To adjust washing machine feet, you'll need the following:

❑ Short length of 2"×4" lumber

❑ Torpedo level

❑ Adjustable wrench

If you can tilt the washer forward with your own strength, fine. If not, ask a friend to help. If you want to take the lazy person's approach to a washer that walks, level the back feet (see the following instructions) and put a rubber mat under the front feet. I have friends who swear this cures the problem.

1. You need to level the back legs of the appliance, which is easy. They are self-leveling, so if you tilt the washing machine forward, lifting the back legs off the floor a few inches (no more than 4), and gently drop it back down, the back legs will be level.

2. Now, tilt the machine *back*. To make it easier to access the front feet, prop the 2×4 under the center front of the washer, and loosen the locknuts on the machine's feet with the adjustable wrench.

3. Pull out the 2×4. Make sure the machine is positioned where you want it to be when you're done. If it's out of place, push it back where it belongs.

4. Take your torpedo level and lay it horizontally across the top front edge of the washer, to check if it's level from side to side. If it's not, adjust the right and left feet so it is.

5. Then place the level along the top of the machine so it's at a 90 degree angle (perpendicular) to you, lying front to back on the machine. If the machine's not level front to back, you should tilt the machine forward again and drop it as in Step 1. Now it should be level.

6. Retighten the lock nuts.

Jammin' with Your Garbage Disposal

I've never had a relationship with a garbage disposal. There were none in any of the apartments I lived in, and my homes in New York and Maine are serviced by septic systems; disposals are a no-no.

So I researched fixing one with my sister, who had an old, extremely loud disposal in her last house. With three kids who put all kinds of things in the sink, hers often jammed. I don't want to publish the long list of stuff that got stuck in her disposal, but the appliance was still working when her kids were finally grown and she moved to a smaller house. So, she's a disposal repair expert!

Occasionally, something that shouldn't will drop into the disposal: a spoon, a coin, a plastic action figure. The grinder starts up, but the motor will just hum, because the grinder blades won't turn. Or the thing shuts off completely via its built-in circuit breaker (which protects the motor from self-destruction).

To fix a jam, you'll need the following:

- ❑ Allen wrench set

- ❑ Long tongs or tweezers

- ❑ Broom handle (the worst case)

1. In order to do any work on a garbage disposal, you *must* first shut off the power. You can do this by turning off the switch, or unplugging the disposal if it plugs in under the sink. However, I am in awe of this appliance's noise and grinding capacity, so my advice is to shut off the disposal's circuit at the main electric panel. I would take no chances with this noisy set of "jaws."

2. Once the power's off, use a flashlight to see if you can see what's jamming the disposal. If it's a big item, use the tongs, tweezers, or if you're brave, like my sister, your hand to get it out.

3. A really small item may go through if you put some ice cubes into the disposal and run cold water through the disposal. You can turn on the machine (press the reset button after you turn on the electricity) and try it.

4. If you can't see what's causing the jam, you'll have to spin the grinding machinery by hand.

5. A newer disposal will have a small hexagonal recess at the base of the disposal (get out the flashlight and *squeeze* yourself underneath the sink) that can be turned with an Allen (hex) wrench. If you're lucky, the wrench that came with the appliance will be under the sink or (jackpot!) taped to the disposal.

   Insert the wrench and turn it back and forth, clockwise and then counterclockwise to free the mechanism. Pay attention, you may hear the obstruction drop down the drain. Or the offending jammer may pop up into the cavity above the grinders. You may have to work the wrench a couple of times to free the jam.

Keep checking the disposal cavity with the flashlight until you're successful.

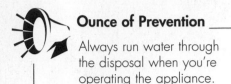

Ounce of Prevention

Always run water through the disposal when you're operating the appliance.

6. If your disposal is an oldie, with no hex slot at the base, you'll need the broom handle to try and free the grinder blades. Put the handle into the cavity and set the end of the handle against the blade. Push it clockwise, then counter-clockwise until you free the blades. Remove the source of the jam, restore power, and turn on the disposal.

Service Calls and Replacement

Sometimes, appliances just wear out. In Chapter 18, you'll see a listing of various appliances and their life expectancies. While a new appliance may be pricey, professional repair is also costly, and you have to weigh the value of a repair against the potential costs/benefits of replacement.

Many appliances—washing machines, dishwashers, and especially refrigerators—have become much more energy efficient. The money you can save by retiring an old, energy-gobbling appliance and replacing it may justify the added expense over the cost of repair. See Appendix B for some helpful information on making the replace/repair decision.

The Least You Need to Know

♦ Repair is much easier when you hang on to the use and care manuals for your appliances. If you don't have them, you can download them from a maker's website.

♦ Manufacturers' 800 phone numbers and websites are bountiful sources of information and parts for DIY repair.

♦ Keeping refrigerator parts clean—the gaskets, the drain, the coils—goes a long way to keeping the appliance cool.

♦ Have a healthy respect for power (the electric kind) when you try to clear a garbage disposal jam.

Chapter 16

Heating and Cooling

In This Chapter

- Learning about your heating and cooling systems
- Facts about gas, oil, and electric heat
- Tips for troubleshooting your heating system
- Maintenance you can do yourself
- Getting to know your water heater
- Central air conditioning systems

Most residential central heating systems are fueled by gas, oil, or electricity. In hot climates, this arrangement is replaced by central air conditioning. And some folks in places where winters are cold and summers are hot have both.

No matter where you live, keeping warm when it's cold and cool when it's hot is a high priority for most of us. It's important to take care of the equipment that makes it happen.

Because there are hundreds of brands and models of furnaces, boilers, and other heating components, this chapter will give you basic information that anyone with a heating or cooling system should know. For specifics, you should check with your system service company and/or your use and care manual.

Maintenance of Heating/Cooling Equipment

Let me begin with one basic piece of advice. The best way to keep your heating and cooling equipment working well is to have it checked annually by a service professional. For heating systems, that means a fall checkup before the peak heating season begins. For central air, spring is the season for this work.

> **What Pros Know**
>
> It's all timing. Systems going bad often fail the first time they are turned on in any heating/cooling season. The professional who services your equipment, and test-runs it during his maintenance call, will help you avoid this sad scenario.

Nothing is more frustrating than having equipment fail when you need it. Anyone who's had the experience knows that a furnace man is hard to find on the first very cold day of heating season. Likewise, the air conditioning specialist disappears during a heat wave; the demand for his services may put your repair at the back of the line.

If you've never had your heating system serviced before, it's worth doing for two reasons:

♦ Your equipment will be ready to run when the season starts.

♦ You can learn how your system functions, including how to turn it on and off, what any dials and gauges mean, the location of parts you need to take care of between service calls, and how to take care of them. Since you're paying for the service call, ask the pro to show you how the system works.

You should take notes on the operation of your system for your home workbook:

♦ Location(s) of emergency shut-off switches, and where applicable, supply shut-offs for gas and water

♦ Directions for restarting the system; for a gas system, how to light the pilot (if it's not automatic), and for oil, the location of the restart button

♦ The normal readings for temperature, pressure, and other gauges so that you'll know if something is going wrong

Gas Heat

More than half the households in the United States are heated with gas, so we'll address this furnace type first.

While gas furnaces have few moving parts, they should be checked annually. Most companies that provide your gas supply will also, for a monthly fee, offer a contract to service your furnace.

Among the things a service pro will inspect:

◆ Heat exchanger

◆ Gas pipes

◆ Electronic ignition system

◆ Fan, motor, bearings, belts, pumps

◆ Air filter

◆ Air cleaner

◆ Pilot and its safety system

◆ Furnace controls

◆ Exhaust

◆ Flame pattern, venting, chimney

◆ Thermostat

Gas furnaces do not usually need annual cleaning (every couple of years is fine), and this can be done via the gas company service people (usually this requires an additional fee), or a certified heating/cooling specialist.

Every 5 years or so, the ductwork should be cleaned. Over time, these heat passageways become collection centers for dust, and sometimes mold or mildew, if your home has a humidity problem. All of these pollutants can be bad for your and your family. This is also a job for a specialist.

Between the annual checkups, your only important task is to change or clean your furnace filter regularly. See Chapter 14 to learn how it's done.

Oil Heat

Only about 7 percent of the country heats with oil, but oil heating systems are more complex than gas furnaces or electric units. If you heat with oil, an annual maintenance appointment should be a given.

Ounce of Prevention

If your heating system vents into the chimney—oil systems do—you should have a chimney sweep clean the chimney before your heating system is serviced. Normally, the heating pro will clean the smoke pipe that vents into the chimney. If the sweep shows up *after* the system maintenance, he'll dirty the pipe with the soot he dislodges from the chimney!

When the pro performs the annual tune up for your *furnace*, he'll do a lot of things:

♦ Test and adjust the oil burner for maximum efficiency; determine an efficiency rating.

♦ Inspect the combustion chamber.

♦ Clean and check electrodes and nozzle assembly.

♦ Change filter and nozzle.

♦ Check all motors, fans, circulator, pump.

♦ Check all the safety features and operating controls.

♦ Vacuum the furnace and flue pipe.

Some service pros will also balance a heating system (steam), or bleed radiators (hot water). Actually, you can do the bleeding yourself (see the section later in this chapter).

Like many households in the Northeast, we have an old, oil-fired hot water *boiler*. It's been running for quite a long time, because it is serviced and cleaned every year. We repair and replace anything that's needed to keep it running. In fact, we've replaced so many of its components my repair guy jokes that, at this point, we've got all-new equipment!

def•i•ni•tion

The heating plant for forced-air systems—the majority of systems in the United States—is called the **furnace**. The heating plant for systems that heat and move water or steam through pipes is called a **boiler**.

We've also got a service contract, an agreement with our oil delivery/service company, that has probably saved us thousands of dollars over the 25 years we've lived in our house.

Our service contract is like an insurance policy. It pays the company a certain amount of money to cover the costs of an annual cleaning. It also covers any emergency service calls that might be made in the course of that year, and it provides for replacement of certain parts, which can be a big savings if you should need them. It's not very costly.

On the other hand, without a contract, midnight runs by oil furnace repairmen, purchased à la carte, can be very expensive. If you have oil heat, a relationship and a contract with a full-service company that delivers oil and does repairs is well worth the price.

Electric Heat

As the cost of electricity rises, electric heat becomes less and less of a bargain, especially in parts of the country with a long heating season. Many of the systems installed in the 1960s and 70s, when *kilowatt hours* (kWh) were cheap, have become very expensive to run.

In places where freezing temperatures are rare, a backup system of baseboard heaters, or a pump that can be controlled to provide both heating and cooling, makes sense. But if you live in a frigid area and have electric heat, I have a word for you: sweaters. Wearing them inside will help keep the bill down.

def•i•ni•tion

A **kilowatt hour** (kWh) is a unit of energy equivalent to one kilowatt (1 kW) of power used for one hour (1 h) of time. To illustrate, if you ran a 1000-watt bulb for one hour, you would use 1 kilowatt hour of energy.

Baseboard electric heaters have their own heating elements that connect directly to your home's wiring system. While using them constantly is very expensive, most of these systems have thermostats in each room; you can turn off the heat in unused spaces.

Because these baseboard heaters collect dust, debris, and animal hair, they can smell very funky when you first turn them on in cold weather. Be sure to dust and vacuum these units before using them, to avoid the smell and to prevent a fire hazard.

Another type of electric heat is generated by a furnace that will warm air and, via a mechanical blower, will push the air through a system of ducts and registers, or to baseboards. While the system is configured like a gas furnace—with electric-powered heating elements instead of the gas flame—heating air this way is inefficient and very costly.

No combustion takes place in this type of furnace, so there's no flue. And only the blower unit of an electric furnace has moving parts, so servicing of the equipment is fairly easy. Filter and humidifier (if there is one), need to be maintained according to manufacturers' directions.

Troubleshooting Your Heating System

If you call for heat by turning up the thermostat—and nothing happens—don't panic. Here are the steps you can try for each type of furnace before calling your professional heating company for service. If you have a good service company, they may walk you through these steps, anyway, before sending someone out.

Gas Furnace

Before picking up the phone to call your repair service, try these fixes in this sequence:

1. Make sure you've turned the thermostat above the current temperature of the room where it is located.

2. If you have a programmable thermostat, be sure it has fresh batteries. If in doubt, change them.

3. Check the emergency switch, usually identified with a red switch plate. It is often located at the top of the stairs or next to the furnace. Someone may have turned it off by mistake.

4. Check your electrical panel. If the breaker is tripped or the fuse blown, replace the fuse/flip the breaker back to on. Follow the manufacturer's instructions for restarting the furnace. If you don't know these, call for service (and learn the startup routine!) If you know how startup works, try it, and if the breaker flips to "off" again, or the fuse blows, call for service.

5. Some newer furnaces are vented directly through the wall with plastic (PVC) pipe. If there is any blockage on the exterior of this pipe, the system will shut down. You can try checking this if it applies to your system.

> **Ounce of Prevention**
>
> If you're in a new house or condo, the builder may have put in an ordinary switch plate over your emergency switch. Change to a red plate that says "Emergency" right away. Unmarked switches can cause a lot of confusion when it's time to power up the heat.

Lighting the Pilot—or Not?

If you have an older, standing pilot furnace (you should know this before you start playing around with it), if the pilot has gone out the burner will not light. *Do not light the pilot yourself if you are not sure how your own system works!* Put on a sweater, call for service, and wait for the pro to arrive.

In general, to light the pilot on a gas furnace, you will find instructions near the pilot control knob on the furnace. You'll need a long match or a long, tubular grill lighter to do the lighting.

◆ Set the control knob to the pilot position. Hold a long match to the gas port for the pilot.

◆ Press down on the control knob; sometimes you must press down for thirty seconds or more until the gas burner starts up. If this makes you nervous, don't hesitate to call the pro. Let them walk you through the process until you're comfortable doing it yourself. It's worth a chilly night to learn your system and be confident of your own ability.

Electric Heat

Electric baseboard heat will not work in a power outage. If you have baseboard units with heating elements and they're not getting warm, and your lights are on, try these actions:

1. If the thermostat is programmable, change the batteries unless you know they are fresh. Then try turning on the heat.

2. Check the electrical panel. First, turn the thermostat that controls the baseboard heat to off.

At the main panel if the breaker that controls the baseboard heater(s) is flipped to off, turn it back on. If you have a fuse panel and the fuse is blown, replace the fuse with a fresh, identically sized fuse. Then turn up the thermostat that controls the baseboard heat. If it still doesn't work because the breaker has flipped or the fuse has blown again, you need to call an electrician.

If you have an electric furnace, you can try Steps 1 and 2 above, first. Also make sure, if your thermostat controls both heating and cooling, that the selector switch is on heat mode.

Call for service if the furnace fails to start.

Oil Furnace/Boiler

First, check that the emergency switch has not been flipped off. Also check the electrical panel to see whether or not the breaker or fuse that controls the heating system has flipped off or blown. Flip the switch to on, or change the blown fuse.

You can turn on the furnace if you know the location of the restart button. This is a red button located in one of two places:

◆ On or next to the motor that starts the oil burner.

◆ On older systems, there may be a switch on the smoke pipe that connects the furnace/boiler to the chimney.

Press this control *only once*. Pressing it repeatedly is dangerous. If the system doesn't fire up immediately, call for service.

DIY Heating System Maintenance

I hope you understand from this chapter that the maintenance that keeps your heating equipment in top running shape is best done by a trained professional. However, that doesn't mean that there's nothing *you* can do. In fact, there are a few important things that you should do.

Filtering Forced Air Systems

Any forced air heating system is equipped with a filter, usually located next to the blower on your equipment. Have your service pro show you the filter, or refer to your equipment manual. Disposable filters should be replaced, and the old ones discarded, every month during heating season.

If you have an *ionizing filter*—an air-cleaning device that gives tiny particles a charge that makes them stick to the surface of the filter until they are cleaned off—it is not disposable, but needs to be cleaned regularly. For information about furnace filters, check out Chapter 14.

What Pros Know

Is your furnace filter dirty? Hold it up to the light. If you can see through it, it's fine. If you have no pets, carpets, or upholstery, your system may not draw up as many pollutants that will clog a filter. But most people need to replace their filter every month.

Ducts, Vents, and Registers

Warm air (and cool air, if you have a central air system that uses the same ducts) comes into your living spaces through vents and/or registers. These need to be clean and unobstructed by furnishings and drapes.

Before any heating or cooling season, make sure that no furnishings block the vents or registers. Vacuum any dust, debris, or pet hair that accumulates on these outlets; remember the forced hot or cold air will blow this stuff around your house if you don't remove it!

Every couple of years you should have your heating/cooling ducts professionally cleaned. This process not only vacuum-cleans these passageways, but also removes any pollutants such as mold or mildew.

Cleaning Radiators

Use the brush or the crevice tool of your vacuum cleaner to keep your radiators and baseboard heaters clean. Be careful not to bend or damage the little aluminum fins on modern baseboard units. And don't use the tops of radiators for storage! Let the heat flow.

Bleeding Radiators

Hot water heating systems often have radiators; ours are old, heavy cast iron. When these units are partially filled with air, the radiators will not completely fill with water, creating cold spots. Completely cold radiators are full of air.

To fill the system uniformly, you need to bleed each radiator, usually starting at the radiator farthest from the boiler on the supply loop of your system. It sounds gruesome, but it's really easy, and painless to all (if you take care not to scald yourself with the very hot water from the radiator).

The bleed valve on each radiator may be operated by a standard screwdriver tip, a key (you can trace the shape of your valve and bring it to the hardware to get a replacement key—these tend to disappear), or, if you're lucky (we are), a little knob at the end of the valve.

You'll need the following:

- ❏ The right tool to open the bleeder valve

- ❏ Cup

- ❏ Rag

1. The heat must be turned on to bleed the system, so turn on your heat and run it so that the radiators start to get warm. Start with the radiator at one end of the pipe run.

2. Hold the cup underneath the valve; if the control is a handle, use the rag to insulate yourself from the heat.

3. Open the valve; if water comes out, the radiator is fine. Close the valve, and go to the next one.

4. If air comes out when you open the valve, let the air escape until water starts pouring out of the valve, then close it.

5. Bleed every radiator in the system so that no air remains in the units.

Bleeding a hot water radiator.

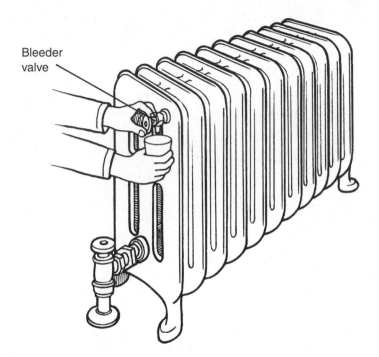

Bleeder valve

Steam Heat

These systems are uncommon, but they're out there, especially in houses built between about 1920 and 1940. While there are some gas-fired steam systems, most are powered by an oil burner. Like other heating plants, steam systems need an annual tune-up. To keep the steam flowing into every radiator, the system needs to be balanced, and every radiator must have a working vent; these cost around $20 each. You'll recognize the steam vent because it will probably whistle a little happy tune when the steam escapes! Most vents look like a larger version of a metal pen cap.

Make sure your service pro shows you all the fine points of steam heat. This will include how to flush the sediment from your system so that its safety mechanism, which shuts off the boiler should the water level get too low, will operate properly.

Usually this feature needs regular (weekly, during heat season) flushing. But most steam-heat homeowners love the incredibly fast, efficient heat provided by their system.

Water Heaters

Few things will make your family as grumpy as being without hot water for a shower when they want it. Water heaters, which are powered by gas in about half the homes in the United States, and by electricity in the other half, are hardworking members of your heating/cooling equipment brigade.

Most water heaters will last about ten years, but you can help prolong their life by knowing a little more about them.

Basic Water Heater Anatomy

A gas water heater differs from an electric model (shown in the following illustration) because it has a vent pipe (at the top of the tank), and a gas supply pipe with a supply valve (stop).

Electric water heater.

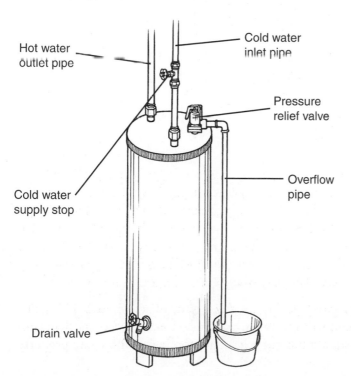

Hot water outlet pipe

Cold water inlet pipe

Pressure relief valve

Cold water supply stop

Overflow pipe

Drain valve

Whether your water is heated by gas-fired or electric heating elements, both types of water heaters have certain parts in common, and a couple of differences.

A gas unit must be vented, so it will have a vent pipe, usually located at the top of the heater. The pipe vents into a chimney, or (with more recent models) through the wall. An electric model has no vent.

The gas unit also has a combustion chamber inside the bottom of the unit; electric water heaters usually have heating elements inside the top and bottom of the tank.

Warm water is able to dissolve minerals that are not soluble in cold water. For this reason, the hot water in the tank is corrosive (a good reason not to drink hot water from the tap). Inside both the electric and the gas water tanks are rods, called sacrificial anodes, that act like mineral magnets. They will corrode so that the mineralized water will not go to work corroding the tank and shortening its life. Some homeowners will have the anodes replaced after a few years to lengthen the life of the water heater.

Other parts shared by gas and electric models include the *drain valve*. This is used to drain the water in the tank. Because the tank collects sediment from the water at its base, it's a good idea to drain the tank every couple of years (see the instructions later in this chapter).

You'll also want to pay attention to the *pressure relief valve* (see the previous illustration). This valve will automatically discharge water from the tank should pressure build up inside from an overheating element. These valves go bad on occasion and you can replace yours with an exact duplicate part, as described later in this chapter.

Testing the Pressure Relief Valve

Once a year, you should make sure this valve is working the way it's supposed to. Unless you have a floor drain close to the water heater, you'll need a sturdy bucket (remember, the water inside the tank is *hot*; a cheap plastic bucket might soften from the heat). Position the bucket beneath the overflow pipe that is connected to the pressure relief valve.

Lift the handle on top of the valve; the overflow pipe below the valve should expel hot water. If water doesn't come out, the valve is not working. Replace it at once. (You should also replace this part if it is leaking.)

Ounce of Prevention

Remember, water heaters contain hot water! Wear gloves and use caution when you test the pressure relief valve.

You will need an exact replacement valve and overflow pipe. If you have the use and care manual for your water heater, you can find the part number in the manual. Or call the manufacturer with the model number of your heater (find this info on the tank); they may be able to give you the number, and even sell you the part!

Replacing the Pressure Relief Valve

If the pilot for your gas water heater does not relight automatically with a restart device after the gas has been turned off, be sure that you know how to relight the pilot before you try replacing the pressure valve or draining the water heater (see next section). Do not do these repairs if you are unfamiliar with the gas pilot!

You'll need the following:

- ❏ Bucket
- ❏ Locking pliers
- ❏ Pipe wrench
- ❏ Replacement valve
- ❏ Teflon tape

1. Turn off the gas at the supply stop; turn off the electricity for an electric unit at the electrical panel. Close the shutoff valve (supply stop) at the cold water inlet pipe. If there is no supply stop, you'll need to shut off the water at the main.

2. Drain water from the heater tank to below the level of the pressure relief valve— usually a couple of gallons. You can do this from the drain valve, by filling the bucket a couple of times.

3. Wearing work gloves and safety goggles, hold the valve with the locking pliers. First remove the overflow pipe, then the pressure relief valve, by turning them counterclockwise with the pipe wrench.

4. You may notice that the valve is covered with sediment; this is a major reason for the valve to go bad. It also indicates that you need to drain the water tank more frequently (see the following section).

5. Cover the threads of the new valve with Teflon tape, and screw the valve into the tank. Make sure it's tight. Then cover the threads of the overflow pipe with Teflon tape, and screw it into the new valve.

6. Turn on the water and electric/gas supply. Test the valve to make sure it runs when the handle is lifted, but does not leak.

Draining the Water Heater

You'll need a sturdy bucket (water may be hot!) or a hose that you can thread onto the drain valve and discharge in a floor drain, sump hole, or outside.

1. For electric water heaters, turn off the electricity for the water heater at the electrical panel. If you have never drained the water heater before, and you have a gas heater, you may want a pro to do it the first time. Or follow the instructions in your model's manual.

2. Turn off the cold water supply stop on the inlet valve.

3. Open a hot water faucet anywhere in the house.

4. Open the drain and allow it to empty. If you have a floor drain, this will be easy. If not, you'll be a one-person bucket brigade.

5. When the tank is empty, shut off the drain valve and turn on the cold water, to loosen up any sediment remaining in the tank. Let the tank partially fill, and then drain it again. If the drain water is running clear, you're done.

6. Shut off the drain valve, open the cold water supply stop, and allow the tank to fill.

7. Once water comes out of the hot water faucet you opened (Step 3), your tank is full. You can turn on the electricity or the gas supply to heat the water.

Central Air

Ah! The beauty of a central air conditioning system is something I'll never experience in my two old homes. The cost of installing the ductwork in either house is prohibitive. Besides, our home on the Maine coast needs air conditioning only about three days a year.

Anyway, most central air systems are best served by a maintenance and tune-up appointment with an air conditioning service company. Do this every year, before cooling season.

Basically, there are four main parts to any air conditioner (even the little room air conditioners that are mounted in a window opening):

- A chemical refrigerant

- A condenser

- A compressor

- An evaporator coil

During your first service appointment, have the pro show you all the parts of the system, its controls, and how to start and stop your unit. Have him or her also go over any troubleshooting you can do yourself to diagnose problems.

Keep all this information in your home workbook.

The Least You Need to Know

- Owners of gas-fired heating systems are the majority of households in the United States, and should know how to change the furnace filter.

- Bleeding a hot-water system's radiators sounds scary, but is easily accomplished with the turn of a valve, key, or screwdriver at each radiator.

- Sediment is the enemy of water heaters; draining yours every year or two can extend its life.

- Problems with a central air conditioning system are best left to professionals.

Part 5

Preventive Maintenance: Safety and Upkeep

One of the things that surprised me when we moved from a rental apartment to our own house was the amount of maintenance needed to keep up with our big investment. While it was kind to us in the first, cash-strapped year that we owned it, after that our house developed problems with pipes, the furnace, lights, dead appliances—everything that makes a first-time home-owner wish for the good old days of renting.

The biggest realization for me was that we had to take a proactive stance and go looking for trouble before it surprised us with inconvenience and a large bill. Inspecting the house every spring and fall, I'd notice small flaws: trees that needed trimming, little drips, and cracks. Timely repairs of little things saved lots of money. And when my first child was born, I became more aware that safety, as well as upkeep, requires a similar "do it before it goes bad" mind-set. After 25 years of home ownership, I'm convinced that a little prevention is worth a ton of cure. Part 5 will help you apply this strategy, too.

"Can't we just put a painting over it?"

Chapter 17

Safety Must-Haves

In This Chapter

◆ The most important device to install and maintain

◆ Facts about carbon monoxide detectors and fire extinguishers

◆ Creating a family emergency escape plan

◆ Critical information to leave with caretakers/caregivers while you're away

With your newfound repair skills, you ought to be able to keep your place running pretty smoothly. But unless you're equipped for *real* emergencies, all the repairs in this book will not keep you, your family, or your home safe. You need to have the right safety equipment in your house, and know how to use and maintain it. You also need to train your family members how to exit the house in an emergency, and know where everyone will meet up once they're out. Finally, when you have someone watching your home while you're away, you need to give them the critical emergency and repair information, should they need to address a problem with your house in your absence. It's probably true that you don't keep your plumber's phone number in your pocket when you go on vacation!

Your #1 Safety Device: Smoke Detectors

The modern smoke detector was patented in 1969; since then, this simple, inexpensive household device has saved countless lives. And it can save yours.

There's only one thing to remember once you've installed smoke detectors: *you must maintain them*. This is critical; a smoke detector that's not working because of a tripped circuit breaker or a dead or removed battery is worthless.

Chirpy Smoke Detector

Sometimes folks get annoyed because their smoke detector is chirping. This can mean a couple of things:

♦ **The batteries are losing their charge**. Test the alarm; if it doesn't sound, replace the batteries immediately. Battery-operated smoke detectors and most hard-wired detectors (connected to your electric system, with battery backup) use 9-volt alkaline batteries. Keep a supply of 9-volt batteries just for this purpose.

♦ **Dust and debris are confounding the detector and making it chirp.** If the test shows that the alarm is still working—the batteries are good—check the instructions that came with the device, if you have them. You may need to vacuum the detector with the soft brush attachment of your vacuum cleaner. If you can't stop the chirping, replace the detector. Do not remove the battery and leave a nonworking detector to protect your family. Many people have been injured or died in fires because they removed a battery rather than replacing the detector— usually an inexpensive (under $12) item.

What Pros Know

The instructions for your safety equipment should be filed in your personal home workbook with other use and care information. It will help you maintain the protection that safety gear in working order affords to you and your family.

The National Fire Protection Association recommends replacing smoke detectors every 10 years—even if they don't chirp!

Testing the Smoke Detector Alarm

The ear-splitting beep of the detector is its life-saving feature; this alarm is designed to rouse even the heaviest sleeper.

Every month, test every detector in your house by pressing the test button on the surface of the detector for a few seconds. If the beep doesn't sound, replace the battery. If the new battery doesn't make the alarm go off when you test it, replace the detector.

If your smoke detectors are hard-wired (connected to your electrical system), and they don't sound when you press the test button, check to see that the circuit breaker on your electrical panel that controls the detectors is in the "on" position. If it is not, flip it on. If the detectors still don't beep when tested, call an electrician.

Test your alarm monthly.

Replacing the Batteries

In general, fresh batteries last at least a year. However, most safety organizations recommend that you change the batteries in the smoke detector every time you change the clocks (spring ahead, fall back) as an extra precaution—it's a routine that's easy to remember.

Smoke Detector Placement

Smoke detectors should be installed on every level of the home, and near sleeping areas. If you or your family members sleep with bedroom doors closed, install the smoke detector inside the bedroom. Smoke rises, so install the detectors on a ceiling, or on the wall close to the ceiling.

Avoid installing detectors near heating appliances, windows, or close to ceiling fans, which can foil the effectiveness of the detector, or cause conditions that make it sound when no smoke or fire conditions exist.

Smoke detector locations.

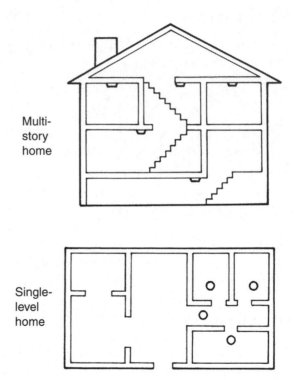

Multi-story home

Single-level home

Carbon Monoxide Detector

Carbon monoxide (CO) is a colorless, odorless gas that is the product of incomplete combustion from any device that is not electrically fueled: gas ranges, ovens, clothes dryers, furnaces, grills, space heaters, water heaters, fireplaces, and vehicles. Open flames produced by ovens and ranges are the most common sources of carbon monoxide; vehicles cause the most carbon monoxide poisoning.

Because you can't see or smell carbon monoxide, it is potentially lethal. Carbon monoxide detectors with an audible alarm have been around for the past twenty years.

> **Ounce of Prevention** _____
>
> While smoke detectors, if maintained, will last ten years or more, carbon monoxide detectors do not have similar longevity. CO detectors should be replaced every two years. Mark the date of installation on the cover of your CO detectors when you put them up.

Installing the CO Detector

Carbon monoxide detectors can be mounted on the wall at least five feet above the floor, or mounted on the ceiling.

Place a CO detector in the sleeping areas in your home. Because it is impossible to detect, a lethal dose of CO is most dangerous to sleepers.

Because CO is often produced by heat sources, do not install the detector close to gas appliances or near a fireplace; it will often give you a false alarm when placed in these locations.

Replacing the CO Detector Battery

Replace the battery when you replace smoke detector batteries; like smoke detector batteries, check the CO detector alarm once a month. You may have to hold down the tester button for 5–10 seconds to sound the alarm.

If the CO Alarm Goes Off

Don't ignore this alarm. Get all members of your household (including pets) out of the house immediately and call 911. Know the symptoms of CO poisoning:

- Low-level CO poisoning prompts flu-like symptoms: mild headache, nausea, slight shortness of breath from mild exertion.
- Higher levels of poisoning cause dizziness, mental confusion, severe headache, nausea, and fainting.

If the alarm sounds and any members of the household have these symptoms, call 911.

Fire Extinguisher Facts

You always hear the caution to keep a fire extinguisher in the kitchen and the garage, and any place else where there's danger of a sudden fire. But how much do you really know about fire extinguishers?

Do you know how they work?

Do you know what types of fires your fire extinguisher will put out?

Is your fire extinguisher in good working order? How can you tell?

In fact, unless a fire is quite small—in a frying pan, or a wastebasket—most fire prevention authorities would prefer you to leave the house and leave the firefighting to the professionals.

But here are some things you should know:

- Household extinguishers are labeled A, B, or C; these letters indicate the type of fire the device can extinguish. *Class A* fires are ordinary combustible materials—paper, cloth, wood, rubber, and many plastics; *Class B* fires are fires caused by flammable liquids—oils, gasoline, paints, grease, solvents, and the like; *Class C* fires are electrical—in wiring, fuse boxes, electrical equipment, computers, etc.

- Home fire extinguishers labeled ABC will work on all three classes of fires, and are known as all-purpose extinguishers.

- If you look at the fine print on extinguishers, you'll see numbers next to the letters A and B. These numbers refer to the amount of fire suppression available in the extinguisher. In general, the higher the numbers, the more extinguishing power is available (and usually, the more expensive the unit). There are no numbers associated with the C designation; the dry chemicals contained in an extinguisher labeled C do not conduct electricity.

- Home fire extinguishers are either disposable or rechargeable; generally, disposable models have plastic valves, rechargeable models have metal valves.

- Purchase at least three extinguishers of the correct type (three ABC for the most versatile equipment) to keep in the kitchen, basement if applicable, and garage. If you use flammable materials in other rooms, then have one for each of those spaces as well.

Using the Extinguisher

Don't try to use an extinguisher to put out a fire if you are not familiar with its operation. The contents of this device are under pressure and come out with some force. Practice using the extinguisher *before* you need it so you will know how it works. That said, when you use an extinguisher—even to try it—it must be recharged right away (if it is rechargeable) or discarded. A partially discharged extinguisher is useless. Yes, it's an expense to have to discard a non-rechargeable extinguisher after practicing with it, but it's worth it.

What Pros Know

Many fire departments offer training in extinguisher use; if you are unsure how to work these devices and don't wish to practice with your own, get some instruction!

To use the extinguisher, remember the acronym P.A.S.S.:

Pull the extinguisher's safety pin.

Aim low, pointing the extinguisher's nozzle at the base of the flames; stand away from the fire—6 feet or more.

Squeeze the extinguisher handle to release the extinguishing agent. Keep the extinguisher upright.

Sweep from side to side at the base of the fire until the unit is fully discharged

Storing the Extinguisher

Don't put the extinguisher in the back of a closet or cabinet. Fire can spread rapidly, and you may endanger yourself or others while trying to get to the extinguisher in an emergency. The wall near the entry to the kitchen, garage, or basement is a logical place to mount a fire extinguisher.

Maintaining the Extinguisher

When you check your smoke and CO detectors every month, put your extinguishers on the safety route, too. Check the following:

◆ The needle in the pressure gauge on the extinguisher is in the green (charged) zone. If not, have it recharged or replace it.

◆ The unit is not blocked by anything that would interfere with access in an emergency.

◆ The pin and seal (if there is one) are intact.

◆ The unit shows no signs of wear, such as rust, leaks, corrosion, or dents.

Emergency Exit: Your Family Plan

Emergencies that happen can be scary for everyone in the family—children and adults. If the smoke or CO alarm goes off in your house, does everyone know what to do? You all should.

Getting cooperation on making an emergency escape plan can be difficult; it sounds like chores! Make it into a contest; dream up a prize for whoever can perform the drill in the least time. Serve a treat when you finish practicing. Do what you have to do so that your family knows what to do if there's an emergency and they have to leave the house quickly.

Here are the procedures that you need to review with your family members. Be sure to cover all the points:

1. Find two ways out of every room. Obviously, the first route is the door. Make sure everyone can open the door easily. Teach everyone to feel around the door frame with the back of their hand; if their hands feel warm when they check, it means fire is near. They need to use the second exit.

    ◆ If the second exit is a window, can you get to it easily? Remove anything blocking it. Does the window open easily? If not, you'll need to unstick it so it does (see Chapter 8).

    ◆ Is a room with a window exit on the second floor (or higher)? You will need a safety ladder for window egress from *every* room where a window more than 3 feet above the ground is the second exit. These ladders are an investment you should make *right away*.

    ◆ Practice using the escape ladder from a first-story window with your children, so they are familiar with how to set it in the window.

2. Once everyone knows two ways out of each room, practice the exit routes. Figure out if there are any obstructions along the way that would impede children or elderly family members, and remove the obstructions.

    Practice a "smoky exit." When there's smoke, you need to crouch low in order to breathe more easily. Have the family do a crouching exit, for practice.

3. Decide together on a meeting place away from the house. We made our meeting place our kids' swing set; it was away from the house, and easy to see from most vantage points.

4. Run an emergency drill. You can do this on a weekend night when everyone's home. Press the test button on the smoke detector, and look at your watch. When everyone has arrived at the family meeting place, check your watch again to see how long it took. Figure out any problems with your plan and then fix them:

   ◆ Doors hard to open? (Fix locks and latches.)

   ◆ Hard to see? (Put a flashlight on every bedside table.)

   ◆ Bumping into things? (Clear all obstructions.)

Run through your escape plan every couple of weeks until it's automatic. Then do it at least twice a year—perhaps when you change your smoke detector batteries.

Your Little Red Book

When you're away and someone else is watching your home, or more important, taking care of your children and/or pets, your caretaker/caregiver needs to know how to use your home's main controls, and whom to call if things should go wrong in a hurry. Get yourself a notebook with a red cover (red is easy to see and broadcasts "important").

In addition to standard emergency info—numbers where you can be reached, emergency service numbers (police, fire, ambulance), doctors (for your children)—you should list the following:

❑ Gas, electric, and phone company emergency contact numbers

❑ Plumber and electrician phone numbers

❑ Any friend or neighbor's phone number who has a spare key

❑ The location of shutoffs for gas, water, and electricity

❑ Your emergency exit plan and meeting location

❑ Pet veterinarian and emergency vet numbers

Making the safety preparations detailed in this chapter takes only a little time, and it's time well spent. Doing everything that's within your power to protect your home and family is its own reward. My wish to every reader is that none of this equipment will ever need to be put to use in your home. But you'll feel good just knowing it's there and ready.

The Least You Need to Know

◆ Keep fresh 9-volt batteries in stock for your smoke detectors; test smoke and CO detectors once a month.

◆ A fire extinguisher labeled ABC will extinguish all three types of common household fires: ordinary combustibles like paper, flammable liquids, and electrical fires.

◆ Do *not* try to extinguish a blaze larger than wastebasket size yourself. Call 911.

◆ Prepare your family for emergencies by creating and practicing an exit strategy from your house, including a meeting place outside.

◆ Keep important information and contact numbers in a notebook for caretakers/ caregivers to refer to while you're away.

Chapter 18

Preventing Repairs: Inside Maintenance

In This Chapter

◆ Tools for the house detective

◆ Using an inspection checklist

◆ Water- and pest-proofing

◆ Planning ahead

If you're like me, there are lots of things you'd rather do than home repairs. So, to avoid having to use this book much more than you'd like, this chapter will help you become a house detective, starting with your home's interior. (I'll cover exterior repairs in the following chapter.)

Good maintenance begins with regular inspection. You can do this every season, or in spring and fall, after your home has endured the months of most extreme weather. Spring and fall are probably the times when you schedule your most intense cleanup efforts anyway. So, while you're at it, take a good look at things as you go through the house. Be brave, grab a flashlight, and examine the nooks and crannies in the basement and your attic. If you know what to look for, you'll save yourself time, money, and grief by stopping any deterioration of your home before it becomes a big and expensive problem.

Your House Detective Tool Kit

If you like detective novels, you know that a good p.i. (that's private investigator for the uninitiated) notices *details:* the color of a car, the sound of a voice. That's how he or she comes up with clues that will help solve a mystery by the end of the book.

To do a good home inspection, you need to focus on the details of your house, looking for clues that it's running fine, or on the downside, that it could use a little TLC in some areas.

Tools

Inside the house, you won't need too many tools to do a thorough inspection. But you will need the following:

- ❏ Flashlight
- ❏ Standard screwdriver
- ❏ Clipboard and pencil
- ❏ Small lamp (to check outlet receptacles)
- ❏ Piece of chalk
- ❏ Safety goggles (attics and basements can be messy)
- ❏ Work gloves
- ❏ Stepladder (if you've got vaulted ceilings or need to climb into the attic or look in the backs of closets)

Without going to the tool bag or the supply closet, you already have the best resources for checking your house: your senses. Observing, listening, touching, smelling—the only one of the five I don't recommend using during an inspection is your sense of *taste*—all of these faculties will alert you when something is going wrong with your house. Use them.

The Lists

In Appendix C, you'll find two sets of checklists that will help you zero in on the fine points of your house: one for interiors and one for exteriors. They list just about everything related to your home's structure and systems that you should check out regularly.

Inspection Checklists: How to Use Them

Each part of the checklists is organized very much like this book. It proceeds from surface elements (walls, floors, ceilings, etc.) to the systems and appliances you'll find in the various rooms.

For interior inspections, there are individual checklists for rooms with heating, cooling, or plumbing fixtures, appliances, or system controls (basement/utility/laundry room; kitchen; bathroom). There is also a general checklist for rooms without these more complicated features (bedrooms, family room, living room, dining room). Start the process by making copies for performing your first inspection, as directed in Appendix C.

When you use each checklist, there are spaces for you to note the condition of each element. You can also note whether the item is something you can handle yourself, or something that needs professional service/repair.

Basement/Utility/Laundry Room

If you don't have a basement, you may have a utility room where the electrical panel, heating equipment, and other service controls are located. Laundry equipment is also listed on this checklist, if you have a separate laundry room.

Surfaces: First check surfaces—walls, floors, ceilings, stairs—for signs of deterioration or water intrusion. Note any damage or defect that needs repair. You will probably be able to do some yourself, using Chapters 5–7. If a surface needs attention or repair, you might want to mark the area with a chalked "x" so you can find it later (chalk will wipe off). Pay attention to the basement ceiling, if the joists are exposed. If there is any evidence of water damage or other deterioration, you can try sticking the tip of your screwdriver into a joist that doesn't look "right." If the screwdriver goes in easily, you may have a problem with rot. Call a pro.

Windows and doors: If your basement or utility room has windows or doors, operate these. Windows should open and close smoothly; the door or doors should also open/close properly. Note any cleaning or lubrication necessary for these moving parts. Repairs described in Chapters 8 and 9 may help here.

Electrical: DO NOT TOUCH THE PANEL IF THE FLOOR IS WET. Open the panel door (remember, only use one hand at the panel; the other should be at your side). Look for any signs of damage. Operate all light switches. Plug the lamp into every receptacle outlet; switch on the lamp to see that the outlet is working. Chapter 13 may come in handy.

Ounce of Prevention _____

Your circuit breakers need exercise! At least twice a year, you should turn every circuit breaker in the electrical panel from the on to the off position, and back to on. By doing this, you'll know that all breakers are operating freely; none are "frozen." If you have any difficulty flipping the breakers on and off, consult a licensed electrician.

Plumbing: Look for any signs of leaks or corrosion at the main water shutoff and at any pipe junctures. The signs are rust, crusty deposits, and of course, any standing water. Address leaks immediately. Chapters 4 and 10 apply.

Gas supply: If you have an inside main, check that the valve is in good condition, with no sign of deterioration or corrosion.

Heating/cooling: Your furnace or boiler, and your central air conditioner (if you have one), should be inspected and serviced by a professional every year. Note the date of the last service. If you are doing your interior inspection in the fall, make a note to call your heating professional now, before the heating season starts. If you have a water heating system, fall is a good time to bleed your radiators (see Chapter 16).

Hot water: If you have never drained your water heater, please see Chapter 16 to find out how to do this, and how to check the pressure relief valve.

Laundry equipment: Check that the valve that links the washing machine hoses to the water supply turns on and off easily. When it's not used for years, this shut-off can freeze up—a big problem if the water's on and your washing machine hose starts to leak! Also check the dryer vent and the back of the dryer for evidence of lint. Lint is highly flammable; if you haven't cleaned the dryer vent recently, see Chapter 14.

Safety equipment: You should have a smoke detector near the entry to your basement or utility room. Check that it is operating, and also check the fire extinguisher, if you have one in this area (see Chapter 17 if you don't know how to run this check).

Bathrooms

Surfaces: Bathroom surfaces may include tile, grout, and caulk (sealant). Check all of these for signs of deterioration, mold, or mildew. Because water pipes may go through walls and under floors in the bathroom, check for any sign of water infiltration: bubbling or lifted wallpaper seams, stained paint, popped nails (see Chapters 5 and 6).

Openings: Check doors and windows for ease of opening/closing. Since humidity can be a problem in bathroom environments, look at metal parts: hinges, doorknobs, locks, strikes. Note any rust. You can clean rust with a wire brush, but rusting metal is a sign of too much humidity. You may need a dehumidifier or a more powerful exhaust fan in your bathroom.

Electrical: Check the operation of all lights and outlets. Test the GFCI receptacles (see Chapter 13).

Heating/cooling: Check that heating and cooling devices (baseboard heaters, heating or a/c vents, radiators) are clean and unobstructed by furnishings.

Plumbing: Operate tub and sink faucets and stoppers; make note of any leaks or mechanical problems. Check the condition of all drains; water should flow out freely. Check under the sink and behind toilet for signs of leaks. Operate the showerhead; check its spray and pivoting mechanism. Flush the toilet. Note any weak flush or running. (Refer to Chapters 11 and 12 for simple repairs.) Check the surfaces of all fixtures—sink, tub, toilet—for scratches or chips. Make note of any needed repairs. Make sure that supply stops for sink, toilet, and tub/shower (if accessible) turn on and off freely. Note any stops that need lubrication.

Kitchen

Surfaces: Because everything is susceptible to cooking grease and smoke that are by-products of kitchens, note any surfaces that need cleaning, particularly light fixture covers, exhaust fan parts, and little noticed places like the top of the refrigerator and the tops of cabinets. (You'll need the stepladder; don't climb on the counters!) Note the condition of floor coverings and any polishing, cleaning, or repair that might be necessary. Pay attention to the points where kitchen flooring meets other flooring; make sure screws, nails, or sills are tightly in place.

Openings: Note any drawers or cabinet doors that don't open and close smoothly. Make a note to lubricate any hinges or drawer glides that are balky. Make sure hardware is secure (use a screwdriver to tighten loose knobs or pulls now). Shine a flashlight in the backs of cabinets and around openings for pipes and vents; this is the area where unwanted critters can enter the kitchen (mouse droppings look like small bits of graying rice—yuck!—see the later section of this chapter for what to do about it). Make sure windows and doors operate smoothly; note if they don't. Refer to Chapters 8 and 9 for easy repairs you can do yourself.

Appliances: Note any problems you have with these, so that you can troubleshoot and call for repairs if necessary. Review Chapter 15 if you're not sure what you're looking for.

Heating/cooling: Check that heating and cooling devices (baseboard heaters, heating or a/c vents, radiators) are clean and unobstructed by furnishings.

Plumbing: Check faucets, sprays, and spouts for leaks or problems that require maintenance (see Chapter 11); check pipes under the sink for any evidence of leaks; try the supply stops and note if they need lubricating (they should open and close freely).

Electrical: Check that light fixtures, switches, and receptacles are operating; test GFCI receptacles (see Chapter 13).

Safety: You should have a smoke detector and fire extinguisher installed near the entrance to your kitchen. You should check these monthly, and during this inspection (see Chapter 17 for how to do this).

Attic/Under Roof Crawl Space

Access: Make sure the drop-down hatch or steps are operating properly.

Surfaces: Use your flashlight liberally to examine the *ridge, rafters,* and attic insulation for any signs of water penetration. Discolored or degraded insulation (possible mold) and water marks on the roof framing (leaks?) are cause for further investigation. Check that roof vents are screened, and that the screens are intact (this is a place where critters—rodents, birds, bees or hornets—can enter, and cause a *lot* of damage). If you see evidence of bats or flying, stinging insects, don't try to handle this problem yourself. Leave the attic immediately, close the door or hatch, and call a pro.

def•i•ni•tion

The **ridge** is the long, straight center timber at the joint between the sloping sides of a gabled roof. The **rafters** are the sloping supporting timbers or boards that run from the ridge to the edge of the roof.

Heating/cooling: Check that the attic fan (if you have one) is operating properly, and is unobstructed and clean. Shine a flashlight on heating/cooling ducts; check that seams in these ducts are intact.

General Inspection

For rooms without plumbing and appliances, you will be checking surfaces, openings, and heating and cooling units or vents.

Electrical: Check that switches and receptacles are all operating. Plug in a lamp to each outlet of every receptacle.

Plumbing/heating: Don't forget to check closets; often, the *chase* where plumbing and heating pipes run from floor to floor is located in such an out-of-the-way place; you want to make sure there's no evidence of water damage or critter entry.

Keeping Out Water and Critters

If you find evidence of leaks or pests that have infiltrated your home from outside, you'll have to plug any outside gaps to control these problems. See Chapter 19 for outside inspection and maintenance information.

If you've got insects that seem to have taken up residence indoors, or a mouse problem that won't quit, you'll either have to use insecticides or traps yourself, or call someone to do this unpleasant task.

Because professional exterminators are licensed to apply pesticides and remove critters (rodents, bats, wild birds), my advice is to get a company that is recommended by someone you know, and use them on a regular basis to inspect your home and remove any pests when and if a problem occurs.

It is in *prevention* that your DIY skills can be most effective. Here are some ideas to keep the inside of your home pest-free.

First, use common sense to avoid problems with bugs and critters:

◆ Keep food in closed containers with tight-fitting lids.

◆ Do not leave food out in the open.

◆ Clean up food spills (including pet food) immediately.

Here are two DIY projects that can make two frequently overlooked areas of your home impervious to pests.

Screening Attic Vents

The vents that allow air to circulate in the attic spaces and along the ridge of your roof are usually large enough to admit many small creatures, as well as providing an entryway for flying and crawling insects to come in and build a nest in the rafters—not something you want!

Be sure you don't have insects or critters already in residence. If you do, you'll have to have an exterminator remove them. If you've got a resident critter and you don't want to harm the little guy, you or your exterminator can try the live-trapping method before taking more extreme or lethal measures. Home supply stores sell live traps for this purpose.

To screen the vents you'll need the following:

- ❏ Measuring tape
- ❏ Hardware cloth
- ❏ Straightedge
- ❏ Scissors
- ❏ Staple gun
- ❏ Duct tape

The edges of hardware cloth are very sharp. Wear gloves when you work with this material. Also wear safety goggles and cover your body when you work in the attic. If your house is insulated with fiberglass bats, you should avoid handling this material.

1. Measure and cut the hardware cloth to cover each vent to its perimeter.

2. Staple the hardware cloth to the perimeter of the vent. Space the staples close together so pests cannot push or crawl through the barrier. You may also want to seal the perimeter with a layer of duct tape, for an extra-tight critter barrier.

Rodent-Proofing Gaps

Rodents are especially attracted to areas of your home where there is a food supply. Although in desperation they'll eat soap and other usually unpalatable items, your kitchen is where they want to be!

Mice can squeeze through very small spaces. If you notice gaps in the seams of your kitchen cabinet interiors, or spaces between pipes and the surfaces through which they come into your kitchen, you can make them less vulnerable.

You'll need the following:

- ❏ Standard screwdriver
- ❏ Steel wool or insulating spray foam

Wearing work gloves, use the screwdriver to work chunks of steel wool into the cracks noted above. Or you can spray these gaps with insulating spray foam (the foam will keep drafts out, too!). Mice and other critters will not be able to gnaw through these two substances.

Planning Ahead for Maintenance

In addition to the cost of your mortgage, homeowners' insurance, and real estate taxes, homeownership makes other demands on your pocketbook. You should try to set aside money on a regular basis for keeping up your house. Doing some of the small repair and maintenance chores outlined in this book will save you a lot, and help you set money aside for equipment, appliances, and other major elements of your house that may need extensive repair or replacement as the years go by.

I've read advice to put away 1 or 2 percent of the purchase price of your home, every year, so you'll have money when something big breaks down. I think this is a good guideline.

Here's a list of large household items and their average life spans:

- ◆ Heating system: 25 years
- ◆ Roof: 20–25 years
- ◆ Refrigerator: 15–20 years
- ◆ Range/oven: 18 years
- ◆ Room air conditioner: 12–15 years
- ◆ Clothes washer: 13–15 years
- ◆ Clothes dryer: 12–18 years
- ◆ Dishwasher: 10–12 years
- ◆ Water heater: 10–13 years

The Least You Need to Know

- ◆ When it comes to home repair, take a proactive stance; look for small problems before they become big ones.
- ◆ Spring and fall cleanup seasons are good times to inspect your home, inside and out.
- ◆ Inspection checklists will help you set DIY priorities and create a "to-do" list for hired professionals.

◆ Pests are most likely to infiltrate your kitchen and attic spaces; you can create defensive barriers.

◆ Plan ahead. Be aware of equipment life spans, and set aside 1 or 2 percent of the purchase price of your home every year for replacing things that wear out.

Chapter 19

Preventing Repairs: Outside Maintenance

In This Chapter

- ◆ Figuring out your home's weaknesses
- ◆ Reinforcing your home's defenses
- ◆ Redirecting water flow
- ◆ Necessary outdoor repairs
- ◆ Tips for finding and using a pro

We all like to think of our homes as *shelter:* from the troubles of the world, from the hustle-bustle of daily life, and certainly from anything outside that we might find threatening.

The major enemies of an intact house—structurally, that is—are water and other weather-influenced conditions. By paying attention to your home's exterior, and maintaining its protective "skin"—siding, roofing, trim, and openings—and the landscape, you'll guard against deterioration that can cause expensive problems outside, and later, inside.

Outside Inspection

Taking a good look around your home's exterior, from the foundation walls to the peak of the chimney, is a helpful way to spot small defects before they become big problems.

As with Chapter 18, which shows you how to check out your home's interior, turn to Appendix C for a checklist for an outside inspection of your home. It will take you through all of the details you should look at. When you're done, you'll have a to-do list for your home's exterior.

You'll need the following:

- ❑ Flashlight
- ❑ Screwdriver
- ❑ Work gloves
- ❑ Stepladder (for inspecting hard-to-reach places)
- ❑ Binoculars (to inspect roof, shingles, and chimney)
- ❑ Clipboard
- ❑ Pencil/pen
- ❑ Inspection checklist (see Appendix C)

Foundation

Clear perimeter: Start with your house where it meets the ground; this is known as "at grade." Walk completely around the building. If there are any obstructions between the house and the ground within a foot of the walls—branches or shrubs, piled-up wood—these need to be removed. A good border to install on the first foot of ground surrounding your home is a layer of pea gravel. Anything stacked or growing against the house wall creates a "bridge" for insects and critters to get to your home and find their way in. Don't provide this opportunity! If branches are growing close to the house, make a note to cut them.

Crawl space vents: If you don't have a full basement under the house, and the house isn't built on a concrete slab at grade, you may have crawl spaces beneath the house. Crawl spaces are usually vented. Be sure your vents are screened and secure.

Foundation cracking: If you see cracks in the masonry foundation, note their location and size. If they have grown larger, wider, or deeper the next time you inspect your home's exterior, contact a pro. If the cracks extend to the interior foundation wall, remember that mice can enter the home through cracks as small as a pencil's diameter. Have a masonry repair person address this problem.

Insect evidence: If you see any signs of insect infestation—grayish mud tubes, sawdust, insect wings—contact a professional exterminator immediately. Remediation for wood-eating insects is not a job for an amateur.

Basement windows: If you have basement windows, be sure the area around them is clean and free of debris. Clean out window wells, if basement windows are below-grade. Note any cracked or broken basement window glass; the panes need to be replaced.

Ounce of Prevention

Secure your crawl space openings! A couple of years ago, an injured skunk crawled under our house and chose to depart his/her life there; it had entered through an opening in our crawl space vent that no one had noticed! The fix for this one wasn't fun; we ran an exhaust fan in the first floor den for nearly two months, and no one could use that room (above the skunk's resting place!) until the odor dissipated. Our wildlife removal expert was helpful but expensive—and even he couldn't get the critter out!

Walls, Windows, and Doors

Masonry/brick walls: Check this type of wall for cracked or missing mortar, which need to be addressed to prevent water penetration.

Siding: Check for loose or missing pieces; warping; signs of mold or mildew.

Painted surfaces: Look for blistering, cracking, peeling, chipping, or a chalky appearance. These indicate your paint finish may need touch-up or repainting. If paint is dirty, washing the surface may extend the life of the finish.

Caulking: A well-maintained exterior is caulked wherever two surfaces meet. Check the integrity of caulking between foundation and siding, between siding and trim boards, between siding and window and door trim.

Examine window glass and screens: note any panes/screens that need to be repaired/replaced.

Check operation of doors (you already checked the windows and doors inside if you did an interior inspection; see Chapter 18).

Examine weather stripping, especially around doors. Make sure there are no small gaps that will permit pests to enter the house.

Roof

Obstructions: Notice whether any tree branches are overhanging or scraping against the roof. These can damage shingles, create a fire hazard if they're near the chimney, and form a "bridge" for animals to access your roof. Make a note to trim them, and have this done as soon as possible.

Shingles: Survey the entire roof. Note any curled, damaged, loose, or missing shingles. They will need to be replaced before the roof starts to leak.

> **Ounce of Prevention**
>
> Climbing onto the roof is not recommended for DIY 101-ers! Use your binoculars to check the details of your roof's condition. If repairs are indicated, call a pro.

Flashing: Usually copper sheeting, flashing is installed around chimneys, vents, dormers, and skylights, and at any other roof seams. Use your binoculars to see whether the flashing appears intact, or whether there are signs of deterioration of the materials above or below the flashing. If you have had interior leaking, and the roof shingles look fine, poorly installed or deteriorated flashing may be the culprit. Call a professional roofer.

Gutters: Examine paint on gutters to see if it needs touching up. Check gutter runs and note if any gutters have slipped from their mountings—they will need to be rehung if they've fallen. Even screened gutters need to be cleaned at least once, if not more, in the fall and spring. See how to do this a little later in the chapter.

Also if gutters end right next to the house, they are dumping hundreds of gallons of water next to the foundation. You will want to address this potential problem by adding extenders to the gutters (described later in this chapter).

Landscape

Check driveways and walkways for cracks, breaks, or wear. You need to kill or pull weeds growing between the cracks of bricks or pavers. Check fences and gates for cleanliness, gate operation, and need for paint and repair. In spring, check the condition of exterior water valves (hose bibs); remove covers if frost danger is past. Make sure outside heating/cooling equipment is not obstructed or damaged. Have it serviced professionally if needed.

Maintaining Your Home's Exterior

Once you've done an exterior inspection, you've got a ready-to-use work sheet for what needs to be done. If you have the time, the skill, and the tools necessary to perform a chore or repair, then do it. If not, you need to find someone to help you get it done.

While some people (myself included) don't have time to do the weekly yard work, seasonal and occasional maintenance and repairs fit within my scope of time and capability. And I like to save the money! Here are a couple of chores you may find doable on your own schedule.

Gutters and Drainage

Water is the great enemy of a house; along with its companion—foul weather, especially high winds—water can do more damage to a structure than any other factor.

When shingles fail and need replacement, leave the job to professionals. Roof work is tricky and dangerous; most construction companies assign their youngest and most agile (and lowest-paid!) employees to the strenuous job of removing and attaching shingles, and walking on the slippery, steeply pitched roof surfaces. Enough said to scare you away from roof repair? I hope so.

If your gutters are not dizzyingly distant from the ground, cleaning them seasonally and installing leaf guards are jobs you can do. I recommend that any work involving ladders outside be done with a helper.

How Gutters Work

Gutters collect rainwater and melted snow and ice that drains from the roof, and carry the water to the ground by means of downspouts. When too much debris—falling leaves, dirt, twigs—clog the gutters, this gunk can clump over the downspout holes and shut down the system. The water then spills out of the gutters, front and back. At worst, the water backs up and damages the roof or leaks into the walls.

There is a large variety of leaf guard products for gutters. Hundreds of inventors have put their minds to the task of a convenient design that helps keep gutters running free. The screens (and other devices, too) fit on top of the gutter, usually attached or fitted to the gutter edges, and prevent leaves from clogging up gutter runs. Depending upon what your gutters look like and how they are attached, you can buy and install an appropriate leaf guard, or hire someone to do this.

What Pros Know

One leaf guard I like—because it's very easy to handle—is constructed like a large bottle brush, with big bristles that have a diameter as large as a standard gutter. These come in manageable three-foot lengths and can be laid end to end in the gutter. They prevent leaves and debris from becoming lodged in the gutter, and are easily lifted out, hosed off, and replaced.

Cleaning Gutters and Downspouts

To clean gutters, you will need to climb a ladder. Please review the ladder safety rules in Chapter 2. They're important.

If your gutters are higher than you can reach with a stepladder, you'll need to use an extension ladder. If you are not afraid of heights, fine. Just follow these rules:

- Make sure that the base of the ladder is firm and level.

- The bottom of the ladder should be one foot away from the wall of your house for every four feet of its length. If the ladder is extended 12 feet up, for example, you'll need to place the base of the ladder 3 feet from the wall of the house.

- Do not stand on the top three steps of the ladder.

- Keep your hips between the vertical rails of the ladder. Climb down and move the ladder; don't extend your body beyond safety range.

- Have a friend hold the ladder at its base.

To clean gutters, you'll need the following:

- ❏ Plastic or metal trowel

- ❏ Plastic trash bag or a bucket

- ❏ Hose, attached to outdoor faucet

1. Position the ladder at one end of the gutter. Wearing work gloves (it's messy up there!), use the trowel to scoop the debris into the trash bag. Remember, do not stretch beyond the rails of the ladder; move the ladder to reposition yourself along the gutter. When the bag or bucket is full, descend the ladder and empty the trash.

2. Once you've cleared the debris, climb the ladder with the spray end of the hose. Have your partner help you so the hose does not tangle in the rungs of the ladder. Spray water toward the downspout of each gutter. When you get to the downspout, flush it with water. Clear every gutter.

After removing debris, hose out each gutter and down-spout.

Directing Water Flow: Extenders and Splash Blocks

Downspouts are generally connected to an elbow piece near the ground, with an angled extender that helps deflect water away from the foundation of your house. Attach extenders to your downspouts if they are not so equipped. If water from the downspout is pooling within five feet of your house after a rainstorm, you can add a longer extender to the downspout (simply detach a piece of downspout and bring it to the hardware for a match).

Or you can purchase a plastic or concrete splash block that will also run the water away from your home's foundation.

The splash block acts like a waterslide and helps keep your home's foundation dry.

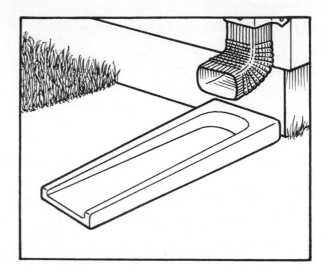

Small Gutter Repairs

If your gutters are bent, rusted out, or otherwise seriously degraded, you should replace them. However, caulking them with silicon sealant can repair leaky joints between sections of gutter. Also if you notice a little hole or two in the gutter, you can patch the holes with a thin coat of roofing cement, applied with a putty knife.

Driveway Repair

Our driveway is as long as a football field, and resurfacing it is more expensive than I want to think about. In our northern climate zone, water always finds its way beneath the asphalt, and sooner or later cracks appear.

Filling the cracks when you notice them is the best way to make your driveway last longer, sparing you the painful cost of replacement.

You'll need the following:

❑ Ice-chipping tool

❑ Connected garden hose

❑ Broom

❏ Driveway cleaner

❏ Bucket

❏ Heavy-duty scrub brush

❏ Rubberized asphalt crack filler

❏ Putty knife

❏ Cold patch blacktop

❏ Small shovel

❏ Piece of 4" × 4" lumber to tamp down patch material

1. Use the ice chipper or a similar tool to scrape away weeds or anything else grow-ing in and around the cracks.

2. Clean out the cracks with the hose spray. Sweep away any debris—dirt, plant matter, chunks of asphalt—and discard.

3. Scrub the area around the cracks with driveway cleaner. You want to get rid of any oil spills and residue. The crack filler needs a clean surface to adhere to.

4. Let the area dry thoroughly.

5. For small cracks less than $\frac{1}{2}$ inch wide, pour asphalt crack filler into the gap. Smooth it with a putty knife.

6. For larger cracks or holes, prepare the area as described in Steps 1–4. Shovel in the cold patch, compact it with the end of the 4 × 4. Overfill the hole a little, and compact it again.

Finding and Using a Pro

No matter how handy you find yourself to be, you'll eventually need to find someone with expertise that you don't have. The best way to find professionals (for outside *and* inside work) is to get recommendations from people you trust. If you don't know the kind of pro you're looking for, ask prospective contractors for references, and *check them*. Problems with hired contractors can be avoided if you follow these tips:

◆ Get a *written* estimate of the scope, timing, and cost of a repair.

◆ Check references. If your job is a large one, visit the site of one of the pro's com-pleted jobs, and talk with the homeowners.

◆ Never pay for a job in advance. Agree in writing on a deposit and then bench-marks (stages of completion) for further payments, with the last payment (at least 10–15 percent of the cost) to *follow* the finished job.

◆ Don't leave money details "for later." Time and again, I've overspent on a job because I didn't itemize and know the budget for everything before a job began.

◆ Trust your gut. If a little voice inside you keeps telling you to hold on, instead of trusting a smooth-talking contractor, listen to that little voice. Check one more reference; read the contract one more time. Don't be afraid to back away from a deal if it doesn't feel right.

The Least You Need to Know

◆ A close inspection of your home's exterior, twice a year, will alert you to small problems before they become big ones.

◆ Trim away any shrubs or tree limbs that brush against, or overhang your house. They're a natural bridge for critters and insects to make themselves at home—at your expense!

◆ Route water away from your house with downspout extenders or splash blocks.

◆ When you need a pro, get references you can check and an estimate in writing.

Appendix A

Glossary

amps (amperes)   A unit of measurement for the speed of the flow of electrons in electric current.

assembly   A set of components before they're put together.

bleeding   Removing the air from a hot water heating system by releasing air from individual radiator valves. This provides consistent heat throughout the system.

boiler   The heating plant for systems that heat and move water or steam through pipes.

caulk   A material used to create a watertight seal between two adjoining surfaces.

chase   A channel in the wall of a structure that holds pipes or wires, providing space for them to run from room to room or floor to floor.

cheesecloth   A light, gauzy fabric originally used to strain and hold cheese. When it comes to home repair, cheesecloth is a great applicator for various liquids.

circuit   A loop through which electrical current can flow, beginning and ending at the same point. Household electrical circuits begin and end at the electrical panel, which receives its current from electric utility service lines that enter at the top of the panel.

circuit breaker   A device that stops the flow of electricity in a circuit if there is too much current for safe operation. Both the toggle switches and the fuses used in the two types of service panels act as circuit breakers, but only the toggle switch type are commonly referred to as circuit breakers.

conductor   A medium that allows heat, electricity, light, or sound to pass through or along it. Copper wire is a good conductor of electrical current.

drywall   The most common type of base wall material. It is made by sandwiching a gypsum core, which is fire resistant, between layers of paper. Also known as Sheetrock, wallboard, or gypsum board, this material is also made in a water resistant variety for use in damp areas.

electricity   The flow of electrons through a conductor.

fenestration   The architectural term that refers to the design and placement of windows in a building.

furnace   The heating plant for forced-air systems—the majority of systems in the U.S—that heat air and then move it, by means of a blower, through a system of ducts.

furring strips   Thin, narrow pieces of wood used to provide backing to support a finished surface.

filament   A slender strand of fiber or other material. The thin wire that is the light-producing element of a bulb when electricity passes through it, and the element that emits electrons in a vacuum tube when current is passed through it, are also known as filaments.

gasket   A material that creates a seal between two surfaces—for example, a door and its opening—that prevents the passage of liquid or gas. Many home appliances have rubber gaskets around their doors.

gauge   The sizing system for the diameter of wire. The smaller the gauge number, the larger the diameter of the wire.

grade   The level at which the ground meets a structure.

ground fault circuit interrupter (GFCI)   A device used in code-compliant electrical receptacles near water sources. The GFCI almost instantly cuts power to a circuit if it detects a leakage of electric current.

grounding   When he or she grounds your electrical system, the electrician has connected it to the earth. Grounding provides a safe path for any loose current—from a defective fixture or appliance, or exposed wire touching metal somewhere in the system.

grout   Thin mortar used to fill gaps between tiles or other surfacing materials.

grout saw   a small hand tool that looks like a knife with an offset handle. It's great for cutting between tiles so that grout can be easily removed, without scratching adjacent tiles.

header   The top horizontal part of a door or window frame.

ionizing filter   An air-cleaning device that gives tiny particles a charge that makes them stick to the surface of the filter until they are cleaned off.

jamb   The vertical part of the frame of an opening, either a window or a door.

joint   In carpentry, the intersection of two pieces of wood. There are many different kinds of wood joints.

joist   The framing that supports a floor or ceiling.

kilowatt hour (kWh)   A unit of energy equivalent to one kilowatt (1 kW) of power used for one hour (1 h) of time.

lath   A framework of thin wood strips, or, more recently, wire mesh, that is used as the foundation for plaster or sometimes for tile.

load   The amount of electrical current that is drawn from a source. An excessive load on a household circuit will cause a fuse to blow or a circuit breaker to trip to "off."

mastic   A flexible cement used as an adhesive for affixing tile to an underlying surface.

mortise   A hole or slot cut into wood or other material, so that a projecting piece (called a tenon) can be precisely inserted. Mortise-and-tenon joints are a very sturdy joinery technique used in woodworking and carpentry.

packing   A material, often string, that is used like a washer in the assembly of a compression faucet.

pneumatic   A tool or machine that is operated by compressed air.

rafters   The sloping supporting timbers or boards that run from the ridge to the edge of the roof.

rails   The horizontal framing pieces of a window sash or door.

ridge   The long, straight center timber at the joint between the sloping sides of a gabled roof.

sash   The part of a window that holds one or more panes of glass or other transparent or translucent material.

shim   A thin, wedge-shaped piece of wood, metal, plastic, or cardboard. It's used to help position something properly by filling a gap, or to protect a surface from something that may scratch or mar it.

stiles   The vertical framing pieces of a window sash or door.

sidelight   A window positioned next to a door.

solvent   A substance in which other substances are dissolved.

spirit level   An instrument designed to indicate whether a surface is level (horizontal measure) or plumb (measured vertically).

spline   A piece of wood, metal, or plastic that is used as a connecting or framing piece between two sections of material. Spline can be used to hold a screen in its surrounding frame; the material that frames caning in a chair seat where it meets the wood or metal part of the seat is also known as spline.

spline tool   A hand tool for installing spline; it has a wheel at each end. One wheel has a convex (∪) rim, for pushing the screen into the spline channel; the other wheel has a concave (∩) rim, for pushing the spline down over the mesh and into the channel.

supply stops   On/off controls found along household utility supply lines, managing the flow of gas or water to individual fixtures and appliances.

tempered glass   Glass that has been heated and cooled repeatedly in a controlled environment to give it more strength than conventional, single-layer window glass.

vise   A tool with two jaws, closed by a screw or a lever to hold objects immobile.

volt   A measure of the force with which electrons move in electrical current.

watt   A measure of electrical output.

Online Resources

Chapter 1: Your Personal Toolkit

If you want to learn more about hand and power tools, consider a hands-on, education vacation! Volunteer with Habitat for Humanity (ladies, Habitat's Women Build program is a great way to learn your way around a house). Go to www.habitat.org or www.habitat.org/wb/ (for Women Build). Or, sign up for a weekend or more at a school that offers hands-on training; this is a more expensive option, as you will pay tuition, plus the cost of a local room and meals. But the courses are great fun, and introduce you to other folks who like to work on their houses. Here are a couple:

Yestermorrow Design/Build School, Warren, VT: www.yestermorrow.org

Shelter Institute, Woolwich, ME: www.shelterinstitute.com

If you're shopping for tools, try tag sales, especially estate sales. You may find some very good buys. And if you're traveling in the state of Maine, check out one of the three stores owned by the Jonesport Wood Company. You can fill a bag with tools for very little money! Info at: www.jonesport-wood.com/jwabout.htm.

Chapter 2: Your Most Important Tool: The Safety Drill

For information on safety glasses with magnifying (reader) lenses, go to www.aosafety. com, click on "eyewear," and look for the "Readers" product.

Chapter 3: Your Supply Closet

WD-40 is such a popular lubricant, with so many uses, that its manufacturer started a fan club where users can post some of the nifty ways they've used the product around the house and at work. Register for all this helpful DIY info at http://fanclub.wd40. com.

Chapter 4: A Map of Your World

If you have a well and septic system, rather than municipal or private water and sanitary service (sewer system), these websites will give you more information than you'll probably ever need:

For water wells, the U.S. Environmental Protection Agency has a huge amount of information you can access through www.epa.gov/safewater/privatewells/.

For septic systems, www.inspect-ny.com/septbook.htm is comprehensive and easy to navigate.

Chapter 5: Walls: From Trash Talk to Smooth Talk

Plaster walls are tough to repair. If you've got an old house with lots of plaster and lots of damage, you'll probably need professional help to repair it. The National Park Service, part of the U.S. Department of the Interior, publishes a vast amount of how-to information for preserving and repairing old buildings—not only plaster, but old windows, roofing materials, floors, and so on. Check out their online resources at www.cr.nps.gov/hps/tps/briefs/presbhom.htm.

Chapter 6: Floors and Ceilings: Beneath Your Feet and (Not Really) Over Your Head

For further information about hardwood floors, visit the website of the American Hardwood Information Center: www.hardwoodinfo.com.

A good general website for flooring information: www.floorfacts.com.

The Carpet & Rug Institute (an industry organization) has a large website with a spot-cleaning section: www.carpet-rug.com.

Chapter 7: Stairs: A Few Steps to a Happy Landing

The Consumer Product Safety Commission has an extensive website and many downloadable publications that address safety issues for children and seniors: www.cpsc.gov.

Chapter 8: Getting Clear About Windows

If your windows are beyond repair, you'll need the latest information on replacements. Pay particular attention to energy efficiency, and get windows that can save you money on heating and cooling your house. Here are two helpful sites to check out:

The Efficient Windows Collaborative: www.efficientwindows.org

National Fenestration Ratings Council: www.nfrc.org/windowshop/

Chapter 9: Doors: An Open-and-Shut Case

The Old House Parts Company has been salvaging old mantels, woodwork, doors, windows, and hardware from antique and just plain old houses for many years. You may be able to locate parts for old doorknobs and locksets here, if you can't find them anywhere else. They'll be happy to work with you by fax or e-mail:

1 Trackside Drive, Kennebunk, Maine 04043
Phone: (207) 985-1999
Fax: (207) 985-1911
www.oldhouseparts.com

Chapter 10: Solving Pipe Problems

If your home is old and has never been re-plumbed with new copper or PVC (plastic) pipes, there may be lengths of lead pipe, or lead solder used in connecting other metal pipe. For more information about pipes, lead, and drinking water, visit this address at the Environmental Protection Agency's (EPA) website: www.epa.gov/safewater/.

Chapter 11: Controlling the Flow: Faucets, Sprays, and Showerheads

Most large home centers and well-stocked hardware stores have extensive inventories of faucet parts. Danco is one company that provides a huge range of parts, plus a helpful in-store guide to help you match your originals to their replacements. For more information and listing of the company's retailers: www.danco.com.

Chapter 12: Tub and Toilet Techniques

Small repairs on porcelain tubs and sinks will not provide an ultra-smooth, like-new finish. But there are companies that specialize in refinishing tubs, which are expensive to replace when you factor in the cost of the fixture, removing the old tub, and labor for both removal and new installation, including plumbing. One national company has franchises that do this work, which is comparable to auto-body repair and painting. Visit the website: www.miraclemethod.com.

Also check your local business phone directory under "Bathtub Refinishing." Be sure to get references for professional service companies with which you are unfamiliar.

Chapter 13: In the Loop: Understanding Your Wiring

Edison Electric Institute, the national association of shareholder-owned electric utility companies, provides a wealth of information about using energy wisely at www.eei.org/wiseuse.

Chapter 14: Smooth Transitions: Cleaning and Replacing Filters and Hoses

Your electrician can install a device that can turn off the water supply to the washing machine automatically (lots of people forget, with disastrous and expensive results). Called an IntelliFlow, it's available from a company called Watts. See the website: www.watts.com/pro/divisions/watersafety_flowcontrol/learnabout/learnabout_intelliflow.asp or call at (978) 688-1811.

Chapter 15: Appliance Repairs

Nearly every major appliance manufacturer has a toll-free customer service number, plus a web site that provides comprehensive information on maintenance and repair, including downloadable use and care manuals, and a parts department. Here is contact information for some major producers:

GE Appliances: www.GEappliances.com; 1-800-626-6005

Sears: www.Sears.com; 1-800-469-4663

Whirlpool: www.whirlpool.com; 1-866-698-2538

Maytag: www.maytag.com; 1-800-688-9900

Bosch: www.boschappliances.com; 1-800-921-9622

Jenn-Air: www.jennair.com; 1-800-688-1100

If you can no longer repair your appliance, consider finding a new one that will cost you less to run. Go to the government's Energy Star website: www.energystar.gov.

Chapter 16: Heating and Cooling

More than half of the homeowners in the U.S. heat with natural gas; about a third use electric heat; seven percent use heating oil; and about five percent use propane. Here are some information packed websites for learning more about your system:

Natural gas: www.aga.org/Content/ContentGroups/Public_Relations2/Natural_Gas_Heating_Systems.htm

Electric heat: www.energyguide.com/library/EnergyLibraryTopic.asp?bid=austin&prd=10&TID=17212&SubjectID=8372

Oil heat: www.oilheatamerica.com

Propane heat: www.usepropane.com/select/furnace?categories=heating&products=furnace

Chapter 17: Safety Must-Haves

The National Fire Protection Association (NFPA) has a website packed with information about safeguarding your home and family from fire dangers: www.nfpa.org.

NFPA also has a well-known mascot, Sparky the Fire Dog, who guides you through a child- and family-friendly website with illustrations of fire safety tools and techniques: www.sparky.org.

You can get safety decals from your local firehouse to mark children's bedroom windows so that the fire department can get to them quickly. But many people also worry about their pets being left in the house when there's an emergency. You can find decals to put on your door that indicate you have pets, and how many you have: www.petalertdecal.com.

Chapter 18: Preventing Repairs: Inside Maintenance

Doing major repairs and replacing equipment is expensive. As part of its fundraising operation to enable more people to become homeowners, Habitat for Humanity operates ReStores in many locations throughout the United States and Canada. Builders and homeowners can salvage good quality building materials and household equipment from renovation projects (that would otherwise wind up in a dumpster and in a landfill), and donate them to ReStores, which will resell these at bargain prices.

My niece, who's just setting up her home, has shopped the ReStore in her area and found a number of bargains. You can too. Check out the website, which has links to a list of ReStore locations: www.habitat.org/env/restores.aspx.

Chapter 19: Preventing Repairs: Outside Maintenance

The American Society of Home Inspectors offers a virtual tour of what a professional covers in a home inspection, inside and out. You'll need a flash plug-in to play the video (it's free to download): www.ashi.org/customers/vhi_tour.asp.

Home Inspection Checklists

How to Use This Appendix

Use this appendix to inspect your home on a regular basis. Spring and fall are the best times to give your home a thorough going-over. These are usually the seasons when we tackle cleaning and maintenance in a big push.

For interiors, copy the checklists for all the rooms in your home. For example, if you have a basement, a kitchen, two bathrooms, two bedrooms, a living room, and dining room, you can make one copy of the basement list, one of the kitchen, two of the bathroom, and four copies of the general checklist, which covers any room without special fixtures or appliances. For exteriors, simply photocopy the exterior inspection list. Then do the following:

1. Date your lists.

2. When an element is in good condition, check it off.

3. If there's a problem and you can fix it yourself, write "DIY" next to the description of the problem.

4. If there's a problem and you need to call someone to fix it, write "Pro" next to that entry.

As you complete the maintenance and repairs on your inspection sheet, note the date completed, and the cost—either for materials if you did it yourself, or labor plus materials if you hired a pro.

Once you've completed your inspection, you'll have a complete to-do list for repairs and maintenance around your house. It's a convenient, simple way to keep your home in order, in timely fashion. These completed inspection sheets become excellent documentation of what you do, and how much you spend, in the years you own your home. Keep your inspection checklists in your home workbook (see Chapter 4).

Inspection Checklist: Interior   Date: _____

Room: Basement/Utility/Laundry

(Make additional copies if these functions are in separate rooms/spaces.)

Note the condition of the following in the space provided:

Surfaces

❏ Floors _____

❏ Walls _____

❏ Ceilings _____

❏ Stairs _____

Openings

❏ Windows _____

❏ Doors _____

Electrical

❏ Service panel _____

❏ Circuit breakers (test) _____

❏ Light fixtures _____

❏ Receptacles _____

❏ Switches _____

❏ Visible wires _____

Plumbing

❏ Main shut-off _____

❏ Visible pipes _____

Gas Supply

❏ Inside shut-off _____

Heating

❑ Last pro service date _____

Hot Water (Check one:) Gas _____   Electric _____

❑ Drain check _____

❑ Pressure relief valve _____

Laundry Equipment

❑ Clothes washer _____

❑ Hoses _____

❑ Water inlets _____

❑ Dryer *(Check one:)* Gas _____   Electric _____

❑ Vent _____

Safety Equipment

❑ Smoke detector _____

❑ Fire extinguisher _____

❑ Other _____

Other/Notes

_____

_____

_____

_____

Inspection Checklist: Interior   Date: _____

Room: Bathroom (Location: _____)

(Make one copy for each bathroom.)

Note the condition of the following in the space provided:

Surfaces

❏ Floors _____

❏ Walls _____

❏ Ceilings _____

❏ Tile/stone _____

❏ Grout _____

❏ Sealant _____

Openings

❏ Windows _____

❏ Doors _____

Electrical

❏ Light fixtures _____

❏ Switches _____

❏ Receptacles _____

❏ GFCI (test) _____

Heating/Cooling

❏ Vents _____

❏ Radiators/baseboard heaters _____

Plumbing

❏ Faucets (tub/sink/shower) _____

❏ Stoppers (tub/sink/shower) _____

❑ Drains (tub/sink/shower) _____

❑ Showerhead _____

❑ Toilet _____

❑ Fixture surfaces (tub/sink) _____

❑ Supply stops _____

Other/Notes

_____

_____

_____

_____

Inspection Checklist: Interior

Date: _____

Room: Kitchen

Note the condition of the following in the space provided:

Surfaces

❑ Floors _____

❑ Walls _____

❑ Ceilings _____

❑ Cabinets _____

❑ Countertops _____

Openings

❑ Windows _____

❑ Doors _____

❑ Cabinet doors _____

❑ Cabinet drawers _____

Appliances

❑ Range _____

❑ Cook top _____

❑ Wall oven _____

❑ Microwave oven _____

❑ Exhaust fan _____

❑ Refrigerator _____

❑ Dishwasher _____

❑ Garbage disposer _____

❑ Trash compactor _____

Heating/Cooling

❑ Vents _____

❑ Radiator/baseboard unit _____

❑ Room a/c _____

Plumbing

❑ Faucet _____

❑ Sink sprayer _____

❑ Under-sink pipes _____

❑ Supply stops _____

❑ Dishwasher connection _____

Electrical

❑ Light fixtures _____

❑ Switches _____

❑ Receptacles _____

❑ GFCI (test) _____

Safety

❑ Smoke detector _____

❑ Fire extinguisher _____

❑ Other _____

Other/Notes

_____

_____

_____

_____

Inspection Checklist: Interior   **Date:** _____

Room: Attic (Under Roof Crawl Space)

(Make one copy for this space, if applicable.)

Note the condition of the following in the space provided:

Access

❏ Stair or hatchway _____

Surfaces

❏ Roof ridge _____

❏ Rafters _____

❏ Vents _____

❏ Insulation _____

❏ Flooring _____

Heating/Cooling

❏ Ducts _____

❏ Attic fan _____

Other/Notes

_____

_____

_____

_____

Inspection Checklist: Interior   Date: _____

Room: General Interior Space: Living Room/Family Room/ Bedroom/Hallway

(Make one copy for each of these rooms.)

Note the condition of the following in the space provided:

Surfaces

❏ Walls _____

❏ Floors _____

❏ Ceilings _____

❏ Stairs _____

❏ Closets _____

Openings

❏ Windows _____

❏ Doors _____

❏ Fireplace (if applicable; have this cleaned and inspected by a professional
    every year) _____

Electrical

❏ Light fixtures _____

❏ Switches _____

❏ Receptacles _____

Heating/Cooling/Plumbing

❏ Vents _____

❏ Radiators/baseboard heating units _____

❏ Pipes (if any) _____

Other/Notes

_____

_____

Inspection Checklist: Exterior   Date: _____

Note the condition of the following in the space provided:

Foundation

❏ Foundation at grade _____

❏ Crawl space _____

❏ Crawl space vents _____

❏ Foundation walls _____

❏ Basement windows _____

❏ Basement window wells _____

❏ Pest evidence (if any) _____

Surface and Openings

❏ Masonry or brick face _____

❏ Wood siding _____

❏ Stucco/plaster _____

❏ Paint _____

❏ Caulking _____

❏ Window/door trim _____

❏ Shutters _____

❏ Window hardware _____

❏ Window glass _____

❏ Window screens _____

❏ Door _____

❏ Door hardware _____

❏ Weather stripping _____

Roof

❏ Obstructions _____

❏ Shingles/tiles _____

- ❏ Chimney _____
- ❏ Chimney mortar _____
- ❏ Vents; other roof projections _____
- ❏ Flashing _____
- ❏ Gutters _____
- ❏ Downspouts/extenders _____

Landscape

- ❏ Driveways _____
- ❏ Walkways _____
- ❏ Exterior faucets _____
- ❏ Heating/cooling unit (should be serviced once a year) _____
  _____
- ❏ Other: trees, plantings, etc. _____
  _____
  _____
  _____

Other/Notes

_____
_____
_____
_____

Index

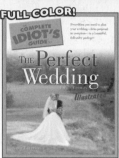
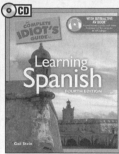